LIVES, WIVES AND LOVES
OF THE GREAT COMPOSERS

FOR INGRID

on our 20th Anniversary 1996

Fritz Spiegl

LIVES, WIVES AND LOVES OF THE GREAT COMPOSERS

MARION BOYARS
LONDON • NEW YORK

First published in the United States and Great Britain in 1997
by Marion Boyars Publishers
24 Lacy Road, London SW15 1NL and
237 East 39th Street, New York, N.Y. 10016

Distributed in Australia and New Zealand by Peribo Pty Ltd
58 Beaumont Road, Mount Kuring-gai, NSW 2080

British Library Cataloguing in Publication Data
  Spiegl, Fritz
    Lives, Wives and Loves of the Great Composers
    I. Title
    780.922

Library of Congress Cataloging-in-Publication Data
  Spiegl, Fritz
    Lives, wives, and loves of the great composers / Fritz Spiegl
    Includes index
    1. Composers—Anecdotes. 2. Composers—Sexual behavior
  I. Title
  ML390.S6885 1995
  780'.92'2–dc20
  [B]   95.41452

ISBN 0–7145–2917–6

Typeset in 10/12pt Nebraska
by Ann Buchan (Typesetters), Shepperton
Printed by Redwood Books, Trowbridge, Wiltshire.

CONTENTS

FOREWORD

Don Giovanni: *Zitto! mi pare sentir odor di femmina!*
Leporello: *Cospetto, che odorato perfetto!*
Extract from Mozart: *Don Giovanni*, Act I, Scene iv.

In the 1980s Piers Burton-Page of the BBC Music Department asked me to write and present several series of 'Wives of the Great Composers' and 'Loves of the Great Composers,' broadcast on Radio 4, BBC World and Transcription Service. It was his idea, and I gratefully acknowledge it as the starting-point for this book. However, it soon became clear that short programmes padded out with musical illustrations were inadequate vehicles for some of the astonishing information that emerged during my researches; and that musical reference works and biographies focus on composers' works rather than their private lives.

That is why I have concentrated on their wives, mistresses and other predilections, rather than their music. Sometimes I felt a little like a scandal-seeking gossip columnist, but it was almost thrilling to realize, for example, that Beethoven, the genius of the *Missa Solennis*, was also a leering womanizer ('When you look at her sideways she's got a magnificent arse!') and that, like Brahms, he visited brothels. Beethoven's (as yet untranslated) Conversation Books, which the deaf man carried to 'speak' with his friends, also yielded exciting material, providing more startling information that biographers have revealed. They suggest the possibility that an illegitimate daughter born in 1820 to his supposedly hated sister-in-law may have been his. Why else would she have been given the unusual name Ludovica? Which biographer has troubled to relate the incident in the Helenental near Vienna, when Beethoven is told how Caroline Unger (the original contralto soloist in the Ninth) lost her virginity? Or of Beethoven the serial bed-hopper? Equally surprising is the revelation that Janacek and his Kamila made the 'earth move' some thirteen years before Ernest Hemingway did in *For whom the Bell Tolls*; and who would have guessed that the saintly Anton Bruckner of the monumental symphonies and masses pursued teenage girls, making Leporello-like lists of candidates? Stranger still, his fascination with corpses, which he always wanted to inspect in mortuaries. There was the young Brahms, with his Beatle-cut a century before its time, who adored women but found loving relationships difficult; who almost became Clara Schumann's toy boy and *may* have produced a child with her. His pockets were always filled with sweets to give to street children — an innocent pursuit that would raise dark speculation today.

Posthumous homosexual 'outing' is now fashionable, and the spotlight recently fell on Schubert. Admittedly not a single love letter of his exists, but there are several references to love affairs with Viennese girls ('the chamber-maid is extremely willing. . .,' he wrote). He sent them songs instead — sort of one-night *Ständchen*. In Biedermeier Vienna it was unremarkable that a 31-year-old man remained a bachelor. His elder brother Ferdinand, a schoolmaster and part-time composer, made up for it by producing 29 children by two wives. One might suppose Vienna would now be brimming with Schuberts, but while the surname still occurs, the musical line seems to have died out. Yet the genius of Schubert, Beethoven, Brahms and the rest might still lie dormant in the descendants of illegitimate offspring, the result of illicit flings. Whereas Johann Sebastian Bach led a quiet, respectable life with two successive wives and twenty children, his youngest son Johann Christian set up a free-and-easy *ménage* in Soho, in the West End of London, with the composer C.F. Abel and the singer Cecilia Grassi; and they were later joined by another Bach, so a potential Kevin Philip Emmanuel might yet lurk in Neasden, a Tracy Magdalena in Tooting.

Tchaikovsky, Fauré, Mahler and Saint-Saëns all married late — for different reasons: Tchaikovsky because he hoped marriage might 'cure' him of his pederasty; Fauré and Mahler because they loved too many women too much to commit themselves to one (which also made Sir Arthur Sullivan remain a promiscuous bachelor); and Saint-Saëns, whose mysterious disappearances to warmer climes were thought to have been related to a quest for Arab boys in Algeria. Debussy — more predictably — was fascinated by blondes — and quickly tired of them. Percy Grainger went so far as to peroxide his own hair, but was possessed by demons of sado-masochism — with a touch of incest. There were two love-related suicides — Jeremiah Clarke shot himself and Haydn's harpist Krumpholtz leapt into the Seine; and one death by erotic strangulation: Kotzwara's — included here more for forensic than musical reasons. George Frederick Handel remained a bachelor and lived with his male cook, yet not a whisper of scandal has come down to us. A case, perhaps, of the dog that did not bark. As the most celebrated operatic composer in England he had the pick of all the voluptuous singers for his casting couch — but was apparently not tempted. We can only speculate: his biographer Christopher Hogwood did — and drew the obvious conclusion. Case not proven. Carlo Gesualdo grievously neglected his wife because he preferred drinking and music-making with his male friends, then murdered her and her lover — a blood-and-thunder tale that would have delighted today's tabloids.

Tantalizingly little is known about Henry Purcell's wife Frances — except that she was blamed for his death — of a cold he caught when she locked him out of their house after he returned home one night '. . . heated with wine from the tavern at an hour later than that she prescribed him.'

Two composers were murdered — Alessandro Stradella and Jean-Marie Leclair, the latter on his own doorstep. Almost like John Lennon, 'he fell a sacrifice to his own fame, for . . . being abroad in the streets of Paris, in the evening of the twenty-second day of October 1764, and returning to his own home, he was assassinated.' The mystery remains unsolved, though his nephew, with whom he had quarrelled, was suspected, as was Mme Leclair, a model wife who learned music-engraving to help publish her husband's works.

Some provide only footnotes — like Isidore De Lara, not a great composer but a great lover, whose *Amy Robsart* was produced at Covent Garden in 1893. He lived at Claridge's Hotel but did not always sleep there, dividing his nights between ladies at whose houses he was welcome. One night a rival chalked on a mistress's front door the words, *Ici dort De Lara!*

To keep the book to a manageable size I have restricted it to heterosexual couples: 'Mothers of the Composers' would make an big book of limited appeal. No one could improve on the televised interview in which the tenor Sir Peter Pears movingly acknowledged his lifelong relationship with Benjamin Britten — artistically more fruitful than many a marriage between creative, procreative couples, in spite of Britten's bitchy nature. If Haydn was the 'Father of the Symphony,' Britten must be the 'Mother of the Boys' Choir,' so much did he hanker after unbroken trebles. The Britten-Pears love was mirrored by Francis Poulenc and Pierre Bernac, life-long partner and singer of his songs; and with ne'er a financial headache for them, as Poulenc inherited the Rhône-Poulenc aspirin fortune. Sir Michael Tippett 'told all' to an interviewing psychiatrist on BBC radio, 'outing' an eighteen-year affair with a music critic (what would the world have said had it emerged that Brahms had been sleeping with his staunch hagiographer Eduard Hanslick?). Satie never married, though he had one weekend-long love affair; but while the word *Gymnopedie* means 'naked boys' no conclusions are to be drawn, just as we may be reasonably certain that Britten's fascination with small boys remained legal — just.

The ambiguously-sexed Dame Ethel Smyth figures only peripherally — a fine composer whose work effortlessly synthesizes the styles of Wagner, Brahms and English Pastoral (known as 'the Cowpat School') — an amusing chronicler and author of nine books and a frank cross-dresser ('Sir Edward Elgar in drag'). Her books reveal more about herself than she intended: she unselfconsciously recounted her photographic adventures with an Arab hermaphrodite whom she persuaded to pose naked; and was so frank about her love for women-friends that she was probably a lesbian without knowing that such things existed. But as she lavished much love on her dogs she appears in my chapter: 'Pets of the Great Composers'.

Richard and Pauline Strauss were happy only when fighting like cat and dog: she the cat, he the good-natured dog; and Sir William Walton's admirers are referred to the biography his widow wrote in which she reveals what few had guessed; her husband's tireless pursuit of other women.

The Schumann story tells of a great husband-and-wife partnership in which the wife is gradually emerging as the more remarkable of the two geniuses. Another underestimated woman composer waiting in the wings is Mendelssohn's sister, Fanny. She was taught music by her mother, knew Bach's 'Forty-Eight' from memory by the age of thirteen, and went to music college at fourteen. Musically, intellectually and emotionally she and Felix were extraordinarily close: both married, but neither achieved with their spouses the bond they had with each other from early childhood. Felix died less than six months after her, some said of a broken heart. Her surviving compositions are almost as assured as her brother's, but their father decreed domestic virtues were more important for a girl than composition. Another great loss is that of Nadyezhda Purgold, strikingly beautiful and supremely gifted, a pupil of Dargomizsky and Rimsky-Korsakov. She wrote much music and became almost a sixth finger of the 'Mighty Handful' ('the Five'). But after she married Rimsky in 1872, Nadyezhda Nikolayevna Rimskaya-Korsakova was content to be his editor and proof-reader — and mother of their seven children. Weep also for Helen Riese, born in Berlin in 1796. She studied composition with Beethoven's pupil, Ferdinand Ries, and glowing contemporary reports are confirmed by her gloriously Mozartian Cello Sonata op. 11; but most of her other works are lost; and after she married a man called Liebmann in 1814 little more was heard of her. She died some time after 1835, her death apparently unnoticed.

The Glasgow-born Eugene d'Albert and the Venezuelan Maria Carreño were composer-performers married to each other — more remarkable for their many marriages than opus numbers. Between them they married eight times, chiefly fellow-musicians; and when at a party d'Albert called to Brahms 'Would you like to meet my new wife?', Brahms is said to have replied, '*Danke, aber diese überspring ich*' — 'Thanks, but I think I'll skip this one.'

The inclusion of performers' as well as composers' love lives would have taken several volumes the size of telephone directories. Stokowski, Paganini, Rubinstein and Toscanini (to name only four) would have required a volume each, the last-named a hypocrite who preached probity to his players but groped everything in skirts (how the sexual harassment writs would have flown today). Leonard Bernstein was engagingly drawn equally to men and women, and the number of conductors who exercise(d) their *droit du seigneur* over their players is exceeded only by that of inter-orchestral liaisons — a constantly shifting kaleidoscope of affairs facilitated by frequent touring, which have produced several steamy novels. Nor is there room for all the celebrated singers who fell for their Svengalis. Of the English tenor Sir Steuart Wilson I know only that he married the former Mrs Adrian Boult, taking over the sainted conductor's numerous children; and that at the ceremony the organist Sir Walford Davies played Handel's '*He* shall feed *his* flock.'

Adelina Patti makes only one scandalous paragraph, for allegedly keeping a dwarf — the ultimate in toy boys — to minister to her needs: perhaps as a reminder that there was none greater than herself.

In projects like this it always pays to bore one's friends with work-in-progress, because they usually say, 'I expect you knew that. . . .' Usually I didn't, so my thanks go to the many who offered ideas and pointers — especially those experts in their fields, Roger Nichols, Professor Robert Orledge and Dr Caroline Potter, who all helped with matters French. Hanny Hieger was a tireless searcher-out of German sources in Vienna; and Aviva Sklan in New York. Belated thanks to my former colleague, the oboist Mary Murdoch, whose father's library of German biographies formed the nucleus of mine; to the broadcaster Peter Spaull and to James McKeon. I have never received a postcard from Professor Arthur Jacobs, or had a conversation with Julian Budden, that did not convey some bit of fascinating information. Ray Abbott, Andrew Lyle and Andrew Mussett all had a hand, with Piers Burton-Page, in producing various editions of my BBC 'Wives' and 'Loves'; and Patrick Lambert was a mine of information about Czechs — though he will not approve my purging that language of its ludicrous diaereses: my computer does not possess them, and few readers know what they mean. Most of all I am grateful for the devoted and tireless help of my wife, Ingrid.

Liverpool, 1996   Fritz Spiegl

JOHANN SEBASTIAN BACH

Born:	Eisenach, 21st of March 1685
Married:	1st (1707) Maria Barbara b.20th of October 1684 (d. 1720)
Married:	2nd (1721) Anna Magdalena Wilcke, b. 22nd of September 1701
Children:	Twenty surviving, by both wives
Died:	Leipzig, 28th July 1750

The Bachs' family tree, as given in Grove's Dictionary of Music, (where it occupies two whole pages of small print), contains no fewer than 86 male Bachs, going back to Hansl and Veit in the late middle ages. Music governed the Bachs for nearly 300 years — and they in effect governed north German music, especially in Thuringia, where they seemed to have what amounted almost to a monopoly. 'He's a Bach' was tantamount to saying 'He's a musician.' Only nine of the 86 were not in the profession — though that excludes female members of the family, who were all probably schooled in the art but did not go into the family trade: it was not the done thing. Their job was in the home, cooking, washing, cleaning and ironing — and breeding more musicians. No one was more aware of the phenomenon than Johann Sebastian, the most renowned member of the family, and, in 1735, he himself declared that he was of the fifth generation; which would make Veit Bach (named after St Vitus, who could not stop dancing) the first. He — Johann Sebastian — drew up a comprehensive survey of all the musical members he knew of. Some of these spread all over Germany and as far as Sweden. In 1728, in a letter to a friend, he casually mentions that all his sons were *gebohrne Musici*, 'born musicians'.

According to J.N. Forkel's biography of J. S. Bach, published in 1802 but which he began compiling soon after the death of the youngest of the 'great' Bachs, Johann Christian, the family held annual reunions, in Arnstadt, Erfurt or Eisenach. These were huge musical parties at which they would exchange personal and professional news, literally comparing notes as to what kind of music or perform- ance styles were fashionable or desirable in different localities. These parties invariably began with a devotional chorale but soon descended into Breughelian feasting with vulgar songs and musical romps, including games and contrapuntal improvisations, with different tunes 'fitting' together as if they were each others' accompaniments. The Bachs called these improvised pieces *quodlibets* ('[sing] what you will') — and in a modified form they are still familiar to the musical Welsh, who call them *penillions*. An amusing example occurs at the end of J.S. Bach's *Goldberg Variations*: the words are *Kraut und Rüben/Haben mich vertrieben . . .*: 'Cabbage and turnips have driven me away — if you'd cooked me better grub, I'd have stayed at home.'

Most members of the family belonged to the artisan class: professional musicians who followed the guild-bound callings of town pipers, tower trumpeters, municipal waits, organists and music teachers in schools. Most were poor as church mice. *Their* treasure was invested in the family, not banks. For the Bachs, intermarriage was the rule rather than the exception. They never got closer than cousins, however: the Church would not have permitted it, and they were all God-fearing folk. Centuries before genes and genetics were understood, the Bachs must at some point have realized that by intermarrying they could almost at will produce musicians — as they must also have noticed that when their neighbours intermarried they were likely to make village idiots. It was unthinkable that a Bach offspring would *not* follow the trade (just as it is traditional among brass band families in the North of England that sons follow fathers into the band). The young Bachs were as a matter of course taught music by their father, by elder brothers or uncles. The girls' training was less intensive, but they were obliged always to be available for copying music and for singing.

The young J. S. Bach acquired a reputation for rebelliousness and insubordination and had a way of alienating authority. When he was an apprentice organist at Arnstadt, congregations complained that he upset them by introducing strange variations and additional notes into his accompaniments — clearly showing off — and was also accused of being high-handed with the choir. Worst of all, what was he doing in the organ loft with a strange young woman? He had allowed her to *sing* — and did he not know that women were not permitted to sing in church? He was too hot-headed, and did not mince his words, but at the same time was himself quick to take offence. On the 4th of August 1704 (aged nineteen) in Arnstadt he was with his cousin Barbara when they had some verbal altercation with a group of more senior fellow-students. Trying, no doubt, to impress Barbara he made some offensive remarks to a bassoonist, J. H. Geyersbach (who was three years older than Bach) to the effect that he made his bassoon bleat like a goat. At this Geyersbach took offence and struck Bach across the face with a stick, whereupon Bach drew his sword but was prevented by other students from doing Geyersbach a mischief. The case came before the Consistory Court and was settled amicably, but soon afterwards Bach transgressed again. Having asked for four weeks' leave of absence to hear the celebrated but now ageing Danish-German organist, Dietrich Buxtehude at Lübeck (he needed a month as he walked there), he stayed almost three months. The great organist was in his last years and Bach could have had the post, but he discovered that the organist's 30-year-old daughter went with the job. A few years earlier both Handel and Mattheson had turned her down — and with her Buxtehude's coveted post.

Johann Sebastian's first known love was his 22-year-old second-cousin, Maria Barbara, daughter of Uncle Johann Michael Bach, organist at Gehren, and they were soon married.

On the 17th of October 1707: the worthy Johann Sebastian Bach, bachelor, organist of the Church of St Blasius, lawfully-begotten son of the honourable and distinguished Ambrosius Bach, deceased, formerly Town Organist and Musician of Eisenach, and the virtuous Maria Barbara, spinster, youngest surviving daughter of the right worthy and distinguished Michael Bach, deceased, Organist at Gehren, here in the House of God, by permission of his Lordship the Count, after banns lawfully called at Arnstadt, were joined in marriage.

The marriage ceremony was followed by a music party, at which the family sang J.S. Bach's Wedding Quodlibet (of which only a fragment remains, as BWV 524). Maria Barbara bore him Wilhelm Friedemann, Carl Philipp Emmanuel and Johann Gottfried Bernhard, who all gained renown as composers. There were altogether six children, among them twins who died shortly after they were born, and, in 1719, Leopold August, who did not live to see his first birthday. Then, to his great sorrow, Maria Barbara herself died suddenly at the age of 35. Bach had gone on a professional trip to Karlsbad, and returned home to news of the kind every traveller dreaded in those days of slow journeys and poor communications. The circumstances were described later by his son Carl Philipp Emmanuel:

> After thirteen years of happy marriage with his first wife, he met with grievous sorrow in the year 1720, when, upon his return to Cöthen, he found her dead and buried, although he had left her in the best of health on his departure. The first news of her having fallen ill and died was given to him as he entered his house.

The woman who became his second wife was Anna Magdalena Wilke, Wülke, or Wülcke (spellings varied). He had noticed her the year before Maria Barbara died, for she was a startlingly pretty woman of twenty with a sweet voice and a sweeter nature. Although not a member of the Bach family she was the daughter of a trumpeter and the niece of an organist. She and Johann Sebastian married without delay. As the church register says:

> On the 3rd of December (1721) Herr Johann Sebastian Bach, widower, Kapellmeister of his Highness the Prince, to Anna Magdalena, spinster, lawful daughter of Herr Johann Caspar Wülcke, court and field trumpeter to His Highness, the Prince of Saxe-Weissenfels, were married at home at the command of the Prince.

At the age of 38 Bach improved himself professionally with a move to Leipzig, where he obtained the post of Cantor at the famous Thomaskirche. Anna Magdalena, still only 22, by this time had five children to look after, including one of her own. As a good father Bach compiled a *Clavierbüchlein*, or *Little Keyboard Book*, for his son Wilhelm Friedemann, and in 1723 and again 1725 assembled two more collections for his wife. Among these she found, together with teaching-pieces for keyboard and morally uplifting Lutheran hymns, a love-song ('Will you give me your Heart?'); and, most touching of all, for he was approaching middle age and his eyesight was beginning to trouble him, *Bist Du bei mir* — 'If you are with me I calmly contemplate my dying day.'

In addition to regular keyboard and composition lessons, Bach also taught Anna Magdalena musical handwriting, so that she could be his copyist: an art she mastered to such a degree that it is sometimes difficult to distinguish her manuscript from his.

Life was not entirely idyllic. Wilhelm Friedemann, the eldest son by Maria Barbara, was considered the most gifted but his mother's death affected him deeply and he failed to settle down.

Johann Gottfried Bernhard, another son by Johann Sebastian and Maria Barbara, also caused Johann Sebastian and Anna Magdalena some distress. He was sent away to take a post of organist, at the same time studying humanities at university, but got into difficulties and left his lodgings without telling anyone his whereabouts. Bach settled his debts for him but wrote, 'My loving care has failed to help him. I must bear my cross with patience and leave my undutiful son to God's infinite mercy.' It soon came to pass: Gottfried Bernhard died while still a student at Jena University and without having seen his family again.

By the early 1840s Anna Magdalena was a sick woman and suffered from an unspecified illness. Yet, in 1742, she bore her husband one more daughter. She was christened Regina Susanna and survived until 1809 — in evident poverty, as she was supported by a subscription opened by the publishers Breitkopf and Härtel: no doubt they were grateful for all the money they had by then made out of the Bachs, and continued to make well into the twentieth century.

In March and April 1750, Bach underwent two unsuccessful eye operations, the result of a cruel deception by an English charlatan, John Taylor, who travelled Europe armed with forged testimonials and called himself 'Chevalier' Taylor — no doubt trying to pass himself off as a knighted English surgeon. Bach's eyesight would probably have failed anyway, even without intervention, but Taylor's operations only made it worse.

Johann Sebastian Bach died on Tuesday, the 28th July of 1750 and was buried in a grave so carelessly marked that he nearly suffered the same posthumous fate as Mozart; an uncertain resting-place. Only after intensive research by German scholars was Bach's grave properly identified in 1894. When his body was exhumed, the sculptor Carl Seffner measured Bach's skull and extremities to enable him to achieve as close a likeness as possible for the Bach memorial which stands outside the South front of St Thomas's Church, Leipzig.

Anna Magdalena followed him on the 27th of February 1760 at the age of 59, worn out by hard labour — puerperal, domestic and musical. At the time of her death the official documents described her as an 'almswoman', so she must have fallen on the charity of the town. It was a sad end for a dynasty.

LUDWIG VAN BEETHOVEN

Born: Bonn, baptized 17th of December 1770
Son of: Johann van Beethoven and Maria Magdalena Leym, née Keverich
Died: Vienna, 26th of March 1827

Beethoven was a reluctant bachelor, like Johannes Brahms; and like Brahms he made a habit of falling in love with women he knew were unattainable, either because they were other men's wives or of such high social status that their marrying a musician — even a famous one — would have been out of the question. It seems that he wanted it that way, and besides, like Brahms, he preferred the uncomplicated services of prostitutes, believing that sex with a respectable woman somehow defiled her. Diary entries mentioning certain places have shown that whenever he recorded having 'conquered a fortress' he afterwards felt disgust and remorse. One day someone wrote down the question, 'Where were you going today at seven o'clock near the Bauernmarkt?' and he replied by writing the answer in Latin: '*Culpam trans genitalium*' or 'Blame it on my prick!' In his Diary there is an undated entry in which he reminds himself, 'Sensual gratification without a spiritual union is and remains bestial; afterwards one has no trace of noble feeling but rather remorse.' In another entry he resolves, 'From today onwards never go into that house — without shame at craving something from such a person' (*eine Person* is a derogatory way of referring to a woman).

Another attribute Beethoven shared with Brahms was a carefully cultivated gruff manner, which they perhaps hoped would frighten women away. In truth no one, of either sex, could have lived with either for long. Beethoven wrote, rather plaintively, to his friend and pupil Ferdinand Ries on the 8th of May 1816: 'My best regards to your wife. Unfortunately, I have no wife. I found only one woman, whom I shall never possess, but that has not made me a misogynist.' That woman was presumably — but not necessarily — the Immortal Beloved, of whom so much has been written.

Franz Wegeler, a Privy Councillor and doctor who had known Beethoven from the composer's twelfth year (Wegeler was five years older: 'hardly a day passed when we did not see each other') revealed in his reminiscences that Beethoven 'was never without a sweetheart, and was mostly smitten to a high degree.' His first love (according to Wegeler's recollections of 1838) was Jeannette d'Honrath from Cologne, 'a beautiful, vivacious blond girl of pleasing disposition and friendly demeanour, who took much pleasure in music and had a pleasant voice.' She would tease him by singing popular songs with slightly suggestive words, but the relationship came to nothing and she married a merchant from Cologne. There followed what was described as a 'Werther love' (i.e. an unhappy one) for a Fräulein von Westerholt. Wegeler added, 'I should also say that all the women he loved were of a higher rank than he.' Then there was Babette, daughter of 'the Widow Koch', who did not return his love either; and Magdalena Willmann, whose hand he asked in marriage but who turned him down.

'In Vienna, at any rate during the time I was living there,' Wegeler recalled, 'Beethoven was always entangled in love affairs and sometimes made conquests that might have been difficult, or even impossible, for an Adonis.' The composer himself, in a letter to his friend Ignaz Gleichenstein, dated the 18th of March 1809, described the kind of woman he was looking for: 'She must be beautiful, nothing other than beautiful, otherwise I would have to love myself [!].' Ugliness offended him, both in men and women. The violinist Ignaz Schuppanzigh and the publisher Carlo Boldrini, who were both fat, had to endure barbs of his cruel humour, sometimes expressed in witty songs. (He nicknamed both of them 'Falstaff', Schuppanzigh usually 'Milord', which he said and wrote in English). If he was in some public eating-house and an ugly person sat opposite him, he would move to another table (forgetting that his ill-tempered scowl and messy eating might equally well have offended *them*). According to another Beethoven scholar, Theodor Frimmel (1853–1928), Beethoven was constantly inspired (i.e. not commissioned) by beautiful women to write compositions for them; and Beethoven's pupil Karl Czerny (1791–1857), reported to Frimmel that he was 'seriously in love' with a pupil, Anna Louise Babette (Barbara), Countess Keglevich. To her he dedicated his Piano Sonata op. 7 in about 1796 (it was at one time nicknamed 'The In-Love Sonata'), as well as the Variations on *La stessa, la stessissima* from Salieri's opera *Falstaff,* but in 1801 she married Prince Odescalchi. Nevertheless, Beethoven continued dedicating works to her under her new name — the most important being the C major Piano Concerto. She died young, in 1813. Beethoven's favourite doctor, Johann Malfatti, had a beautiful niece, Therese, with whom he is thought to have had 'an amorous interlude'. She is the dedicatee of the best known of his piano pieces, *Für Elise* — a misreading of *Therese.* The autograph manuscript belonged to her but has not been seen since 1867 and is unlikely to turn up again. Another Therese, the Countess Brunsvik (only five years his junior) was another object of his affections, and a putative Immortal Beloved, and her younger sister, Josephine has also been mentioned in that context. Josephine died in 1821, Therese lived until 1861 — and could have saved posterity much speculation had she been inclined to talk about her famous admirer. Beethoven was also in love with Giulietta, Countess Guicciardi (born 1784), when he was about 30 and she his teenage pupil — a pert-looking girl, exceedingly pretty, with a wild look and light-brown ringlets falling over her face. She became the dedicatee of that most romantic, serenade-like of the composer's Sonatas, the 'Moonlight', but in 1803 married Count Gallenberg and moved to Italy. When she returned and tried to re-establish contact with Beethoven, he ignored her. She, too, has had a good run as one of the contenders in the Immortal Beloved stakes. Among his maturer women friends — Beethoven usually went for youth — the Princess Lichnowsky (née Countess Thun) was said by his — not always reliable — amanuensis Anton Schindler to have been 'a second mother' to him. Frau Nanette Streicher, scion of the well-known Viennese piano firm who as a girl had enchanted Mozart with her keyboard playing, carried on a long-running correspondence with Beethoven instructing him in the arts of housekeeping and how to deal with servants. She carefully replied to his questions on how *little* food he could get away with giving them. She expressed sincere affection, while he shamelessly treated her as a convenient advice bureau. One letter to her reads, in its entirety, 'I've got only one emetic powder [;] must I wash it down with plenty of tea? I beg you for a tin spoon in haste y[our] friend Beethoven.'

Ferdinand Ries described a less attractive trait: 'Beethoven liked very much looking at women, especially those who had beautiful young faces. If we passed one in the street, he would leer at her intensely through his eyeglass, and if he thought that I'd noticed, he'd laugh or grin. When I teased him once about some conquest of a beautiful lady, he confessed that she occupied him more strongly and longer than all the rest — a full seven months!' One young woman sounds like a chance pick-up. Ries described the occasion: 'One evening . . . when I came for my lesson, I found a lovely young lady sitting on the sofa by him. As it seemed to me that I'd come at an inconvenient moment I prepared to leave, but he kept me back and said: "Play something for us." He and the lady sat behind me. After I'd been playing for a long time, he suddenly called out: "Ries! Play something in love." And shortly after that, "Something melancholy". And then: "Something passionate". From what I could hear [i.e. going on behind Ries's back] it seemed to me that he had offended the lady in some way and wanted to make it up to her. At last, he leapt to his feet and cried: "These are all compositions of mine!" . . . . The lady soon left, and to my amazement Beethoven didn't know who she was. Afterwards we followed her, to try and find out where she lived and who she was. We saw her, from a distance, in the moonlight, then suddenly she had disappeared. We strolled for an hour and a half . . . and when he left, Beethoven said, "I must find out who she is, and you must help." A long time afterwards I came across her in Vienna and discovered she was the mistress of a foreign prince.' In view of such casual encounters it is perhaps not surprising that among the books Beethoven had on his shelves (at any rate on his book list — we cannot be sure that he actually bought them) was a newly-published treatise, *How to Guard Against and Cure Sexual Diseases*; though he also bought, or meant to buy, *The Art of Healing Diseases of the Ear*, books on Homœopathy, and on Macrobiotics.

Several of Beethoven's female admirers begged him for a lock of his hair, as was the custom of the time: not necessarily a token of love but akin to a request for a signed bar or two of music. On one occasion, his friend and sometime secretary, the violinist Karl Holz, played a trick on a lady by mischievously sending not Beethoven's grey hair but a tuft he cut from the beard of a billy-goat. She treasured it until someone revealed the truth to her, and she angrily confronted Beethoven. There and then he took a pair of shears, cut off a handful of hair from the back of his head and gave it to her: much subdivided, it still survives. The event is amusingly described in the Conversation Books which he used also for writing down notes, musical ideas and important shopping lists that throw light on his domestic habits. He also employed these 'Magic Books' for telling his friends and visitors things he did not want others to hear. Like many deaf people, he could not judge the volume of his own voice and often spoke so loudly that his friends wrote down messages telling him he was disturbing bystanders — or embarrassing them (usually fellow-diners, as many conversations took place in eating-houses). Entries like 'Not so loud please — everyone can hear!' and 'Please keep your voice down, the place is crawling with police spies,' abound. One day Beethoven wrote down a comment on the figure of the young wife of a conductor sitting at a nearby table: 'If you look at her sideways she's got a magnificent arse!' On another occasion he scribbled a note about (presumably) a waitress: 'I like the little fat one.' His dining companion then took the exercise book from him and wrote: 'I will procure her for you.' Even stranger is the evidence that at least one, probably two, of his close friends and drinking-companions, invited him to share their wives. Before *Hofrat* (Court Counsellor) Peters goes off on a trip to Italy, he says to Beethoven: 'Would you like to sleep with my wife [while I'm away]? It's so cold.' He explains: 'When I'm not at home, my place is taken by amenable friends.' Similarly, a singer called Antonia Janschikh, the 29-year-old, soon-to-be-estranged, wife of another friend and drinking-companion, Franz Janschikh (Janscheg, or Janitschek — spellings vary) writes, 'Why don't you come and visit me? My husband is away.' Admittedly, the interpretation depends on the circumstances, the nature and tone of the conversation; but after what was clearly a rather drunken, late-night party at the Janschikhs' house where they all had to stay the night because of the lateness of the hour, Mr Janschikh makes the same kind of generous suggestion as Peters had done during another meeting, writing down for him: 'She says I can't sleep with her. The bed's too small. We'll have to draw lots.' Fanny del Rio, who was the daughter of Beethoven's nephew's teacher, kept a diary in which she described Frau Peters as 'very promiscuous'.

In light of Beethoven's constant preoccupation with young women one might legitimately wonder whether his pioneering use of a solo vocal quartet in the Ninth Symphony might not have been influenced by his deep attraction to the soprano, Henriette Sontag, *and* the contralto, Karoline Unger — he fancied them both, but was more taken with the vivacious Unger. Many of the entries in the Conversation Books during the preparations and rehearsals for the symphony cast light on his relationship with them. Both at times exasperated him, mainly because of their reluctance to rehearse (one made the excuse of a toothache) and they giggled and joked all the way through rehearsals. At one point in the Conversation Books someone writes: 'Surely you don't think they're laughing about *you*, or you *work*? You know perfectly well that Unger is a crazy girl, full of fun and teasing, even when it's out of place?'

Caroline Unger continued to flirt outrageously with Beethoven. When she and

Sontag said goodbye to him and kissed him on the cheek, he wrote down (because he did not wish to say it aloud): 'I'd rather you kissed me on the mouth.' Unger was at the time 'going out' with a young man, and Beethoven, in his 50s, was jealous. Someone tried to reassure him by writing down: 'She asks me to tell you that she cares more for *you* than any 23-year-old.' In 1826, Karl Holz, who always liked to report gossip and scandal to Beethoven, regaled him in an entry in a Conversation Book with a juicy tale about Unger. In this he suggested that Unger, when still in her teens, had lost her virginity *al fresco* to the 30-year-old French flute virtuoso Louis Drouet (1792–1873) and moreover, that he (Holz) was an eyewitness to her embarrassment after the event. Holz recalled a concert in Baden near Vienna on the 4th of August 1822 in which Unger and Sontag had also taken part, as well as the Frenchman and Holz himself: 'We all had a meal together, and afterwards went for a walk in the Helenental [a nearby beauty spot]. Drouet and Unger fell behind and disappeared into the mountains. The rest of us went on, and we waited for them at the entrance to the valley for more than an hour. At last she and Drouet reappeared, both looking hot and embarrassed, and she had a big blood-stain on her white dress.'* At the time of the première of the Choral symphony Unger had only just turned twenty, Sontag was even younger — nineteen years and four months. Their voices would therefore have had a 'white', childlike quality (girls matured later than they do now, Unger's adventure notwithstanding), yet this is not reflected by organizers of today's 'authentic' performances, who, while insisting on using 'contemporary' instruments, invariably give the solo vocal parts to singers with powerful, mature, vibrato-throbbing voices.

Among the numerous papers Beethoven left at his death three letters were discovered, together with some stocks and shares, in a secret compartment of his writing-desk — letters to an unknown woman whose identity has been the subject of endless speculation. They have been much quoted, and used as the basis for novels, plays and even films, so a few quotations will suffice: 'My Angel, My All, My Very self. Only a few words today, and in pencil (with yours) . . . ,' followed by some 300 words of love, mixed with more prosaic passages about the state of the roads, the post-coach and the lack of horses; and ending: 'My heart is too full to say much to you. There are times when words are inadequate. If our two hearts could only beat as one, there would be no need for words.' The second letter opens without superscription: 'You suffer, you, my dearest creature,' and ends, 'However much you love me, I shall love you more. Oh God. So near and yet so far! Is it not a heavenly edifice, our love?' The third letter which, almost distraught, ends with: 'Be calm. Love me — today — yesterday — what longing for you, what tears for you — you — you — my Life, my All — farewell. Oh continue loving me, never misunderstand the most faithful heart of your beloved, Ludwig.' Postscript: 'Eternally yours, eternally mine, eternally ours.' The letters were probably written in 1812, but according to an entry in the diary of Fanny,

---

* The other possible reason for such a stain would not have detained the pair for an hour and more.

daughter of Karl's new headmaster, Giannatasio del Rio, the affair continued for a long time — longer than those seven months mentioned by Ries. Fanny confided to her diary that she had overheard a conversation between Beethoven and her father, who had asked him, as male friends might, whether 'he had anybody, etc.' 'I listened with the utmost attentiveness,' wrote Fanny, 'and heard that he was unhappily in love. Five years ago he got to know a person, and to be united with her he would have considered the greatest happiness of his life. But it was unthinkable, an impossibility, a chimera. "I have not been able to get it out of my mind" were the words which so painfully affected me [i.e. Fanny as she overheard them].'

There is a twist to Beethoven's love life which has not yet been sufficiently explored but which inescapably suggests itself after close reading of the Conversation Books. On the 25th of May 1806 Beethoven's younger brother, Kaspar Anton Karl, a clerk, married the already pregnant Johanna Reiss, the daughter of a wealthy Viennese *Tapezierer* (literally this means a paperhanger, but he would now be called an interior decorator). Five months later she gave birth to a son, Karl. When the boy was nine, Kaspar Anton Karl died, allegedly of a consumption he was said to have contracted in 1813. He had been chronically sick for some years, during which Beethoven supported him. In 1815, Ludwig tried to procure for him from Graz some young peacocks to eat, which Benvenuto Cellini also had prescribed for him, as a supposed cure for syphilis; and Schubert, too, asked for some.* Kaspar Anton Karl's will, witnessed by his brother Ludwig and a friend and dated the 12th of April 1813, stated: 'Inasmuch as I am convinced of the openhearted generosity of my brother Ludwig van Beethoven I desire that after my death he assumes the guardianship of my surviving under-age son Karl. I therefore request the Court to confer the guardianship upon my said brother after my death and beg my dear brother to accept the office and aid my child like a father . . . .' On the 14th of November Kaspar Anton Karl added a qualifying codicil stating that 'I by no means desire that my son be taken away from his mother, to which end his guardianship is to be shared by her as well as my brother . . . .' This codicil was not witnessed by Ludwig, and he may at first not have been aware of its existence, for it gives as a reason for the amendment: '. . . as the best of harmony does not exist between my brother and my wife . . . God permit them to be harmonious for the sake of my child's welfare. This is the last dying wish of the dying husband and father, Karl van Beethoven.' On the following day he died.

That there was not 'the best of harmony' between Johanna and Ludwig is an understatement. As soon as his brother was dead, Ludwig started a long and bitter lawsuit against her, to have the codicil declared null and void and to try to wrest the child from her. He published a stream of insults, allegation and downright calumnies against her, called her a loose woman, a prostitute, a frequenter of

---

* So far as I know, this connection has never been pointed out, nor the significance of the peacocks understood. See also the Schubert chapter, in which the allusion is even clearer.

dance-halls, and 'The Queen of the Night.' He put it about that she had been in trouble with the police (she was briefly under 'house arrest' after a domestic dispute about money during which her husband had wielded a knife and slightly injured her hand), and that she had been saved from prison only by his, Ludwig's, intervention. Beethoven kept up a barrage of hate, and his letters as well as the Conversation Books are filled with attacks on the poor woman. Indeed, after his brother's death he insisted that his body be examined in case Johanna had poisoned him. He persuaded his friends to spy on her, tried to prevent Karl from seeing his mother, and even incited him to say bad things about her. Nobody spoke up for her or remonstrated with him for his appalling behaviour: on the contrary — he had enough influential and aristocratic friends to move mountains in the corrupt police-state that was Biedermeier Vienna. Eventually, on the 9th of January 1816, the Court decided in Beethoven's favour, appointing him as joint guardian with Councillor Peters (the man who had invited him to share his wife!). Karl in effect became his son — at any rate *de jure* — for Beethoven wrote to a friend, Councillor Dr Johann Nepomuk Kanka, in Prague, on the 6th of September 1816: '. . . I am now the real and bodily father of my deceased brother's child, and in this connection I could also have produced the second part of the *Zauberflöte*, seeing that I too have a Queen of the Night to contend with.' Beethoven addressed the boy not merely as 'My son' (as any uncle might his nephew, or older person a younger) but also, as he had written to Kanka, as 'My bodily son.' He and Karl set up a strange bachelor-*ménage*, usually with the help of a woman housekeeper and one or two young kitchen or chamber maids. On one occasion Karl told his uncle about a seduction attempt by one of the housemaids, when 'she sat up in bed with her breasts exposed and looked at me in a brazen way.' Some of those who claimed to have seen the domestic arrangements reported scenes of chaos and neglect, which is the now traditionally accepted view as to how Beethoven lived. And yet the shopping lists he noted down in the Conversation Books reveal that he frequently bought articles used by a fastidious, house-proud person: soap, brushes and other cleaning-materials, even mechanical kitchen gadgets.

Beethoven had Karl educated at a private academy, engaged the best music teachers for him, fed and clad him — but between expressions of almost stifling love subjected him to emotional blackmail and incitement against his mother. Old and understanding for his years, Karl joined Beethoven's cronies in writing down conversations which the deaf man could not hear, often spending late nights with them in noisy taverns and eating-houses. In the Conversation Books Karl emerges as an intelligent boy, with a good sense of humour — he used to write down jokes for his uncle which he had picked up and reported comic events at school and college, adding some witty observations of his own. The occasional episode of naughtiness also emerges, but he diligently did his homework and practised the piano, under the tuition of Joseph and Karl Czerny. In many of the replies he gave to Beethoven in the Conversation Books he appears on the defensive, having to calm his uncle's wrath and respond to his niggling and fault-finding. Clearly he was deeply unhappy. He ran away twice, only to be brought back. In the summer of 1826, by then a university student, he hid in the ruins of Rauhenstein castle and attempted suicide by putting a pistol to his head. The ball merely injured his skull, without penetrating it. He was taken to hospital, attended by all the medical experts his now distraught uncle could mobilize and eventually recovered. The entries in the Conversation Books of that period show his friends rallying round Beethoven after breaking the news to him — in writing as usual. Even the hated Johanna came to visit him to talk about the boy, and he seems to have been civil to her. When it became clear that Karl was not going to die the police arrested the youth — suicide being a punishable offence — until Beethoven's influence secured his release. The episode left Beethoven shaken, and for a time brought him to his senses. When Karl was asked why he had tried to kill himself, he replied, 'Because my uncle kept harassing me.'

In spite of the hateful words Beethoven directed at Johanna, there is no evidence that she ever replied in kind, or complained about his behaviour. No one reported that she spoke a single unkind word against him. She simply kept a dignified silence. My theory is that the acrimony on his part, and the patience on hers, represents a classic case of love gone sour; that they had been lovers but quarrelled; and perhaps even that in January 1806 she was pregnant by Ludwig, not his brother, and that Kaspar Anton Karl, already ailing, was persuaded to marry her to save Ludwig, the most celebrated man in Vienna, from scandal. An intriguing — if circumstantial — piece of evidence for that is that when, in 1820, Johanna gave birth to an illegitimate daughter, she chose to give the child a name which was — and still is — most uncommon: Ludovica. Would she have named her child after a mortal enemy? Was Beethoven her lover and made her pregnant, possibly twice, the second time during a reconciliation (one is occasionally hinted at) but then turned against her out of jealousy about her flighty behaviour? In March 1827, as Beethoven lay dying, a heavily-veiled woman visited him. His friends, ganging up against Johanna to the last, put it about that it was his other brother's wife, Therese; but in fact it was later suggested that Therese van Beethoven could not have been there at the time and that the veiled lady was indeed Johanna.

ALBANO MARIA JOHANNES BERG

Born: Vienna, 9th of February 1885
Father: Konrad Berg (1846–1900)
Mother: Johanna Maria Anna Braun (1851–1926)
Siblings: Hermann (1872–1921), Carl 'Charly' (1881–1952), Smaragda (1887–1953)
Married: 3rd of May 1911 to Helene Nahowski (d.1964)
Daughter: Born out of wedlock, 1903 to Marie Scheuchl
Died: Vienna, 24th of December 1935

Berg's first forename was registered as Albano, but his family dropped the *o*, and even as a small child he was known as Alban. He inherited his father's striking looks, grew to more than six foot in height and remained very slim throughout his life. His soft and feminine face, of the type that runs to puffiness and is generally almost beardless, could have been that of a kindly aunt, with a beaked nose set high in the face above a small and rather prim mouth. He was, however, a man's man: a keen athlete, powerful swimmer and a sporting motorist, and when World War I broke out was eager to fight (at any rate under the comfortable conditions which as a member of his class he felt he could expect). Mechanical gadgets and inventions fascinated him (something he shared with Puccini) and he always had to have the latest electric cigarette lighter, the latest motor car and, when these became available, the best Siemens multi-valve wireless sets.

While he was still a schoolboy, on holiday at the family's country estate, he fathered an illegitimate daughter by a Carinthian peasant girl, Marie Scheuch — probably the result of youthful fumblings that got out of control rather than a grand passion, and he was so upset by this calamity that he attempted suicide (without much determination, it appears). However, he took no further interest in either the child or her mother, who was paid off, as was the custom.

He had numerous early love affairs, most notably — though probably platonically — with a sixteen-year-old Austro-American girl, Frida Semler-Seabury: they continued to correspond long after she had gone to America to study at Wellesley College. She was effortlessly bilingual and a gifted poet in both English and German: Berg's early song *Traum* is set to her German words, and in America a play of hers was performed at college.

Berg's early music was lush and romantic, evolving by a natural process from that which had gone before. He was at first content to develop the language of his older contemporaries: Brahms, Richard Strauss, Zemlinsky and Hugo Wolf, and it suited his youthfully romantic nature, especially as he wanted mainly to write songs.

His family was wealthy above average middle-class standards. In a country where rented accommodation and urban flat-dwelling are the norm, the Bergs owned their own house in Vienna as well as a property in the country. His father died when he was fifteen and his subsequent devotion, both musical and personal, to the then 30-year-old painter-composer Arnold Schoenberg has been interpreted as a father-replacement. Although Schoenberg's Twelve-Note method of composing-by-numbers was not officially promulgated until 1923, it had long been simmering in his mind. It appealed to Berg especially, as he was afflicted by a kind of numeromania — not as severe as Bruckner's but it shaped his life as well as his compositions. For example, the numbers 10 and 23 were so important to him that he tried to arrange his life and significant happenings, like the completion of a work, to coincide with such dates. With Berg and another student, Anton von Webern, Schoenberg founded what became known as the Second Viennese School, which devoted itself to a system that laid down strict rules of numeric, Twelve-Note chromaticism (and later an even stricter form called 'serialism').

Towards the end of 1906, when Berg was 21, he encountered a strikingly beautiful, blonde music student, Helene Nahowski, who hoped for a career as an opera singer. They hit it off immediately and decided to marry, but her father, a civil servant, objected strongly — and on much the same grounds as Friedrich Wieck had tried to stop his daughter Clara from marrying Robert Schumann. Berg was not able to convince his prospective father-in-law that he could support himself, let alone a wife and family; he looked thin and unhealthy (a characteristic thought to indicate a predisposition to tuberculosis); and furthermore, Nahowski had discovered that Berg was addicted to opiates, as were many middle-class people. Berg's sister Smaragda had also caused a scandal: after a brief marriage she left her husband and 'came out' as a lesbian, embarking on a number of publicly conducted affairs. She made a half-hearted attempt at suicide, as Berg had done after the scandal of his illegitimate daughter (though Nahowski could not have known about that Berg peccadillo, which was not revealed until half a century after his death). In the self-consciously artistic circles of Schoenberg, Klimt, Kokoschka, the Mahlers, the satirist Karl Kraus and the aphorist Peter Altenberg (all of whom were part of a circle), unconventional behaviour was the norm. The Nahowskis, on the other hand, had a certain — yet dubious — position to maintain. They were middle-class (*bürgerlich*), but it seems their family cupboard, too, contained a skeleton that could be rattled. Vienna was always full of rumours (there was no freedom of speech), and some hinted that the Nahowskis' lifestyle was too grand for a mere *Beamter*, a civil servant; and that the reason for their prosperity was that Helene's mother was one of the Emperor Franz Josef's kept mistresses, with the husband's connivance.

Instead of retaliating (which would have deprived him of Helene) Berg wrote a rather pompous and self-important letter to his prospective father-in-law, attempting to refute each allegation point-by-point, neatly sub-sectioned with use of sarcastic quotation-marks: 'My "Intellectual Inferiority"; My "Impecuniousness"; My "Shattered Health"; The "Moral Depravity of members of my Family." ' When Nahowski finally did give his consent he insisted they marry not according to the Catholic religion both bride and bridegroom shared but in a Protestant church — to facilitate the divorce he felt would inevitably follow. They married on the 3rd of May 1911. Four years later, when relations had been mended, by which time Berg called Nahowski 'Papa' and enjoyed gifts of fine wine from him, Alban and Helene repeated the ceremony according to Catholic rites, as if to affirm that they did belong to each other for life.

To friends and strangers alike, Alban and Helene Berg appeared to be the perfect couple. When they were parted, loving letters, postcards and telegrams flew back and forth, always full of affection and concern for each others' well-being, and they spent much time and money on long-distance telephone calls (usually from post office to post office). If Berg did not have at least one letter a day he went out of his mind with worry. Both were anxious that the other should eat properly, and when Berg was travelling, especially abroad, he often gave an account of the food he ate, with friends or in restaurants. She, in turn, encouraged him to eat only nourishing food so that he would put on weight — the unspoken fear that equated thinness with tuberculosis. Many of his letters are amusingly illustrated and express a longing for the speediest reunion in a matter of days or weeks, and for eternal togetherness in the next life. Berg suffered from hay fever and asthma and had a predisposition for minor injuries like cuts and bruises to become septic — 'the carbuncle-spectre', he called it; indeed septicaemia killed him at the age of 50. He had a childlike, irrational fear of thunderstorms, a reluctance to travel by train in case there was a derailment or collision (this with good reason, because he was once an unhurt passenger in a train accident in which others were killed).

Most of all he suffered from hypochondria, though curiously enough he was aware that many illnesses had a psychosomatic basis. This was not generally understood at the time; but he had 'a sudden idea' in a letter to his wife on the 12th of August 1916, when he was making much of a sore throat, describing every minutely painful sensation of it, page after page: 'Don't look for physical reasons . . . there will be psychological ones! How could I forget this? In the last ten to twenty years (probably more like 30) I've been ill only when there was some kind of emotional disturbance ... the severe rheumatic attacks that began suddenly after Papa's death . . . .' Like Mahler (who underwent psychoanalysis for marital impotence), he was a patient of Sigmund Freud, though only by accident. During a holiday in the Austrian Dolomites, Freud happened to be staying in the same hotel and Berg, worried as usual, insisted that Freud should treat him for a sore throat. For all the good the great man's advice did him he might as well have consulted a doctor of music. During the autumn of 1923 Helene must have gone through a bad patch (though his letters were affectionate as always) and fashionably had herself psychoanalyzed by a colleague of Freud's. Berg was worried and annoyed and not a little jealous of the psychoanalyst, knowing perfectly well that a condition for such treatment is that the patient falls in love with his analyst. He called it a 'bestial science' and wrote to her on the 29th of November 1923:

Don't you go to any more 'sessions'. Tell the doctor I forbade you to have them, and in any case, if it had come to psychoanalytical treatment at all we'd have gone to Professor Freud or Dr Adler, whom we've known well for many years . . . . In a week we shall be laughing about this 'psychoanalysis' nonsense, all this about frustrated desires and sexuality . . . . One day in the snow and the Semmering forest will wash away all this spiritualist muck that's been poured all over your poor, pure little soul . . . . It takes two to make an unhappy marriage [!]. For *me* it's a happy one, the happiest I've ever seen . . . .

After Berg's death in 1935, Helene preserved Berg's study exactly as he left it and could hardly bear to enter it, let alone go through his papers. Several composers had expressed a wish to complete his unfinished opera *Lulu* but she forbade it — probably for a variety of reasons: it is a gruesome tale of sexual sleaze and murder, containing a part for Jack the Ripper; even the incomplete, two-act form was for a time banned by the authorities.

In 1965, 30 years after her husband's death, Helene Berg reluctantly brought out a big suitcase filled with her husband's letters to her, from which she 'selected,' cut and expurgated some 600 (together with a few carefully chosen ones of her own to him), though most had been destroyed. I purposely avoid the word 'edited,' for there is not a word of explanation of any kind, whether of persons referred to, of abbreviations or nicknames: the reader is left to cope with mysterious or private references, and often with the Viennese dialect. Identities are tantalizingly veiled by initials, and many dots in parentheses indicate the omission of doubtless fascinating gossip about celebrated contemporaries. The Bergs and all their friends were given silly nicknames, dozens of them. Outsiders were not excluded from these childish games — and Berg rather tactlessly addressed Gustav Mahler's widow, Alma, by her husband's own nickname for her, 'Almschi'.

Wealth and influence stood Berg in good stead when war broke out in 1914 and gained him a sympathetic medical examination as well as a 'cushy' office job in the War Ministry, followed a year later by a second examination which he failed altogether — having taken the precaution of turning up with a specially-acquired hangover. He was free to return to office duties for the rest of the war.

The Bergs lived comfortably enough, in one of the best neighbourhoods of Vienna, but in 1925 Alban experienced for the first time the luxurious life of the really rich. Alma Mahler had arranged that he should be invited to stay in the Prague mansion of a rich industrialist, Herbert Fuchs-Robettin, his 29-year-old wife Hanna, and their two small children. Hanna was her sister-in-law via Alma's third husband, Franz Werfel, and the Fuchs-Robettins offered Berg hospitality when parts of *Wozzek* were being performed in Prague under Zemlinsky's baton (Zemlinsky had been Alma's lover in her youth and was now Schoenberg's brother-in-law . . . not for nothing did Artur Schnitzler write his famous story of the Viennese sexual merry-go-round of that period, *La Ronde*). Berg's first letter home was filled with excited superlatives, as enthusiastic as that of a schoolboy allowed to stay in the Emperor's palace:

> Goldilocks, how can I tell you about everything? I live here quite simply in the Fuchses' villa . . . a life of luxury that is taken for granted. Oh if only I could pass some of it on to you!!! Every step I take is taken not by me but by motor car — and what a motor car! My hosts spoil me: my room has running warm water, a magnificent view, Roger-Gallet soap, rollerblinds, so that one can sleep nights with open windows. At seven in the morning a breakfast-trolley rolls to the side of my bed, and on it pastries (that would be something for you!) of which I simply couldn't eat enough. At eight o'clock a knock on the door, and in burst the two children, who would not be prevented from seeing the 'famous' composer. A seven-year-old boy and a three and a half-year-old little girl. And they're so sweet . . . .

Berg omitted to mention the real reason behind his excitement: the hostess, with whom he had fallen in love, and she with him. In the autumn he was back on another visit, and fired off to his wife more letters brimming with enthusiasm, raving about the luxurious life, about Herbert Fuchs-Robettin's kindnesses and the quality of his 'incredible' wine (he was reputed to have kept the best cellar in the Austro-Hungarian empire): 'Herbert and I drank a whole bottle'; also enthusiastic descriptions of the children and the exotic menus: ' . . . eggs with lobster, partridge with potatoes, fruit salad, cheese . . . and an indescribable Hennessy [brandy] . . . .' Only in passing did he mention 'Mopinka'; and that alone should have given it away, as Hanna had already been given a nickname. But he tried to reassure his wife that he was so enthusiastic about the hospitality 'not because it's so terrific here (my thoughts are already in Berlin) but to stop you worrying about Mopinka's charms'. There had been talk of Helene's joining him at the Fuchs-Robettins, and at first Berg was in favour of the idea; but then one senses, reading between the lines, that he was trying to put her off: the trip was hardly worthwhile, the journey too arduous — and anyway he would soon be home, etc.

Helene was no fool and smelt a rat. He wrote, in something of a panic, a letter so dissembling that it takes the breath away. Not only was he lying to Helene but at the same time tried to make *her* feel guilty:

> . . . It really is a bit much to have to 'reassure' you about me and Mopinka. Let me tell you, faithfulness is one of my chief virtues (I'm sure I must have been a dog in a previous incarnation and perhaps shall be in the next one, but in any case, to start from the beginning, may I die of distemper if I ever sin against faithfulness!). Faithfulness to you, and also to myself, to Music, to Schoenberg (and *he* makes this really hard for one) . . . . So, being of such conservative disposition, how could I help, my darling, to be anything but faithful to you and remain faithful for ever? Believe me as I believe the same of you . . . .

He was lying through his teeth. At the same time his enthusiasm for Hanna raised suspicions in her husband, too, though there is some indication that he turned a blind eye. She and Berg used 'letter-drops', having their correspondence discreetly conveyed via Berg's friends and pupils, including Hanna's brother, Franz Werfel, who must all have been at least partly in their confidence. None of her love letters survive (presumably Berg destroyed them, as did those other erring husbands, Elgar and Janacek, discard the letters of their mistresses) but fourteen of Berg's to Hanna were discovered by George Perle in the possession of Hanna's daughter, Dorothea, who allowed him to see them. This one was written nearly six-and-a-half years after Alban and Hanna's relationship began:

Hanna, I am using the opportunity of having transmitted to you a letter to write to you once again after a long, long time. I have longed for this opportunity. More than ever! For in the last few months I have been seized, more and more, by a terrible fear: that you might believe my love for you has cooled off, that during the years of 'resignation' the passion dominating my whole being might have turned into indifference. That could never be. For feelings like these which can only be measured in terms of eternity cannot have an end. This will never happen. You must believe me — and should months and years pass by without our seeing each other and without your hearing from me more than such pitiful letters as the one I'm just writing . . .
Not a day passes, not half a day, not a night when I do not think of you, not a week when I am not suddenly flooded by yearning, which submerges all my thoughts and feelings and wishes in an ardour that is not weaker by one iota than that of May 1925 — only still shadowed by a grief which since that time rules me more and more, and which, for a long time now, has made me into a double, or better said, a play-acting person. For you must know: everything that you may hear of me, and perhaps read about me, pertains, insofar as it is not completely false — as, for example, in a Zürich programme: 'A completely happy domesticity with which his wife has surrounded him, allows him to create without disturbance' — pertains to what is only peripheral. But it pertains only to a person who constitutes only an exterior layer of myself, to a part of me which in the course of recent years has separated itself (ah, how painfully separated) from my real existence, and has formed a detached being, the one I appear to be in my surroundings and in the world. In the frame of *this* life everything takes place that a normal life brings with it: vexation and joy, ill-humour and gaiety, interest and indifference, business and pleasure, art and nature— But believe me, Hanna (and now I can finally address you properly: *one* and *only eternal love*), all this pertains to this *exterior* person, the one I have been forced to present myself to my fellow human beings and whom you (thank God) have never known, and who (only in order to characterize him in *some* way) might for a time be fulfilled with the joys of motoring, but could never be able to compose *Lulu*. When I work and take hold of your pen . . . I am with you in my thoughts . . . .

Hanna had presented 'the famous composer' with a gold fountain-pen, which he used for writing *Lulu* and the Violin Concerto*, and of course for his love letters. Helene remained for many years after Berg's death unaware of the relationship, though his pupil Theodor Adorno tactlessly mentioned the affair to Helene eleven years after her husband's death, even boasting about his own role as *postillon d'amour*.

There was probably not a single composition of Berg's which was not inspired by love and friendship, or some amorous relationship. The fact that Marie, the murdered heroine in *Wozzek* (who had an illegitimate child), bore the same Christian name as Berg's mother and the mother of his own illegitimate daughter, as well as his own Catholic middle-name, is probably of no significance — Marie was the commonest girls' name in Catholic Austria. The lesbian element in the opera was doubtless inspired by his sister Smaragda; and, as Berg's biographer Mosco Carner pointed out, his wife Helene inspired all his music between op.1 to op. 6; Schoenberg and Webern the Chamber Concerto; Hanna the *Lyric Suite*; Manon ('Mutzi') Gropius, the tragic teenager who died from polio while he was writing the Violin Concerto (hence its inscription, 'To the memory of an Angel'). Berg was certainly in love with Manon; and the poignant Carinthian folksong in the same concerto recalls Marie, the Carinthian girl who bore his daughter — though mother and child were abandoned by him. A certain part of *Wozzek*, he told Helene on the 27th of May 1922, was *her* work: 'You composed it and I only wrote it down.'

While neither dodecaphonic nor serial methods lend themselves to the kind of old-fashioned romantic melody traditional for 400 years, both the Violin Concerto and *Wozzek* temper these musico-mathematical schemes with traditionally cherished ways of creating musical beauty. In the Violin Concerto Berg made use of the wistful folk melody already mentioned, as well as a J. S. Bach Chorale using Bach's original harmonization. Both provide, for those who do not take easily to what they might consider tuneless Twelve-Note music, welcome emotional relief — a cool spring in an arid desert. In devising his note-rows Berg made constant use of notes spelling out names, with the added advantage that in German notation B is called *H*, while the German *B* stands for the English/American musicians' B flat. This musical game has been played since the time of J. S. Bach (who signed himself with the musical notation B.A.C.H.) — and its rules have traditionally been flexible: thus non-musical letters like *i* can be declared rests, E flat, pronounced 'es' in German, appears as *s*, D flat as 'des' (see Chopin's chapter for an obscene interpretation of this note); and the letter *o* may be made into a kind of 'wild card' whose head can be placed between any spaces or on any lines. Such predestined arbitrariness is ideal for Twelve-Note tone rows (*Tonreihen*) of the kind the

---

*After Berg's death his widow mentioned in her will 'Berg's gold fountain-pen, a gift from Franz Werfel'. In fact it was Hanna's gift: Werfel merely acted as messenger, as he was one of his sister's letter-carriers.

Second Viennese School specialized in — and Berg entrusted his innermost love secrets to it. Researches conducted during the 1970s by the musicologists Mosco Carner and George Perle pointed to interesting encipherments in Berg's works, especially the *Lyric Suite*, which give a clue to intertwining musical and emotional tangles and is full of cyphers relating to his ten-year love for Hanna. The inevitability of the note rows in the *Lyric Suite* and other works was for decades praised by Bergians, unaware that the *Suite* is a veritable alphabet soup of initials and name references translated into musical notation, full of secret ciphers, private messages and numeric references to which only the composer and his secret mistress were party — the 'tunes', therefore, are arbitrary!

Berg did not witness most of the Nazis' evil as he died only two years after they came to power in Germany (and three-and-a-half years before they annexed Austria). They declared the works of the Second Viennese School *entartete Kunst* — perverted art, and as Twelve-Note music was hardly a suitable vehicle for providing the Führer with marching songs, and was the brainchild of the Jewish Arnold Schoenberg, performances were prohibited. In the autumn of 1934, the year the Nazis took over in Germany, Berg found his music banned from an Italian Festival along with that of Jewish composers. A petulant letter to the Italian composer G. F. Malipiero makes uncomfortable reading today, as it suggests that Berg condoned the banning of the works of his teacher Schoenberg and other Jews, yet felt aggrieved when it was his turn:

> Since the Berlin Reichstag fire not a single note of mine has been heard in Germany — although I am not a Jew. For with the present tendency in Austria to glorify the Jews as martyrs, *I am hardly ever performed.*

The italics indicate Berg's underlining, and the translation is Mosco Carner's. In fact it was all a misunderstanding: Berg's music had been removed from the schedules for practical reasons. But it does illustrate the sad truth that when artists want to be performed, or perform, they often forget their principles. Many joined the Nazi party not out of National Socialist conviction but because they hoped for artistic preferment: strange that Berg was one of them. Indeed he was willing to serve as adjudicator on a jury in Munich for the *Deutscher Musikverein*, knowing that any compositions by Jews had been barred from being entered: he confessed to feeling uncomfortable about it — but served all the same. Schoenberg and Zemlinsky left for America, while Webern remained, only to see one of his sons killed in the service of the Nazi *Wehrmacht*, and almost as soon as Vienna was liberated was himself accidentally shot dead by an American soldier. Among those who stayed, the self-excusatory term '*innere Emigration*' was much bandied about after the war: 'inner emigration' — meaning 'we stayed, but emigrated in spirit'.

During World War II, Helene Berg lived quietly in Vienna, feeding her birds and keeping a low profile. Although Berg could be a Jewish name the family had no difficulty in furnishing proof of their *echt*-Catholic, Aryan origins (Berg's mother in fact kept a shop selling cheap Catholic souvenirs near St Stephen's Cathedral). Yet the Nazis *still* banned his music, with that of the rest of the Second Viennese School: they considered the keyless 'equality' of the twelve semitones *Kulturbolschewismus* ('cultural bolshevism'). In 1941, one of Berg's brothers wrote to Helene that if Berg's works were played again she would benefit from the royalties; and suggested she should write a letter to Baldur von Schirach (the Nazi youth leader installed by Hitler in Vienna as *Stadtleiter*), reminding him that Berg had been cleared of all racial taint and asking whether the ban might be lifted. She replied with dignity:

> Dear Brother-in-law!
> Thank you for your letter and the suggestion — well-meant, I'm sure — which, however, I can only decline. Alban Berg's art is part of the eternal beauties of the divine and spiritual world. I could never bring myself to do anything which would have been against his convictions — he who was so untainted, who never made a single concession! It would be a desecration if his work were to be taken up by people who are — and must remain — so utterly alien to his works. Alban can happily rest until this hell-on-earth has worked itself out. His time will come — a more fitting time for him, of that I am convinced. You may argue that if he were performed I would have a less hard life. That I admit. But a concession bought with a sin against the Holy Spirit is for me an impossibility. My one and only purpose in life is to guard his artistic legacy. What else is there for me to do in this godless world? Sincerest regards to you and yours.
> Helene.

Helene did not find out about Berg's illegitimate daughter by the Carinthian girl Marie until shortly before her death at 91. She accidentally came across a faded photograph of a child whose resemblance to Berg was unmistakable and knew the truth at once. Even though the child was conceived and born before she and Alban had met, it must have been a painful discovery (more so even than the Fuchs-Robettin affair) as their own marriage had been childless. What she never found out about was the intimate programme of the *Lyric Suite*, of which almost every bar contains enciphered references to Alban's and Hanna's love. The 'official' dedication of the suite is to Zemlinsky, in gratitude for his having introduced Hanna to him. The movement titles alone suggest that this is no mere act of friendship for a male colleague: *Allegro giovale; Andante amoroso; Allegro misterioso/ Trio estatico; Presto delirando/ Largo desolato.* The 'unofficial' dedication consists of a special score, headed 'For My Hanna', which he annotated and secretly gave to her. She kept it hidden until her death, when it passed to her daughter Dorothea. Of its 90 pages, 82 have careful annotations in coloured pencils: red or blue for himself and Hanna. In the second movement both her children figure as musical ciphers, annotated and explained in green pencil. It has a quotation of the opening bars of Wagner's *Tristan* (the ultimate love opera), which was insinuated as a form of 'liberty' that disregards the strictly numeric nature of Twelve-Note composition. Another 'liberty' occurred in the Adagio, with a quotation from one of Zemlinsky's songs, a passage with the words, *Du bist mein Eigen, mein Eigen*. — 'You are mine own, mine own.' Berg wrote into the score, 'This, my Hanna, has permitted me other liberties! For example, that of constantly secreting into the music our initials, H F and A B; every movement and every section thereof is related to our numbers, 10 and 23. 'I have done this for You (for You alone — in spite of the 'official' dedication) . . . . May it be a small memorial to a great love.' The entire score is filled with detailed programmatic annotations of love, with repeatedly encrypted forms of 'their' numbers 10 and 23 or multiples (the metronome marks, too, are related to these numbers). The names ALBAN BERG and HANNA FUCHS-ROBETTIN have 10 letters and 2 × 10 letters (including spaces), respectively. The children are represented by Dorothea, nicknamed 'Dodo', appearing as two adjacent notes C in the tonic sol-fa naming, 'doh-doh'. The husband, Herbert Fuchs-Robettin, makes an appearance, purely for the sake of his famous wine cellar, in a quotation from Wozzek (*Lauter kühler Wein muss es sein* — 'Only pure, cool wine must it be'). The *Lyric Suite* ends in mid-air, the last bar remaining 'open', without so much as a barline to indicate where the end of the work would be — and it fades out on an interval of a third on the viola, which is directed to be repeated 'for ever', if desired.

In May 1930, Berg wrote to Hanna, 'No-one can take from me the certainty that in the afterlife we shall be united for ever . . . .' — and a few months later, 'How many years more before that eternity envelops us both?' He had not long to wait before he joined the ranks of those who would have been saved if antibiotics had been available earlier. Berg was always prone to trivial infections; and in the summer of 1935 he was stung by a swarm of wasps ('the warning finger of God pointing at me,' he wrote to Helene). Abscesses developed, which led to septicae-mia, and matters were not helped by the way Helene, at his request, lanced them with a pair of nail scissors.

Right up to the end of his life his numeromania haunted him. In December 1935, gravely ill and on his deathbed, he dreaded the coming of the 23rd, certain that the reaper would come on that day (just as he had blessed the 23rd June 1918, when Schoenberg had 'offered' him 'the *Du*- word', that is, suggested they use the second-person singular mode of close friends). The 23rd of December came and passed, and Berg breathed a sigh of relief — but died in the early hours of the 24th, Christmas Eve of 1935.

Helene Berg and Hanna Fuchs-Robettin both died in 1964, the mistress aged nearly 70, the wife 91.

LOUIS-HECTOR BERLIOZ

Born:	La Côte-St-André, Isère, 11th of December 1803
Father:	Louis-Joseph Berlioz (1776–1848)
Mother:	Marie-Antoinette Marmion
Married:	1st (3rd of October 1833) Harriet Smithson, (1800–1854)
Son:	Louis, b. 14th of August 1835
Married:	2nd 1854 Marie Geneviève Martin, alias Marie Recio (1814–1862)
Died:	Paris, 8th of March 1869

Berlioz was born on the '19th Frimaire, Year XI of the Republic' — for he was a child of the French Revolution. 'Year XI' was in fact 1803, the year Beethoven composed his *Eroica* symphony. Berlioz's parents were well-to-do, his father a prosperous doctor whose wide interests were reflected by his large library of books and music. He was one of five children (of whom three survived into adulthood) and had a happy childhood in the foothills of the Isère that approach the Alps. He learnt to play the flageolet (a descendant of the recorder) and later the flute and guitar. He is thought to have been the only notable composer who did not play the piano, though he must surely have been able to 'pick out' tunes. Some say that this handicap influenced his often startling orchestration and bold harmonic schemes.

Berlioz's first love was Estelle Duboeuf, whom he met one hot summer while their respective families were on vacation near Grenoble, a holiday relationship about which he romanticized all his life. At the time he was twelve years of age, she eighteen or nineteen. He recalled that their affair was ardent — at any rate on his part — and brief. Although they parted when the holiday ended, his feelings remained undimmed all his life. She became his ideal female and sowed in him the seeds for his lifelong, incurable romanticizing and exaggeration — about music as well as love — especially as it was a relationship that remained unconsummated and therefore untouched by sexual *ennui*. To his *Mémoires* he confided this steamy passage (adapted from W. J. Turner's translation) about this first 'affair', a passage Berlioz doubtless reworked many times in the light of subsequent attacks of nostalgia:

The name [Estelle] alone would have attracted my attention; it was dear to me on account of the pastoral of Florian, *Estelle et Némorin*, which I had taken from my father's library and had read secretly hundreds of times. But she who bore it was eighteen years old, had a tall and elegant figure, large eyes full of fire although they were always smiling, a mass of hair worthy of ornamenting the helmet of Achilles; feet, I will not say of an Andalusian but of a thoroughbred Parisian; and — rose-coloured lace-up boots! I had never seen such boots before .... You laugh! ... Well, I have forgotten. Each time I saw her I had an electric shock. I loved her, that's all. An infatuation took possession of me and never left me. I hoped for nothing .... I knew nothing ... but my heart felt a profound sadness. By day I hid myself in the fields of maize or the secret nooks of my grandfather's orchard like a wounded, dumb, suffering bird. Jealousy, that pale companion of the purest of loves, tortured me with every word any man addressed to my idol. I can still hear with a shiver the noise my uncle's spurs made when he danced with her. Everybody at home and in the neighbourhood made fun of this poor child of twelve years overcome by love beyond his powers. She herself was the first to be aware of it and was much amused, I am sure. One evening her aunt gave a party and they played a game in which it was necessary to divide into two groups. The gentlemen chose their ladies; I was purposely made to choose mine before everybody. But I did not dare, my heart was beating violently; I lowered my eyes in silence. Everyone made fun of me. When Mlle Estelle, taking my hand, said: 'No, I will choose! I take M. Hector.' Oh what misery! She also laughed, cruel as she was, looking down on me in all her beauty ....

First love can be a powerful experience, especially when fuelled by holiday euphoria. Berlioz saw Estelle only twice more, but her memory turned him towards composition, and inspired him to write, at the age of twenty, a little opera about young love — *Estelle et Némorin*. He sought her out again when he was 60 and she a widow of 67, his romantic childhood memory intact although she did not remember him .... 'My soul leapt out towards its idol the moment I set eyes on her again, as if she had still been in the splendour of her beauty,' he wrote. By then it was too late for romance.

Berlioz's relationships were all turbulent and, like the inspiration for Estelle, rooted in literature. The most frenzied of his affairs — and artistically the most fruitful — was his pursuit, courtship of, and eventual marriage to, the Anglo-Irish actress Harriet Smithson. It would never have happened had he not been obsessed with English literature and, in particular, the works of Shakespeare, which his father had in a French translation. The combination of William Shakespeare and Harriet Smithson was to him irresistible — though she captivated him more by her beauty than her acting talents, which were minimal. As in his exaggerated relationship (if one can call it that) with Estelle, he seemed to find true happiness only in romantic misery; fulfilled only when frustrated by unfulfilled longing. In the end, when he thought he had conquered her, he failed to see (through tears, no doubt) that in fact it was she who captured him — for she had by then fallen on hard times and was desperate for the security of a supportive man. Posterity owes gratitude to her as the inspirer of Berlioz's *Symphonie fantastique*.

Berlioz's *Mémoires* extravagantly chronicle his every thought and feeling for Harriet during his pursuit — and doubtless numerous thoughts and feelings he only imagined or wished he had had, but afterwards invented and embellished to heighten the effect. Berlioz was besotted — with Shakespeare, with every literary heroine, with Harriet Smithson — but most of all with himself, the amorous romantic. His overheated, overblown literary style is the French equivalent of the German *Weltschmerz*, which got Schumann, too. Berlioz suffered it to excess. For him *Weltschmerz* was not the 'pain of the world' that preoccupied him but his own feelings. He was an incurable *poseur*. Reading his *Mémoires* one gets the impression that he often did things only because he liked the idea of later elaborating them romantically, as if he saw himself as a kind of 'Jean Paul', or the Werther of music — though unlike Goethe's Werther it was not he but his beloved who came to a sticky end.

Berlioz conceived a plan for a symphony which was destined to become the *Symphonie fantastique*, with its *idée fixe* representing Harriet — though in fact the theme had already served its purpose for an eponymous *Hermine* — in an earlier cantata. And no harm in that — for what lover has not used an old turn of phrase (or, in the case of Chopin and Smetana, the same old waltz or polka) to woo a new mistress? For Berlioz the symphony itself had became an obsession for which he needed a subject, and that subject was Harriet. In his *Mémoires* he gives a blow-by-blow, scheme-by-scheme account of his breathless pursuit of her.

> I resolved that although my name was unknown to her I would by a supreme effort make it shine, so that even she would catch a glimpse of it. I would dare to do what no composer had attempted in France before: I would give a concert exclusively of my own works. I would show her, that not only she — that I too — was a dramatic artist.

The concert took place in May 1828, and the response bitterly disappointed him. He reported that the hall was 'only two-thirds full', but the *Revue Musicale* said it was 'almost empty'. Nevertheless, some influential critics liked the symphony, though the event made little impression on the object of Berlioz's chase. Engrossed in his own artistic egotism, he forgot that the woman he was chasing was also a self-obsessed performer, interested only in the impression *she* made on her audiences.

> Had these repercussions been sufficient to reach Miss Smithson and make her pause for an instant in the whirl of her own triumphs? Alas, I learned later that, engrossed in her brilliant career, of my concert, my struggles, my success, she had never heard a word.

It was some years before Berlioz managed to get an introduction to Harriet — his Ophelia, his Desdemona, his Juliet, depending on which Shakespeare play was the obsession of the moment. He had meanwhile won the Prix de Rome in 1830 and spent some time in that city, so his fame was spreading — everywhere except in Harriet's narrow horizon. Another thing had happened. Somewhere beneath the romantic histrionics there lurked a more practical young man. Tired of waiting for his heroine to take notice of him and his achievements, he had formed an attachment to the nineteen-year-old Camille Marie-Denise Moke (1811–1875), on the principle that a bird in the hand was better than an unattainable one on the stage. She was a piano teacher at the *Institut Orthopédique* where Berlioz also taught — not composition but the guitar.

The manner in which Hector and Camille became lovers reflects little credit on either of them, for Berlioz insinuated himself into her life through being a secret messenger, a *postillon d'amour*, between her and her suitor, the German composer Ferdinand Hiller (1811–1885). Having gained closer access to Camille, Berlioz pushed the younger man aside and graduated from postman to lover — though she may well have taken a fancy to him. Camille was later widely regarded as a nymphomaniac, who had flings also with Liszt and Chopin (once using the latter's rooms in his absence for an assignation with the amorous Abbé, and Chopin was not pleased when he found out).

Camille and Berlioz began a passionate affair (could Berlioz ever have had anything less?) which led to their official engagement — though this may have been little more than his marking out of an amatory territory, a do-not-touch warning to others while he went off on a prolonged stay in Rome. By the time he returned she had tired of waiting for him and had started a new affair, with an older man, a fellow-pianist, Camille Pleyel (1788–1855), who curiously shared with his wife-to-be the same forename. When Berlioz found he had been jilted he made an hysterical scene. Overdramatizing as usual, he rushed out to buy a woman's outfit and a wig to disguise himself, and two pistols. His plan was to waylay and 'assassinate' Camille and her mother (whom he had accused of scheming and called a 'hippopotamus') as well as the innocent husband. Then he would kill himself. Needless to say, Berlioz did not get beyond the fancy-dress stage. He extricated himself from the dramatic scenario (which of course he merely fantasized so that he could write about it entertainingly in his *Mémoires*) by claiming that the sheer excitement engendered by the planned deed made him so sick that he 'vomited violently for an hour' — a feat for the medical record books and enough to deter the most determined assassin. But, just to be on the safe side, he left instructions about the completion of his new symphony. He exacted a more subtle revenge on the Moke-Pleyel clan by publishing a novel, *Euphonia*, in which Camille is portrayed as Ellimac and her mother as Ellianac (Camille and *canaille* — 'bitch' — respectively, spelt backwards). All the characters except the hero, Rotceh (Hector reversed) are crushed to death in a steel pavilion, together with the mother's lovers. When Hector and Camille Marie-Denise met again in real life, it was on the concert platform in London, on the 28th of April 1852, when she was playing the solo piano part in Weber's *Konzertstück* and he was conducting. She later claimed that he took revenge on her for having jilted him by crashing in the orchestra too early and ruining her solo.

Camille and Camille Pleyel, incidentally, proved even less happy together than were Berlioz and his successive wives. Four years after they married, Mme Pleyel left the house one evening and announced that she was spending the night with a young man, returning to her husband in the morning considerably worse for wear. Pleyel forgave her, but their reconciliation lasted only a few days, before she left for good and he eventually obtained a legal separation.

In the meantime Harriet, Berlioz's Irish Shakespearean obsession, was as remote as ever. When they finally met, it was not as a result of his theatrical scheming but through the hand of coincidence.

> For two years I had heard nothing of the fair Ophelia. I had no idea where she was, whether in England, Scotland or America; and here I was, arriving home from Italy at exactly the same moment as she reappeared after a tour of Northern Europe. We had just missed meeting each other — and in the same house! I had taken an apartment which she had left the previous evening!

It was clearly the signal as well as the opportunity for setting up a formal meeting. Berlioz began all over again to lay siege to his fair Ophelia, his Juliet, Desdemona. Another concert was arranged, in the hope that this one would make a greater impression on her than the last. Its purpose was to present to the world and, he hoped, to Harriet, the now completed *Symphonie fantastique*, as well as its sequel, *Lélio*. 'The subject of this musical drama,' he wrote, 'was none other than my love for Miss Smithson and the anguish and bad dreams it brought me.' He persuaded friends to insinuate themselves into her company and, almost by force, bundle her into a carriage and take her to the performance.

> On the way she glanced at the programme. The title of the symphony and the headings of the various movements somewhat astonished her. But it never so much as occurred to her that the heroine of this strange and doleful drama might be herself. But when she heard the lines 'Oh if I could only find her, the Juliet, the Ophelia for whom my heart cries out! Oh if I could drink deep of the mingled joy and sadness that real love offers us, and on some autumn evening on some wild heath with that north wind blowing over it, lie in her arms and sleep a last, long, sorrowful sleep!' 'God,' she thought, 'Juliet? Ophelia? Am I dreaming? I can no longer doubt it. It is of me he speaks.' From that moment, she has often told me, she felt the room reel about her; she no longer heard the music but sat in a dream; and at the end returned home like a sleepwalker.

The date was the 9th of December 1832. When Berlioz returned from Rome (where he lodged at the Villa Medici and was given something of a rough time by his fellow-students, who saw in this *poseur* little more than an insufferably vain, affected French fop) he had no inkling that Harriet's fortunes had taken a sharp downward turn. The public had tired of her and her theatrical company was about to go bankrupt. She also had the misfortune of breaking a leg and, worse, the English press all but ignored the accident. Indeed, there were dark hints that her leg was not broken at all and that the whole thing had been a publicity stunt to gain sympathy and ward off a growing band of creditors. To her, therefore, the sudden offer of a safe haven of matrimony, even an uncertain union with a struggling composer, looked decidedly attractive.

In the summer of 1833, Henriette Smithson being bankrupt and still weak, I married her, in the face of violent opposition from her family as well as my own. But she was mine, and I had defied the world.

Not quite his, yet. First he had to defy his father, who objected strongly to his son's marrying an actress, and a foreign one at that; and French law forbade marriage without parental consent. Berlioz had to start a court action against his own father to obtain an injunction. He probably regretted its success. After his marriage to Harriet, on the 3rd of October 1833, Berlioz's *Mémoires* grow decidedly less gushing about his deeper feelings, or indeed his shallower ones. A son, Louis, was born in August of the following year, and he and Harriet were reasonably happy for a few years. Before long he began to find domestic life oppressive. He was doubtless an inadequate house-husband, even by the one-sided standards of the time, and took his art more seriously than his marriage. The Shakespearian ideal he had built up so foolishly round his stage idol collapsed into the boring domesticity of dirty nappies and squalling children. If ever he said 'my wife does not understand me' it would have been close to the truth, for he spoke no English and Harriet never bothered to learn French. She needed his support, and he was unable to give it. What he wanted was a romantic mistress, not a mundane wife. He longed to go on his musical travels — and she tried to prevent him from doing so. There are no further references in Berlioz's *Mémoires* to his Ophelia, Juliet or Desdemona. It is a cold and factual 'my wife'. He planned a trip to Brussels, to earn much-needed money to keep the home financially solvent. He prepared to leave on the comparatively short journey.

Before I could do so, something like a *coup d'état* was needed to enable me to go. On one pretext or another my wife had always been opposed to any plans for travelling. An insane jealousy, for which I had given her no grounds, was her driving motive. I had to smuggle my luggage and bundles of music out of the house, leaving behind a letter explaining my disappearance.

No grounds for jealously? Berlioz did not travel to Brussels alone and had no intention of doing so. He was accompanied by Marie Recio, an old-established mistress and minor opera singer of mixed French and Spanish origin. He tried to explain himself, somewhat disingenuously:

I had a travelling-companion who has followed me in my various expeditions. By dint of being accused of infidelity and incessantly nagged and harassed, always unjustly, I could find no rest or peace at home. I came at last to enjoy in actual fact that which had been so wrongly [!] imputed to me.

Marie's real name was Marie Martin and, although she had a hold over Berlioz, it was not for artistic reasons: as a singer she rated poorly and was able to obtain only secondary roles at the Paris Opéra. When he returned from Brussels he went back to Harriet, but soon left again, this time for Germany, intending to travel alone. Marie, however, insisted on accompanying him, to which arrangement he agreed with mixed feelings. This time the roles in the chase were reversed: she was the pursuer, he the quarry. And although she cramped his style by her presence she made herself useful by acting, in effect, as his manager, cashier and book-keeper. Unlike Harriet the scatterbrained actress, Marie was a good cook and a frugal housekeeper. Berlioz's personal life between 1840 and 1842 is shrouded in some mystery, but his wife played little part in it; and a contemporary wrote of 'the various women of the stage, singers, dancers and supernumeraries who caused such suffering to poor Ophelia'. Harriet's health had gone into a gradual decline, the arduous life as a touring actress having taken its toll; and by 1854 she was dead. To his credit, Berlioz never abandoned Harriet but supported her and retained to the end a touching gratitude for the creative force she inspired in him during his tempestuous youth.

Seven months later, however, Berlioz capitulated to Marie. 'I married again. It was my duty,' he writes, tersely. But Marie, too, died — after eight years of marriage. Soon after Marie's death, a friend gave him a cemetery plot in a grander graveyard. He had her body dug up — and made it his business to witness the exhumation. 'It was a harrowing experience and I was deeply affected by it. But it was nothing to what fate had in store for me.' Not long afterwards the same scene was repeated, when Harriet's body, too, had to be removed, because the cemetery at Montmarte was to be closed. Again he insisted on being present to watch her corrupted remains being uncovered, and described the gravedigger's gruesome work in minute detail. Did he, like Bruckner, have a morbid fascination with dead bodies, or even suppressed necrophiliac tendencies? The charitable view is that he thought of himself as a kind of Hamlet, acting out the graveyard scene.

The two dead women now lie in peace, awaiting the time when I shall bring my own share of corruption to the same charnel-house. I am in my 61st year. Past hopes, past illusions, past high thoughts and lofty conceptions. My son is almost always far away from me. I am alone. My contempt for the folly and baseness of mankind, my hatred of the atrocious cruelty of man, have never been so intense. Shakespeare! Shakespeare! Where is he? Where art thou? I feel as if he alone among all men who have ever lived can understand me, must have understood us both . . . poor unhappy artists, loving yet wounding one another. Shakespeare! You were a man. You, if you still exist, must be a refuge for the wretched. It is you that is our father, our father in heaven, if there is a heaven. I say hourly to Death: ' When you will.' Why does he delay?

He did not delay long; Berlioz died on the 8th of March 1869 in Paris.

ALEXANDRE CÉSAR LÉOPOLD (GEORGES) BIZET

Born:	25th of October 1838
Father:	Adolphe Amand Bizet (1810–1886)
Mother:	Aimée Bizet, née Delsarte, or del Sarte, or Delzart (1815–1861)
Married:	Geneviève Halévy (3rd of June 1869) died 19th of December 1926
Children:	Jean Reiter (illegitimate) June 1862; Jacques 10th of July 1872
Died:	Bougival, near Paris, 3rd of June 1875

Alexandre César Léopold Bizet, always known as Georges though not so christened, was the son of a hairdresser-wigmaker who turned singing-teacher, and who also composed some music. His mother taught him to read both music and words at the age of four (the alphabet and the musical scale simultaneously) followed by more systematic music lessons from his father. In 1846, at the age of eight, he gave the first indication of his phenomenal, almost Mozartian, musical memory; and on the 9th of October 1848, before he had celebrated his tenth birthday, he was admitted to the Paris Conservatoire. At eleven he won First Prize in *solfège* (the curious French adaptation of the Tonic Sol-Fa system by which they sing, and memorize, all music, instrumental as well as vocal), a tribute to parental teaching. After that he carried off one prize after another. Needless to say, Bizet duly won the Rome Prize, with its obligatory three-year residence at the Villa Medici. In September 1860, however, he left Rome hurriedly when he received news that his mother had been taken ill. His return home enabled him to reactivate some of his interrupted Paris love affairs: almost as soon as he returned, he told Gounod that he was conducting two relationships simultaneously (probably trying to make the 'philandering monk' jealous). His mother's condition improved for a while, but she died on the 8th of September 1861, aged only 46. He was grief-stricken, but the Bizets' maid, Marie Reiter, evidently consoled him, for exactly nine months after his mother's death Marie gave birth to a son, Jean, whom Georges, then only 23, was happy to acknowledge as his. It is not known whether he counted Marie as a love affair or, as used to be the custom in middle-class homes, a convenient and safe provider of sex kept on the premises for the benefit of the son of the house. Bizet's father, too, behaved honorably towards her and retained her in service. Little Jean was also accepted into the household and brought up as a 'cousin'. When he grew up he became an army officer, married and had children, and later ran the printing-plant of *Le Temps*. He died in 1939. Marie tended Georges Bizet in his final illness (which must have been poignant for his wife), then looked after Bizet's father, and after his death, remained in Geneviève's household until 1913.

In 1863, Bizet's father bought a plot of land in Le Vésinet, near Paris, and had two small houses built on it: summer residences, one for himself and the other for his son. Two years later an adjacent piece of land was taken by a Comtesse de

Moreton de Chabrillan. On one of her preliminary inspection trips to supervise the building work she and Georges met on a train, he learned her identity and gradually pieced together her story. She was Céleste Mogador, the daughter of a loose-living young woman and an unknown soldier — unknown in the paternity sense, not as an anonymous fallen hero. Céleste was or had been an actress, a novelist, courtesan, circus horsewoman, playwright and author of a volume of memoirs. She had been mistress to artists, musicians and writers, including Alfred de Musset, but finally landed a part-time diplomat, Count Lionel de Moreton de Chabrillan, who died at his post in Melbourne, Australia, as French consul. Bizet probably knew of her already, as she had in the previous year scored a success with a play adapted from one of her novels by Alexandre Dumas the elder. (After her death, a second volume of memoirs was discovered, in which Bizet figures as a rather taciturn and glum figure.) He spent much time in her company, at her piano and in her bed, so perhaps there was little occasion for conversation. She described herself as feckless, moody, sultry and determined to get what she wanted. Several writers, most notably Winton Dean, who wrote the most important English Bizet biography as well as the *Grove* article, have detected in her a prototype for Carmen herself.

In 1867, Bizet announced his engagement to the beautiful eighteen-year-old second daughter of his teacher Jacques Fromental Halévy, but the family forbade the marriage: perhaps they discovered that he had a weak heart, or had heard rumours of his relationship with Céleste Mogador. 'My hopes are dashed,' he wrote. 'The family are insisting on their rights! I am very unhappy.' Later he claimed that the Halévys had described him as a gipsy and vagabond; and felt obliged to assure Mme Halévy that no actress or 'lady of the theatre' would ever cross his threshold again. In the following year, soon after the first performance of *La jolie fille de Perth*, and while working on *Roma*, in effect his second symphony, he suffered from depression and severe attacks of *angina pectoris*, which lasted until and throughout July and August 1868. A year later, the Halévys relented and Georges became re-engaged to Geneviève, who was then still only twenty.

They married on the 3rd of June 1869. Her portrait by Élie Delaunay ('his finest work') is in the Louvre, and shows dark, melancholy eyes, 'gazing like black stars': Maupassant was said to have been infatuated with her. She had a gift for coining Proustian aphorisms, tinged with a sharp wit .

Geneviève's sharp tongue and Georges' bouts of temper, combined with his touchiness bordering on persecution mania, resulted in many quarrels, but apart from one brief episode, they stayed loyally together.

On the 10th July 1872, when Georges was 34 and Geneviève 23, they had a son, whom they named Jacques, after his grandfather, Jacques Fromental Halévy. Apart from the birth of Jacques, it was not a good year for the Bizets. In May, his one-act opera *Djamileh* had failed, and three months after the baby's birth *L'Arlésienne* met with a hostile reception (a work of which Richard Strauss said, 'Seldom has more been expressed in fewer notes'). Bizet never knew Jacques beyond infancy: the child was only three when his father died.

The Bizets' marriage was not a success, and in 1874 Georges and Geneviève had a short trial separation, after which they lived together until his final illness and death. At the beginning of March 1875 Bizet was, in effect, knighted, being created *Chevalier de la Légion d'honneur*. At the end of March he was taken seriously ill. A long and slow convalescence followed, and all seemed well, but in May he complained of a curious double-tinnitus in his head. By the early summer his former ailments erupted — especially his rheumatism. Nevertheless, as a passionately keen swimmer, he went bathing in the Seine. He developed a high fever, suffered two heart attacks on consecutive days and died on the 3rd of June, at Bougival, near Paris.

Debussy, who considered Bizet a greater composer than Berlioz, said that after his death French music was 'like a pretty widow who is too weak to take care of herself and falls into the hands of strangers who maltreat her', and added, 'Ah, to have written *Carmen*!'. Geneviève remained Bizet's beautiful widow for eleven years then, on the 8th of October 1886, she married the noted French lawyer Émile Straus.

JOHANNES BRAHMS

Born:	Hamburg, 7th of May 1833
Father:	Johann Jacob Brahms (1806–1872)
Mother:	Johanna Henrike Christiane Nissen (1789 –1865)
Sister:	Elisabeth Wilhelmine Louise (1830–1892)
Brother:	Friedrich Fritz (1835–1885)
Died:	3rd of April 1897

Numerous women figured in Brahms's life, all either unattainable, or if attained, rejected: Beethoven's story all over again. Brahms's difficulty in forming lasting relationships with women have traditionally been blamed on the fact that he spent his youth as a brothel pianist in Hamburg to earn money and help to feed his family. The experience may indeed have left indelible marks on his personality, but on the other hand, it might equally well have been character-forming, giving him a greater insight into human nature than he could have gained playing the organ in church like Bruckner — and God knows *he* had his troubles, too.

The musicologist Max Friedländer, who knew Brahms well, recalled the composer's own account of how as a child he was befriended by the prostitutes he accompanied and who cuddled him when he rested from his stints as bar pianist:

> When the sailing ships made port after months at sea, the sailors would emerge from them like beasts of prey, looking for women. And these half-clad girls would try to drive the men even wilder, so they used to take me on their laps between dances, kiss, caress and excite me. That was my first impression of the love of women . . . .

It was a love he returned many times over and throughout his life: uncomplicated, uncommitted — and paid for. The wonder is that it did not ruin his health in those days of primitive prophylaxis, as it had Schubert's, Schumann's, possibly Beethoven's and that of many other composers.

Like Mozart, Haydn, Beethoven, Clara Schumann and others, Brahms was a child prodigy. But he was the son of a poor Hamburg tavern musician, a *Bierfiedler,* not a court musician. As soon as he had gained some proficiency as a pianist Brahms followed his father into the dockside *Kneipen,* the taverns which also served as pick-up places for sailors and prostitutes. The family lived in St Pauli, not far from the present *Reeperbahn* in the red-light district, a street popularly known as *Ehebrechergang* (Adulterers' Alley). Prostitutes were not only neighbours but family friends.

Brahms loved women, probably to excess, but was afraid of long-term commitments; and as cynical about marriage as any divorce court judge. One of his favourite sayings was 'I never married, unfortunately — and therefore remained single, thank God!' In the 1920s and early 30s Robert Schauffler carried out researches among the composer's surviving friends and confidants for his book, *The Unknown Brahms*, and tried to piece together fragments of information that had been omitted or smudged over by the official biographers who knew but would not tell. His English biographer, Florence May, who witnessed many of his gruff flirtations, was a piano pupil (and probably the object of his attention), wrote with guarded circumlocution, 'Several quite independant informants have concurred in describing the author as being . . . something less than indifferent to the society of ladies, especially of young ones.' Brahms never trusted women and, even when he formed a potentially loving friendship with one, he always managed to rebuff her with sudden outbursts, blurting out deeply wounding remarks, perhaps about her playing or singing. He longed for 'respectable' women (the appropriate German word is *anständig*, something like 'decent') and frequently fell in love with them, especially if they were singers: of the nine 'respectable' women known to have figured in his love or affections (Agathe, Bertha, Luise, Elisabet, Hermine, Ottilie, Alice, Clara and Julie) five were professional singers, and the rest sang to drawing-room standard. But he kept returning to the unrespectable ones, mostly street-women, to whom he had no obligations. He was unfailingly generous and they knew him by name — sometimes calling out '*Guten Tag, Herr Doktor!*' when he was walking in Vienna with friends, leaving him not in the least embarrassed or discomfited. 'I want you to know that I have never made a married woman or *Fräulein* unhappy,' Brahms said to a friend; and towards the end of his life he recounted with pride that he had never endangered a marriage or seduced a girl 'from a good family'. Yet there were stories, and when the city of Leipzig invited him to become Cantor at St Thomas's, a post formerly held by J. S. Bach, the municipal worthies withdrew the invitation after the mayor had objected to his 'dissolute behaviour'. No further explanation was given.

Brahms feared rejection and dreaded the idea of 'offending' a woman he loved and respected — a not uncommon condition among men, which is why he was drawn to the 'rough trade'. After his death, Schauffler tried to glean information from his housekeeper; but she simply said, 'He was a very naughty old gentleman.'

At 20, Brahms had decided to seek his fortune by travelling, setting out in the romantic, unplanned manner idealized in many of his own songs and those of Schubert. In Düsseldorf he called on the celebrated music journalist and composer Robert Schumann, to find not only friendship but an immediate, attraction to his wife Clara. She, too, was attracted to Brahms, then still a youth with beautiful blond hair. Brahms had admired Schumann from afar, but now it was almost too late for friendship, as the older composer was already showing signs of his advancing insanity. Sharing their concern for Robert, Brahms and Clara almost inevitably fell in love, although both tried to deny it at first, to themselves and to each other. In 1854, having reluctantly continued his artistic travels,

Brahms received news that Robert Schumann had tried to drown himself in the river Rhine. He hurried back to Clara and supported her during Schumann's dissolution. She was 35, fifteen years older than Brahms (almost the same age-difference as between his father and his mother, who was 17 years her husband's senior) and there was certainly a mother-son element in their relationship.

On his suggestion (although German etiquette lays down that it should come from the woman) he proposed they address each other as *Du*, while Clara felt the need to justify this display of intimacy in the presence of others, so that they would not misconstrue their relationship: 'I could hardly refuse him, for after all I love him as deeply as I would a son . . . .' After Robert Schumann had been taken to the lunatic asylum at Endenich, which he was never to leave, Brahms moved in with Clara and the children. He protected her like a husband. The poignant last entry in Robert's *Household Account Book* is dated February 1854 — a few days after he had entered a final 'F-sign' on St Valentine's Day to record that he had made love to his wife, doubtless for the last time. From the 27th of February the Household Accounts are kept in Brahms's hand. There have been suggestions that Clara Schumann's last child, Felix, was really Brahms's, but it seems unlikely.

When Robert died, Clara moved with her children to her mother's home in Berlin, and Brahms in sadness resumed his travels. In 1856 he took her to Switzerland, chaperoned by his sister Elisabeth (Elise). When Clara went on a concert tour of England he wanted to follow but drew back because they feared they might be taken for an established couple. In the summer of 1858, while in Göttingen with Clara, he met and fell in love with Agathe von Siebold, a fine singer and the daughter of a university professor in the city. Most of the songs from his opp. 14, 19 and 20 owe their existence to her, as does his later G major Sextet — cast throughout in a wistfully valedictory mood, as if the affair had fizzled out before it — and the Sextet — even got under way. Brahms's feelings were confused — especially as Clara, now showing signs of jealousy, abruptly left Göttingen and was forced to admit to herself that her love for Brahms was more than that of a mother for her son.

Brahms and Agathe became engaged and exchanged rings; but when, in 1859, Clara played his D minor Piano Concerto in Hanover, he was depressed not only by its cool reception but also its associations with Schumann's suicide attempt (which had inspired him to write it). He suddenly realized that by committing himself to Agathe he might lose Clara and, even while wearing Agathe's ring, wrote a strange love letter to her (Agathe), emotionally spattered with exclamation-marks and containing a cruel escape clause:

I love you! I must see you again! But I cannot bear the prospect of wearing fetters! Write and tell me whether to see you again, to take you in my arms, to kiss you and tell you that I love you!

Agathe took offence and broke off the engagement — which no doubt was what Brahms had hoped: he felt unable to go through with the marriage and handed her the excuse for rejecting him. Six years later they were still pining for each other, and in the second string Sextet, which he wrote in 1864–5, he repeatedly calls her name — in the nearest 'spelling' musical notation allows. The passage where the first and second violins play A - G - A -D - E was explained by Brahms to his friend Joseph Gänsbacher unequivocally: 'At this point I freed myself from my final love affair.'

Brahms had experienced in Hamburg his first attraction to Viennese female charm when he was 'bewitched by a natural, cheerful girl', a singer called Bertha Porubszky. She sang a little Austrian *Ländler* to him, which he later transformed into one of the two Songs op.91 for voice, piano and viola — the lilting *Geistliches Wiegenlied,* the Virgin's Cradle song. The original *Ländler* was far from *geistlich,* with the words, 'If you think you can force anyone into love, think again.'

Robert Schauffler questioned a man called Oscar Ullmann, who used to meet Brahms in Ischl and who told him of a young woman he knew who confessed to having had an affair with the composer. She reported that he was 'a passionate but awkward lover'. After he settled in Vienna he met another singer, Luise Dustmann, a divorcée whose performance in the title role of Beethoven's *Fidelio* he admired. She responded to his first approaches with a letter that betrayed a curiously unladylike forwardness, suggesting a rendez-vous the very next day. She always signed herself 'Fidelio' and was the only person ever to address Johannes with the Viennese diminutive 'Hansi'. The progress, if any, of their affair, is shrouded in mystery but there exists a letter containing a significant double meaning. After a visit during which he had played her piano with great enthusiasm she wrote: 'One day I'll invite that Hamburg fellow not for my piano but for me. Perhaps he'll succeed in making my own untuned strings twang . . . .'

The Luise relationship petered out as the others had done. In Vienna, Brahms formed a Ladies Choir (as he had done in Hamburg) and promptly proposed marriage to one of its members. But having secretly learned that she had just become engaged to a doctor, he knew she would not accept him; so it was another empty gesture.

Brahms was also taken with a sixteen-year-old 'blond enchantress', Baroness Elisabeth von Stockhausen, who had sought him out for piano lessons. It was almost a pre-echo of the Gustav-Alma Mahler relationship, as she was already under the spell of her teacher Julius Epstein, who told Brahms that if he did not fall in love with her he would be breaking a law of nature. Brahms could not cope with someone so young, so beautiful and so gifted (she could play entire symphonies on the piano after two hearings). Something must have happened, for he abruptly stopped her lessons and sent her back to Epstein. Brahms's housekeeper, Frau Truxa, reported that the girl's picture, which had stood on his desk, suddenly disappeared. He gave her the empty frame and growled, 'There — you can put your husband's picture in it instead!' Elisabeth married another composer, Heinrich von Herzogenberg but, sadly, she died young.

Then Brahms told his friend Max Kalbeck that he was once again in love. The lady was another young singer, Hermine Spies, pretty if a little on the dumpy side, with an amiable moon-face, whom he met after she had sung some of his songs. A critic summed her up in a sentence, 'A serious voice but a merry girl.' She had a deep contralto voice of the kind that captivated Brahms, and a number of songs resulted from this friendship, too. He called her 'my songstress', or 'my pretty little Rhine Maiden', and said 'she is like Shakespeare's Hermione but without the o . . . .' Another writer described Hermine as 'a child of nature, full of ready humour' — full of playful facetiousness behind which she doubtless 'tried to disguise the obvious awe she felt for a composer who was very famous and so much her senior'. She herself, four years later, confided to a mutual friend, 'He's a one, that Brahms. Once again I was quite overwhelmed by him, enraptured and carried away and lost my head. How sweet he was! In a really summery, cheerful, youthful mood. He's eternally young.'

Clara Schumann's life as a travelling pianist inevitably meant that she and Johannes moved apart not only physically but also emotionally. Their letters became calmer, if not cooler, and when Brahms heard that she found it difficult to make ends meet he offered her large sums of money ('Here am I, swimming in it, and no-one to use it on . . . .'). In 1893, he wrote to her from his holiday home in Bad Ischl:

Dear Clara . . .
I'm tempted to write out for you a little piano piece because I'd dearly like to know how you'd get on with it. It's seething with dissonances! They may be all right and explainable — but maybe you won't like them . . . . The little piece is exceptionally melancholy, and it's not enough to say 'play it very slowly'. Every bar, every note must sound like a *ritardando*, as if all sadness were being squeezed out, with desire and satisfaction! Lord God what fun you're going to have with this description . . . .

The piece is No.1 of the *Vier Klavierstücke*, op. 119, but Clara did not live to perform it. She died on the 21st of May 1896, after suffering two strokes. News of her death reached him while he was on holiday in Ischl. He hurried to Frankfurt, but in his confusion got on the wrong train and arrived after a 40-hour journey. According to one source he was just in time to see the coffin disappear, and according to another that the mourners had dispersed and that he stood for a long time, alone, staring at her grave.

Then he composed his *Four Serious Songs*. On his return to Ischl from the funeral Brahms developed jaundice, a sign of the liver cancer of which he died less than a year later. His last letter was written to Karoline Brahms, his stepmother, and dated the 29th of March 1897, when he was already on his deathbed, though he may not have known how serious his condition really was. As always he played down his troubles:

> Dear Mother,
> I thought I'd lie down a little, so I'm not able to write very well. Don't worry about me, nothing in my condition has changed, and as usual all I lack is patience.
> From the heart, your Johannes.

He died five days later, on 3rd April 1897, a confirmed but regretful bachelor.

There is hardly a Brahms work that does not express a wistful yearning — from the aching melancholy of the *Clarinet Quintet* and the almost Mahlerian tragedy of the *Four Serious Songs* to the serene slow movements of the piano concertos and symphonies:

> I missed the boat. When I wanted to settle down I was in no position to support a woman in a manner that would have been appropriate. At the time when I most wished to be a married man my things were hissed off concert platforms, or at any rate were received with icy coolness [a gross exaggeration]. I could bear such things quite well. I knew their worth and I knew that eventually my fortunes would turn. When after yet another fiasco I returned to my lonely room I didn't feel so bad about it on my own. Quite the contrary! But if in such moments I'd had to come home to a wife and meet her anxiously questioning eyes, and been obliged to say to her, 'Again — another disaster' — I would not have been able to bear it.

ANTON BRUCKNER

Born:	Ansfelden, Upper Austria, 4th of September 1824
Father:	Anton Bruckner, 1791–1837
Mother:	Therese Helm. Twelve brothers and sisters, five surviving infancy
Died:	Vienna, 8th of October 1896.

A fierce Catholic upbringing made Bruckner into an honest and simple man, deeply religious and free from artifice or sophistication — but left him with a bundle of neuroses that would have had Sigmund Freud whistling through his teeth. Fashions, whether in dress, music or poetry, passed him by. He had no feeling for literature, unlike Brahms, Mahler and Wolf, and set hardly any secular texts to music. His spelling was as haphazard as Mozart's, his pronunciation that of an uneducated peasant. His clothes — always black — were shapeless even for those days of rumpled, unstructured serge: jackets baggy for comfort, like a yokel's Sunday-best, trousers cut wide round the chest. His photographs make him appear like a rather creepy waxwork figure of himself.

As a youth he was sent to the famous monastery of St Florian, to combine organist's duties with farm-labouring, then briefly abandoned monastic life to become a schoolmaster. But he missed its certainties, and at the age of 21 returned, as a low-grade teacher. He was obliged to eat with the labourers, yet thought it no loss of status. Everything was God's will. He devotedly taught general subjects, while in his spare time teaching himself harmony and counterpoint. Ten years later he re-emerged to seek tuition in Vienna (from Schubert's old teacher, Simon Sechter), a village yokel totally unprepared for life in a big city and horrified by the public entertainments. But when he had to improvise an organ fugue at the Conservatoire, the chief examiner exclaimed: 'He should have examined *us*! How happy I would be if *I* knew only a tenth of what he knows.'

Although he abhorred the stage, Bruckner worshipped Wagner. In July 1882 he met him in Bayreuth at the *première* of the pseudo-religious *Parsifal* and was as awestruck as a schoolgirl meeting a pop idol: 'Because the Highest Being held my hand I fell to my knees, pressed the Highest Being's hand, covered it with kisses and said, "O Master, I worship you!!!" ' Like Brahms he admired the waltzes of Strauss, though he would never have entered a dance floor, let alone held a woman in his arms. Brahms thought him a harmless lunatic: 'A poor, crazy man whom the *Pfaffen* [a derisive Austrian word for priests] of St Florian have on their conscience. Have you any idea what it means when one had to spend one's youth in the company of *Pfaffen?*'

Not surprisingly, Bruckner thought sex unutterably wicked. Yet God demanded that man should marry and multiply, so he kept approaching women, in a clumsy way. Towards the end of his life he confessed, sadly: 'Just once in my life I kissed a girl. I have regretted it ever since.'

Among his neuroses was a fascination with corpses — a kind of Platonic necrophilia. When the remains of Beethoven and Schubert were exhumed for reburial he insisted on being there; not for the awe of being in the presence of their earthly remains but curious to see the decayed corpses. Whenever he heard news of a disaster, accident or murder, he hurried along to inspect the victims. After Kaiser Maximilian's assassination in 1867, he wrote to his friend Rudolf Weinwurm: 'I would like at any cost to see the body of Maximilian. Please be so good, Weinwurm, and send a reliable person to Court and ask in the Chief Chamberlain's Office whether the body could be viewed either open in the coffin or through glass; even if I could just look at the closed coffin. Let me know by telegram, so I don't miss the opportunity. I beg this most urgently!' When the *Ringtheater* in Vienna caught fire on the 8th of December 1881 with the loss of 386 lives (a disaster my grandparents are said to have escaped because they could not get tickets), Bruckner, living just across the road, enjoyed a ringside view of the charred bodies laid out on the pavement, but had nightmares afterward: he thought he saw lights flitting past the windows and said they were the restless spirits of the victims. After failing to gain sight of an executed murderer he contented himself by visiting the butcher who had supplied the man's last meal — demanding a cut from the same piece of steak and enjoyed it fried in butter and breadcrumbs — a Viennese Schnitzel. He spent the whole night before the execution on his knees, asking God to save the condemned man's soul — and doubtless that the butcher would be able to save him that steak. A photograph of his dead mother, in her open coffin, hung over his bed.

One of Bruckner's less spooky quirks was numeromania. He had to *count* everything. Not just his toes, or the bars in his scores, but the number of words on the pages of books (even newspapers); every pinnacle, finial or capital of every building, church or cathedral he visited; the repetitions of a wallpaper pattern and anything else countable. He had to get the totals absolutely right and was miserable when he failed to count the leaves on a tree. In small notebooks he numbered the prayers he said, all day and every day. A lady wearing strings of pearls was startled to find this normally so mild-mannered a man shouting at her: '*Please* go away, otherwise I shall feel obliged to count the number of pearls round your neck and I *can't stand it!*' He also listed the girls he fell in love with:

In 1851, Luise (Aloisia) Bogner, aged sixteen
In 1866, Josephine Lang, aged seventeen
In 1869, Caroline Rabl, aged seventeen
In 1885, Marie Demar, aged seventeen
In 1889, Lina Opitz, aged eighteen
In 1890, Fräulein Wiesner (first name unknown), aged seventeen
In 1891, Ida Busch, aged nineteen
In 1891, Minna Reischl, aged eighteen
In 1892, Fräulein Anna (second name unknown)

Only teenagers interested him, and he always asked for permission to declare his love. This procedure continued throughout his life without the slightest chance of success: his failures were as carefully recorded as Leporello listed his master's successes. When a butcher's daughter from Linz, whom he had known since she was twelve, turned sixteen, he wrote a flowery letter in rambling German almost impossible to put into sufficiently clumsy English:

16th August 1866. Very honoured, charming young Fräulein. It is not that I am mindful in the least to trouble you in addressing you with a displeasing matter, honoured Fräulein; no, I write to you out of the conviction that you might have long have been aware of my having quietly, patiently but steadfastly waited for you, I thus take up the pen in order now to pester you, to make a thorough nuisance of myself. It is my greatest, my most fervent request which I herewith take the courage to address to you, Fräulein Josephine, whether Fräulein Josephine would have the greatest goodness to let me have your candid and sincere, your final and definitive, your absolutely decisive reply in writing, so that it may contribute to my future peace of mind, that is to say, in regard to the question of whether I may harbour the hope to be allowed your permission to seek your dear parents' agreement for me to sue for your hand in marriage? Or is it perhaps, by reason of some lack of personal affection you may or may not feel for me, that it is impossible for you to contemplate taking such a step, namely marriage? The Fräulein will understand that the question has to be decided. One way or the other, I implore her to give me her decision, but with certainty, in writing. Please would Fräulein Josephine tell all this to her dear parents (but otherwise to keep it the strictest secret!) and choose one or other alternative of these two possibilities, with the agreement of your dear parents. My faithful friend, your Herr brother, has prepared me for everything and will also have warned you beforehand, in accordance with his promise. Once more I pray you: would the Fräulein write quite frankly and openly and quite decisively: may I sue for your hand or expect a total, final rejection? (No prevarication or consolatory circumlocution because it is high time for me to make a decision and you may not change your mind easily, because the Fräulein is after all so very sensible). The Fräulein may feel quite unconcerned about telling me the absolute truth, because it will help to calm my spirits. I kiss your hand with impatient anticipation of the soonest possible decision. Anton Bruckner.

He enclosed a prayer book and a gold watch. The reply was neither consolatory nor did she prevaricate. She simply returned his presents. He knew exactly what sort of wife he wanted: one in her teens, beautiful (not just pretty); and with parents sufficiently rich to bring a good dowry. He asked Weinwurm to scout for talent:

The other day the Herr Leather Master Turek from Steyr was here and he had with him a dear, pretty girl. The dear creature is called Henriette Reiter, 18 years old. She is said to have a fortune of 3,000 florins but may possibly be in expectation one day of even more. As I'm 42 years old it's high time . . . . But better wait a little rather than take things too hurriedly. I liked the girl very much and as I am without a young woman I do implore you most urgently but in the strictest confidence whether you might not — as the step is so necessary for me — be able to make some enquiries *with a reliable source* as to her virtue, etc. and her pecuniary circumstances. (Don't let her know that I am 42 years old, at least until she has seen me — I still look a little younger than that — she might think I'm 36). What was it you recently wanted to tell me about a girl from Salzburg? Which girl? Pretty? Rich? Please be frank — the moment is nigh. . . . Dearest friend! I have had a bitter week. After I had long given up my old love (on your advice) I cast my eye over the adopted daughter of a respectable house, where they in any case already had their own daughter, but the girl stands to get maybe 6,000 florins. And when I sent the girl a copy of Schubert's Serenade, which she had asked for, my present was returned to me — so, you see even my most modest aspirations bring me no luck. I'm sick of this whole world.

Like many seminary celibates, Bruckner made up for sexual deprivation with gluttony and alcohol, yet never lost his inhibitions. After one drinking session his fellow choristers sent a 'lightly-dressed' waitress to his room. In terror he fled into a corner, knelt before a crucifix and sought God's protection against the Devil.

He would have made a good husband and father for the few years that remained before his child-bride turned into a young widow; and even in old age he considered himself attractive to women. In 1885, he wrote to a friend, Moritz von Mayfeld: 'As to my marrying, I have yet to find a bride. If only I could find a suitable young flame! I do have many girl friends, because many beauties have recently been very much pursuing me . . . .'

To a girl whom he had persuaded to send him a photograph he wrote:

Kindest, noblest Friend, Fräulein Marie! Sincerest thanks for your glorious picture. Those innocent, beautiful eyes! What solace they are to me. Until the end of my life this will be a treasured, priceless relic . . . . Ah, I beg for your precious friendship, dearest Fräulein . . . . Your friend who worships you above all, Anton Bruckner.

He nearly succeeded once — in Berlin in 1891, when his *Te Deum* was performed under Siegfried Ochs. He stayed in the Hotel Kaiserhof and was much taken by the devoted attentiveness of a chambermaid. He was nearly 67, she a simple girl of nineteen called Ida, doing her work cheerfully and kindly. He interpreted this as love, asked her to marry him — and to his joy she accepted. Her parents consented, perhaps welcoming the prospect of a famous son-in-law; she doubtless looked forward to escaping the drudgery of hotel service; or perhaps she did love him — who knows? Bruckner was taken ill, while still at the hotel — and was even more touched by the way she nursed him. As soon as he was fit he hurried to a jeweller and bought a ring. His happiness was shortlived. To his dismay he discovered she was a Protestant, so marriage was out of the question. Ida returned his ring, as all the others had sent back his presents. Alma Mahler had a different story:

> Siegfried Ochs told me a touching tale concerning Bruckner, one in which he himself played a part. Ochs conducted in Berlin a Festival performance of Bruckner's Mass. Afterwards there was a splendid evening held in honour of him. In the afternoon Bruckner telephoned to say he would attend only if his fiancée could come too, else he would refuse. *Fiancée?* Since when has he been engaged? Ochs sensed there was trouble and rushed to the hotel. He found Bruckner totally shattered, almost in a collapsed state. The night before, the hotel chambermaid had come into his room and . . . to cut a long story short, in the morning she howled and cried that he had robbed her of her honour and would now have to marry her. Bruckner had promised it to her and so they were engaged. Ochs called for the girl and asked her straight out — how much money did she demand? It was a considerable sum. In effusive gratitude Bruckner reached out and kissed Ochs's protesting hands.

In the light of what we know about Bruckner it sounds like typical Viennese intrigue — and an unlikely story. Alma Mahler also reported — but discounted — a story that Bruckner had been '. . . engaged as a music teacher in a girls' school but was suddenly relieved of his post because of "certain improprieties". But nobody believed it. It was only his innocence about the female sex that made him appear a brute'.

Whatever the facts, Bruckner was surely incapable of 'improprieties'. Yet he went on looking for his child-bride. Soon after the musical triumph and amatory fiasco of Berlin he went on holiday in Upper Austria and met a merchant's daughter, Fräulein Reischl who — what bliss! — shared her first name, Minna, with Wagner's first wife. A lucky omen? No; her parents politely told him to try someone his own age. Five years later, at the age of 72, Bruckner finally gave up hope and returned to what had been his first and probably only love, the great baroque organ of the Monastery of St Florian. When he died he was buried in a vault below the organ.

FRÉDÉRIC (FRYDERYK) FRANCOIS (FRANCISZEK) CHOPIN

Born: Zelazowa Wola, near Warsaw, 1st? of March 1810
Father: Nicolas Chopin, b. Marainville, 15th of April 1771
              d. Warsaw, 3rd of May 1844
Mother: Tekla-Justina Krzyzanowska (1782–1861)
Died: Paris, 17th of October 1849

Chopin has been the victim of a tug-of-love dispute between the Poles and the French, both nations claiming him as their own. He was of French descent but enjoyed a Polish upbringing, spent much time in France and, like all educated Poles and Russians of the nineteenth century, spoke French. But he was a Polish composer through and through, and was christened Fryderyk Franciszek. His music sounds more Polish than French, its roots in Polish folksong and dance.

Chopin's dates have also been disputed. Many reference books give his birth as the 1st of March 1809, while he maintained he was born on the 1st of March 1810, thus taking a year off his age — a thing not unknown in musical circles. Fifty years after his death a baptismal certificate came to light and confused matters further, with another date: the 22nd of February 1810.

His first recorded love affair took place when he was twenty, with a beautiful Polish girl, Constantia Gladkovska, who was on the threshhold of a promising career as a singer. What is known of the relationship suggests that her love for him was greater than his for her — as tended to be the case in all his later affairs. Not only did he tire quickly of women but he found the act of love debilitating, fearing that it might deprive him of energy he could better spend on his compositions. This was either an excuse brought into play when he was trying to discard a mistress, or a rare condition indeed: the annals of musical relationships are full of exhausting liaisons embarked upon by composers who preferred making love to making symphonies, or managed with ease to combine the two.

Chopin was one of the first composers whose real likeness has come down to posterity, at first on daguerrotypes and then proper photographs, so that we need not rely on the romanticized or conflicting evidence of painters. The photographs show him as slight, pale, sickly and somewhat effeminate, with a beaky nose, his face displaying early signs of the consumption from which he died at the age of only 39. What he needed was probably not mistresses but women who combined the roles of mother and nurse.

In the summer of 1835, in Dresden, he renewed his acquaintance with a family he had known some years earlier, the Wodzinskis. Their baby daughter Marja, whom he used to dandle on his knee, had grown into an attractive sixteen-year-old and an accomplished pianist. They fell in love, but the affair proved too tiring for him and he fell — or pretended to fall — seriously ill. A Warsaw newspaper even carried a premature obituary of him.

Increasing depression about their relationship inspired one of his best-known works — the Funeral March, later incorporated in the B flat minor Piano Sonata. Marja was always heavily chaperoned, so it is unlikely that their love affair went beyond (if as far as) what Schumann called 'finger-games under skirts'. In the summer of 1837, the relationship faded out, without drama or recriminations. Chopin dedicated to her the Waltz *L'adieu*, op. 69 No.1. This piece was to come in useful repeatedly, as farewell situations multiplied — a stock present he kept in readiness for prospective women-friends.

Marja was followed by Delfina Potocka, née Komar, the young wife of Count Mieczyslaw Potocki, a man of many vices, some declared by contemporaries to have been 'unspeakable'. When the marriage collapsed he settled on her a generous annuity with which she set up a salon in Paris. There she acquired and shed lovers as if they were evening gowns: poets, sculptors, painters, counts, dukes, Beau Brummel himself — even the Duke of Orléans, Dauphin of France. The painters Eugène Delacroix and Hippolyte Delaroche also shared her favours (either in parallel or in series). After tumbling with her in bed, Delaroche painted her as the Virgin Mary: the portrait now hangs in the Wallace Collection in London. Honoré de Balzac raved about her grace and beauty; and when Delacroix first met her in Chopin's home he wrote in his diary:

> I have heard her sing twice before, and thought that I had never encountered anything more perfect, epecially that first time, when it was dusk . . . the black velvet dress she was wearing, the arrangement of her hair, everything about her made me think she must be as ravishingly beautiful as her movements were graceful.

Delfina (or Fidelina, as Chopin nicknamed her) inspired him to write his most revealing — and embarrassing — love letters, brimming with over-romanticized nonsense and pseudo-scientific drivel:

> Fidelina, my one and only beloved: I will bore you once again with my thoughts on the subject of inspiration and creativity, but as you will notice, these thoughts are directly connected with you. I have long reflected on inspiration and creativity and think I have gradually discovered the essential nature of these attributes. To me inspiration and creativity come only when I have abstained from a woman for a longish period. When, with passion, I have emptied my fluid into a woman until I am pumped dry, then inspiration shuns me and ideas won't creep into my head. How strange and beautiful it is, mark it well, that the same forces which go to fertilize a woman and create a human being should go to create a work of art! Yet a man wastes this life-giving precious fluid merely for a single moment of ecstasy. The same is true of scholars who devote themselves to scientific pursuits, or men who make discoveries. The formula is apparently a simple one. A man must renounce women — then the forces of his body will accumulate in his brain in the form of inspiration and he may give birth to a pure work of art. Just think of it —

sexual temptation and desire can be sublimated into inspiration! A fool who lives without a woman will merely be driven insane by frustration. On the other hand, a genius's unrequited love and unfulfilled passion that is sharpened by the image of one's beloved and carries with it unbearable frustration, can contribute to creativity. What about Mozart? I don't know, but I think his wife became ordinary food for him, his love and passion cooled, and that is why he was able to compose a great deal. I have not heard that Mozart had any love affairs in his life. Sweetest Fidelina, how much of the precious fluid, how many forces of genius, have I squandered on you! I have not given you a child but only God knows how many musical ideas have been lost for ever! OPERAM ET OLEUM PERDIDI!!!! Who knows what Ballades, Polonaises, perhaps an entire Concerto, have been forever engulfed in your little D flat . . . .

The Latin tag is a transposed allusion to Plautus: *Oleum et operam perdidi* — 'I have wasted both my [lamp] oil and my work.' Later Chopin explains what he meant by his mistress's 'little D flat' — one of those twee lovers' euphemisms which hardly bears discussion in public; and all the more foolish as he must have hoped that his letters would be preserved for posterity. To make it all quite plain he labours the point:

I am unable to imagine what might have been written, because I have not composed anything for a such long time, having been so immersed in you and in love. Works which could have seen the light of day are forever drowned in your little D flat, so that you are filled with my music and pregnant with my compositions! Time flies, life runs its course and no-one can recapture wasted moments. It is not for nothing that saints describe woman as the gate to hell! No, no. I take back the last sentence. I eat my words. I will not erase what I have just written and I haven't got time to start this letter all over again. To me you are the gate to paradise. For you I will renounce fame, creativity, everything. Fidelina, Fidelina, I long for you intensely and fearfully. I am shivering as if ants were crawling up my spine. When you arrive in your carriage I will glue myself to you and for a whole week you won't be able to tear me away from your little D flat — and let inspiration and ideas go to hell. Let my compositions disappear into the black hole for ever.

To another letter he adds a PS:

I would like again to plonk something down your little hole in D flat major. Do not refuse me. Your F.C.

How did it arise, this silly euphemism of Fidelina's little D flat? Two explanations are possible. One is that on the piano the note D flat is a shorter black one between two long white ones — the latter perhaps representing a woman's legs. The other is that in German notation D flat is *Des* — which in dialect pronunciation can mean 'that thing'. Whatever the reason, Chopin blamed Fidelina and her D flat for making him waste his precious energy in it. Then he has another idea:

> Ah — I've thought up a new musical name for the little D flat. Let's call it 'tacet'. I'll explain it to you at once. A tacet is a pause, a hole in the melody. So that's quite appropriate for your little D flat. My pupils will arrive shortly so I must finish this letter, that it can go by today's post. I kiss your beloved little body all over.

> Your most faithful Frédéric, Your entirely faithful Frédéric, Your gifted pupil, who has skilfully mastered the art of making love.

> PS I have just finished a Prelude.

Chopin dedicated to Delfina what was to become his most famous waltz. It is in the key of D flat — a key he rarely used — and better known as the Minute Waltz, op. 64 No. 1, though any attempt to play it in a minute is an impossibility. Perhaps the Minute Waltz was a private joke between Chopin and Delfina, because he was unable to make it last longer.

Chopin's nonsense about wasting precious creative fluid was probably meant as a signal to Delfina that he was ready to move on, for by the previous year, in the autumn of 1836, he had already met his most formidable feminine challenge. Or rather, she had taken steps to meet him; and to describe her as a *feminine* challenge is inaccurate. Her given names could hardly have been more ladylike: Armandine Aurore Lucile Dupin, Baronne Dudevant, but she did things few women dared to do in those days: she wore trousers, smoked cigars and liked to be addressed as George: George Sand, notorious novelist, poet and proto-feminist, who numbered Alfred de Musset among her conquests. She was what is now called a single parent with two illegitimate children, a daughter and a son, Solange and Maurice. In the company of an actress friend, Marie Dorval, she attended one of Chopin's concerts in Paris, at the end of which she sent him a card that read, *'On vous adore'*. Perhaps she intended this to be read as the royal *'on'*, for her friend added, *'mois aussi, moi aussi, moi aussi'*. Chopin was interested but not immediately. He wrote: 'Yesterday I was introduced to George Sand. I found her exceedingly unpleasant.' To the composer Ferdinand Hiller he said: 'What a repulsive bitch this Sand is! Is that really a WOMAN?'

She was determined to win him. But before there was any question of capitulating he expressed deep reservations. He seemed unwilling to commit himself to a full love-affair, and doubtless let her, too, know his theories about wasting precious fluid on any little D flat that happened to come his way. Sand was both insulted and puzzled: no-one had ever resisted her advances; but she blamed not him but his previous mistress:

> I think he said something about 'certain adventures' that might destroy beautiful memories for him. What nonsense! He surely cannot believe this — or can he? Who is this woman who put such ideas in his head about physical

love? Women who thus demean and belittle the most heavenly moments of ecstasy, the most exalted act known to humankind in the entire universe. Women like that should be hanged.

Eventually Chopin was persuaded to put both Delfina and Marja Wodzinska — to whom he was still officially betrothed — out of his mind and become George's lover. Somehow, for she was not beautiful, the force of her personality managed to turn his earlier revulsion into an obsession. In his diary he wrote:

I have now seen her three times. I played to her and she looked deep into my eyes. Our heartbeats moved in unison. Her extraordinary, dark eyes held mine in a spell. She bent down to the piano keyboard. Her glances set me afire and overwhelmed me. My heart was captured. Since then I have seen her twice more. She loves me. Aurore — what a bewitching name.

He still thought of her as Aurore, so clearly she had not yet spoken the magic words, 'Call me George;' though she herself already addressed him as '*Mon petit*', or by her special nickname, 'Chip-chip'. Of Marja, the presumed cause of his initial reluctance, she wrote:

This young person whom he thinks he loves, or thinks he is obliged to love, could she really make him happy, or would she simply add to his sufferings and his sadness? I do not ask whether she loves him, or he her, whether her love is greater than mine . . . . I ask which of us two he wants to forget or renounce in order to find peace in his soul as well as happiness, and to preserve his health — which, after all, is far too delicate to endure any great upsets . . . .

To Delacroix she confided:

I am still as enchanted by him as I was at our first meetings. Not the tiniest cloud darkens our brightest heaven, not a drop of bitter Vermouth sours our wine. I am beginning to believe there are angels who descend to earth to take on human form. You think such happiness cannot last? It is true that when I look on my past experiences and reason with myself, then I have no doubt that it could be so. But if I ask my heart it confirms that this happiness can never end. But is it so important? If God chose to take me to him in the next hour I would not complain, for I have lived through three whole months of unclouded bliss.

Delacroix (who was Chopin's best friend in France) painted a double portrait of him and George, she standing by him, looking admiringly down at him over his right shoulder, while he plays the piano for her. When their affair ended the picture was symbolically cut down the middle to make the rift absolute. Chopin now hangs in the Louvre, Sand in a public art gallery in Copenhagen. Of the letters Chopin wrote to George Sand during their liaison only about ten have survived. They are reserved to the point of coldness, invariably showing more concern for his own health and comfort than hers, or their feelings for each other.

> Paris, Saturday 25th of September 1841. I have arrived in my apartment in the *rue Tronchet* without having unduly tired myself. It is eleven in the morning. Now I am going to the *rue Pigalle*. I will write to you tomorrow morning. Don't forget me. I embrace your children. Chopin.

Chopin loved Sand's son and daughter, helped to educate them and gave Solange piano lessons. When the fifteen-year-old son fell ill with rheumatism, Sand was advised to seek a cure in pure and fresh air, so she packed him and his eight-year-old sister off to the Balearic Islands. The illness may have been a pretext, for Sand's recently-discarded lover, Félicien Mallefille, was about to challenge Chopin to a duel. In making a prudent exit they also hoped that the mild Majorcan climate would benefit Chopin's health, as he was by then consumptive with an incipient tuberculosis. The Majorcan stay turned into a disaster for Sand and Chopin, although the children thought it a great adventure. George described it in an ill-tempered little book which must be the ultimate in anti-holiday brochures: *Un hiver à Majorque.* Chopin is not mentioned by name but described as 'our invalid', 'our patient', or 'one of our party who was sick'. Their misery began even before they landed, when the captain of the steamer forbade 'our invalid' from occupying a bunk in their cabin, for fear of contagion, and had his mattress burnt after he had lain on it. They were charged double the normal rate for the short voyage. Sand wrote:

> We arrived in Palma in the month of November 1838, in a heat comparable to that of the month of June in our country. We had left Paris a fortnight earlier in extremely cold weather. For us it was a great pleasure, after having felt the first touches of winter, to leave the old enemy behind.

Little did they realize that the old enemy had followed them, in different guises. The weather soon turned cold, and for three months it rained non-stop — though the locals, wrote Sand, 'after two months of deluge, still maintained that it never rained in Majorca'. A Señor Gómez leased to them his villa. Its rooms had paper-thin walls, she complained, and no fireplaces, and she felt perpetually cold.

> Our invalid began to suffer and cough. From that moment we became the object of horror and fear to the villagers. We were accused and convicted of pulmonary consumption, which was equivalent to the plague, according to the prejudices of the Spanish medical world terrified of contagion. But a wealthy doctor who, for the modest sum of 45 francs, condescended to visit us, declared that it was nothing, and prescribed nothing.

The villagers' diagnosis was unfortunately correct. Chopin's tuberculosis had taken hold, and it would have been useless for the doctor to prescribe a medicine, as there was no cure. Besides, there were no pharmacies on the island able to dispense anything but folk-remedies.

The illness got worse due to causes which neither science nor care could combat properly. One morning when we were feeling very depressed by the persistence of the rain and our other worries, we received a letter from the frightful Gómez telling us, in the Spanish fashion, that we had a person with us afflicted with a complaint likely to infect his house and prove a source of danger to his family. By virtue of this he begged us to get out of his place as soon as possible. News of our consumptive spread like a flash. But for the hospitality of the French consul, who performed miracles to shelter us under his own roof, we would have been obliged to take refuge in some cavern, like real gipsies.

The function of consuls is to give first aid and temporary shelter, not to take a consumptive, his ill-tempered mistress and her two children by a previous lover as permanent guests in his house. But fortunately:

Another miracle happened: we found asylum for the winter. There was in the *Cartuja*, the Carthusian monastery of Valldemosa, a Spanish refugee who had gone into hiding there for some unknown political motive. We had already visited the Caruja and been surprised by his cultured manners, the melancholy beauty of his wife, and the rustic furniture of their cell. It came about that the mysterious couple wished to leave the country hurriedly, and they appeared to be prepared to hand over their cell to us with as much pleasure as we had in accepting it. For the fair sum of 1,000 francs we acquired, then, a complete set of furniture, but of the sort we could have got in France for a hundred: so rare, costly and difficult to come by are items of prime necessity on the island.

They had shelter, and furniture of sorts, but otherwise the holiday was still unrelieved misery. The rain came down without pause and the cold and dank climate on the top of a mountain almost inaccessible except by donkey, speeded Chopin's deterioration: no amount of fresh air was able to halt, let alone cure, his consumption. Besides, the air was not as fresh as they had been led to expect. Sand complained of a permanent smell of rancid cooking oil as well as pepper, garlic and 'corrosive spices of every kind' — and of the ubiquitous pork being fried in it. She also complained that smelly and noisy pigs ran wild everywhere.

The Majorcan food, and especially the manner in which it was spiced, always caused our invalid a malaise. One day, when we were served with a skinny chicken, we saw hopping about on its steaming back some enormous fleas . . . . My children roared with such infantile laughter that they nearly fell under the table.

The locals shunned the strangers, clearly resenting their presence, convinced that they brought not only ill health but also ill luck. They feared infection, and were offended by their visitors' ways, by turn unconventional and patronizing. Sand also found fault with the local produce — if they could get any. The peasants were poor and in need of any money they could earn, but they felt so strongly about the strangers in their midst that they embarked on an action which would have gladdened the heart of a British shop steward of the 1970s.

They leagued together and agreed among themselves not to sell us fish, vegetables and eggs except at exorbitant prices. It was no use our quoting tariffs or the usual charges. At the least observation the peasant would put his onions or potatoes back into the sack and say to us with the air of a Grandee of Spain, 'Do you not want them? Then you shall not have them.' And he would retire in a highly dignified fashion, without our being able to make him return and come to an agreement. They made us go short in order to punish us for bargaining with them.

In desperation Sand and Chopin bought a pair of goats — but neighbours crept into the garden and stole their milk ('in the end we had to put them under lock and key'). And anyway, the milk had 'a sour rough taste which the Majorcans thought highly of but which to us was awful'. Eventually Chopin managed to have a small Pleyel piano shipped out to the island ('. . . they demanded 700 francs import duty, almost the value of the instrument itself'), which enabled him to embark on a period of intensive creativity remarkable under conditions of such discomfort. On this piano, a small rickety upright which can still be strummed in the Chopin Museum in the Valldemosa monastery, he completed the set of Twenty-Four Preludes and began the C# minor Scherzo and the C minor Polonaise, opus 40 No. 2.

Calamitous holidays can ruin the most promising relationships, and by this time Chopin and Sand must have been ready to murder each other. He was probably secretly glad that the cold, the discomfort and the prying locals absolved him from 'wasting' his creative juices on his demanding holiday companion. The pair began to drift apart emotionally soon after their return to civilization, though they cohabited again in Sand's splendid house at Nohant. After a while, as the children grew older, Maurice turned against Chopin, while Solange took her surrogate father's side, so much so that he soon fell in love with her, as Sand could not fail to observe, especially as Chopin supported Solange after she and her mother quarrelled irreconcilably over the daughter's disastrous marriage. Chopin, for his part, had been violently jealous when Solange got married.

Another close woman friend of Chopin's was Pauline Viardot, a plain but enchanting woman who captivated every man she encountered and whose name was linked with other composers in this book. She was married to the critic Louis Viardot, much older than herself, but was for 40 years the mistress of the Russian novelist Ivan Sergeyevich Turgenev — to whom she was so devoted that she took into her home Turgenev's illegitimate daughter by a servant-girl. She and Chopin certainly often made music together but the precise nature of their friendship can only be guessed. Maurice Sand drew a wicked caricature of them together and Pauline herself amiably caricatured Chopin — they were a multi-talented group. While Chopin was still living in Sand's house she began a relationship with the Paris journalist Victor Borié and proceeded to make other conquests, chronicling each in barely-disguised fiction. But she had had enough of sickly musicians. Chopin and Sand parted for ever, though they met once more, by chance, as fellow guests in a Paris salon. She enquired after his health, he replied briefly and coldly and moved away. She wrote to Pauline Viardot:

> Do you ever see Chopin? Tell me about his health. I am unable to reciprocate his hatred and fury by an equal measure of hatred and fury. I think of him often as a sick child, embittered and lost.

Chopin appears to have kept himself free from further serious — or debilitating — entanglements. There was a close friendship with the singer Jenny Lind and another with a young Scottish woman, Jane Stirling, to whom he had given lessons and who became the dedicatee of his Nocturnes, opus 55. She was devoted to him, while he was — or pretended to be — bored. Meanwhile his consumption raged on, in spite of several remissions, during which he gave numerous concerts.

> My Scottish ladies give me no peace. They are stifling me out of courtesy, and out of courtesy I do not refuse them . . . . I have been ill the last eighteen days, ever since I reached London. I have not left the house at all, I have had such a cold and so many headaches and all my bad symptoms. I don't care about anything. I have never cursed anyone but now my life is so unbearable that it would give me relief if I could curse Lucrezia [his nickname for Sand]. But no doubt she also suffers, suffers all the more because she will doubtless grow old in anger.

Jane, a student of one of Chopin's own pupils, Lindsay Sloper, was in love with the Master, but by 1848, when he visited Scotland, he was far too ill to do anything about reciprocating her love, even if he had wanted to; and she expressed hers in acts of selfless generosity. As a youth he had always hated the English, and the Scots were no better (in the eyes of foreigners 'England' included all four parts of the Kingdom). Fortunately not everything was negative, and Chopin managed to summon up a little gratitude to the piano-maker Henry Broadwood, who had booked an extra, empty seat next to Chopin in the carriage for the journey to Edinburgh, so that he would have more room. But apart from that one expression of appreciation Chopin remained sullenly anti-British. On the 23rd of November 1848 he left 'this hellish London' and returned to Paris to take up residence at No.12 Place Vendôme, now so weak that he was barely able to leave his bed. From Scotland, Jane sent him a large sum of money (approximate present-day equivalent: £10,000); and the soprano Jenny Lind came and sang to him. Delfina, who travelled specially from Nice to be at his bedside, tried to sing, but her voice was choked by tears. Solange was at his bedside when he died, on 17th October 1849. Her mother enquired about him by letter but decided against a visit. The intuitive Pauline Viardot provided the final and most perceptive comment:

In all those love-affairs there was no FRIENDSHIP — for *that* is a passion which cannot diminish. It is the most beautiful of all.

ACHILLE CLAUDE DEBUSSY

Born:	St Germain-en-Laye, 22nd August 1862
Father:	Manuel Achille Debussy
Mother:	Victorine Manoury, b. Levallois
Married:	1. Rosalie (Lily) Texier 19th October 1899
	2. Emma Bardac 20th January 1908
Daughter:	Claude-Emma (Chouchou)
Died:	25th March, 1918

Debussy was born 'over the shop', in St Germain-en-Laye near Paris, where his father sold china while at the same time engaging in revolutionary activities, for which he was imprisoned during the 1871 Commune. Debussy received early piano lessons from a Mme Mauté de Fleurville, who claimed to have been a pupil of Chopin (she was certainly Verlaine's mother-in-law) and knowing Chopin one may safely suspect that there was an amorous entanglement. Debussy started having lessons when he was nine, comparatively late for a child destined to become a renowned pianist. Debussy was a quick learner in love, too, having turned to an older woman to teach him: the beautiful Marie-Blanche Vasnier was 32, an amateur singer, married, with two small children. Her portrait by Jacques-Emile Blanche of 1888 shows a well-rounded woman, with big eyes and a pouting little mouth. Debussy worshipped her and, between 1881 and 1884, wrote for her a large number of songs to sing at the frequent soirées M. and Mme. Vasnier held at their home. They had taken Debussy into their family, in return for which he gave music lessons to their young daughter. They could afford to support the struggling young man, for M. Vasnier was a highly-paid official in the building trade. But it would be rash to condemn Claude for repaying this kindness in the manner of Wagner — by seducing the lady of the house. She started their affair, and for all we know her unfaithful husband may have been a conniving party. In the early 1880s, Debussy set his heart on winning the sought-after *Prix de Rome*, and won it in 1884, at the third attempt. However, by this time he no longer enjoyed the prospect of joining the illustrious band of winners: much as he loved the honour and needed the money, he dreaded a prolonged separation. To leave Marie-Blanche for several years was more than he could bear. But, encouraged by her as well as her husband, he took up residence at the Villa Medici in Rome. If he wrote any letters to Marie-Blanche from Rome, they would have been discreetly destroyed, for none seems to have survived. To her husband, M. Vasnier, he wrote:

> I'm afraid I may come back to Paris rather sooner than you expect. Perhaps that would be very silly of me, but what else can I do? On the one hand I am afraid of going against your wishes and trying your friendship too far, which is the last thing I would want . . . I am not very well and the atmosphere in Rome

does not agree with my constitution. I would willingly work my head off, but the only result is a fever that lays me out and leaves me helpless.

He omitted to send news of a brief affair at the Villa Medici, with 'Loulou', a Mme Hochon, who was the wife of a professor. She helped him overcome his homesickness: various reports tell of their kissing in public. Understandably, the letter contained only a brief, tactfully formal, message for his mistress:

> Please give my best wishes to Mme Vasnier. Is Marguerite well? And is she still studying my songs? Yours most sincerely and affectionately . . . .

Rome kept him only for the minimum two years, and he lost no time in rushing back to Paris and into the arms of Marie-Blanche. But the affair had lost its momentum, and the lovers soon parted. Absence had failed to make Mme Vasnier's heart grow fonder — there were other young men, more conveniently close at hand, on whom she bestowed her favours.

In the summer of 1880 Debussy had made the acquaintance of Nadyezhda von Meck, better known as Tchaikovsky's beloved friend: a recently-widowed millionairess with eleven children. She was an accomplished pianist, fond of music but even fonder of musicians — an avid collector of celebrities and inveterate name-dropper. The world of music is eternally indebted to her, though she never made her subsidies appear like charity: she expected her protegés to work for their money. Only the best was good enough for her, so when she wanted her children to have music lessons she engaged Franz Liszt to be their teacher. Her meeting with Debussy is described in a letter she wrote to Tchaikovsky from the Alpine resort of Interlaken:

> Two days ago there arrived a young pianist, just graduated from the Paris Conservatoire with the first prize in the class of Marmontel [in fact the prize was for score reading, and in the class of Bazille]. I engaged him for the summer to give lessons to the children, to accompany Julia's singing and to play four-hand duets with me. This young man plays well, his technique is brilliant but he lacks personal expression. He is still too young. He says he is twenty but looks sixteen.

He was in fact eighteen, Nadyezhda fifty. Tchaikovsky must have had mixed feelings about his benefactress's new friend, who was not only sharing a piano-duet stool with her, thigh-to-thigh, but playing what Tchaikovsky and Nadyezhda considered 'their tune': his anguish-laden Symphony No. 4 in F minor. She did not, however, support Debussy in the way she sent regular allowances to Tchaikovsky but took him on lavish (and musically educational) holidays and grand tours. After the luxury he enjoyed, first with the Vasniers and then the Mecks, Debussy was reluctant to return to the archetypal French garret in which to accommodate himself and a succession of mistresses. For the time being he was living in the greatest ease. Mme von Meck wrote to Tchaikovsky:

Yesterday for the first time I played our Symphony with my little Frenchman, so I am in a terrible state of nerves today. I cannot play it without a fever penetrating to my very innermost being and am unable for days to rid myself of this feeling. My partner did not play it well, though he sight-read it splendidly. That is his only merit, though a very important one. He reads a score, even one of yours, like an open book . . . composes very nicely, but here, too, he is a true Frenchman.

During his tutelage of Mme von Meck's children, Debussy duly fell in love with the sixteen-year-old Sophie and asked her to marry him. She flatly turned him down. The von Mecks took him from Switzerland, where he had joined them, to Venice to meet Wagner, on a cultural tour of Europe (later also visiting Russia). The first trip ended in Florence, at the Villa Oppenheim, and when Debussy had to leave 'he cried bitterly', Nadyezhda reported to Tchaikovsky. She invited her 'little Frenchman' (alias 'my little pianist Bussy' — a pun: *Bussi* is South German for a kiss) back the following year. On a return visit to Moscow in the season of 1913–14, Debussy, nearly at the end of his short life, had a poignant reunion with his briefly-adored Sophie, by then the Princess Galitzin. Hardly anything is known about Debussy's next companion, except that she left him and he was heartbroken:

> . . . I'm still very confused. I wasn't expecting that business which we talked about to end so miserably and cheaply, with tales being told and unmentionable things said . . . . Precisely as her lips uttered those unforgiving words, echoes of her once loving voice resounded within me. This battle between the wrong notes (not accidental, alas!) and what I heard inside me was so overwhelming I hardly understood what was going on . . . . I've left a large part of me hanging on those thorns and it'll be a long time before I get back to my pursuit of art, the great healer . . . . I loved her so much, but with a sort of despairing passion because it was easy to see she was never going to commit herself utterly . . . . Now I must try to find out whether she really possessed what I was looking for. Or was I chasing a shadow? . . . I'm still mourning the loss of a dream. Maybe it's not so bad after all! Anything rather than those days when death seemed the only way out, and I was the one keeping vigil over the corpse! (Roger Nichols's translations).

That death-fantasy almost came true later, when his love for his first wife cooled. But before he embarked on his first marriage there were still to come a couple of broken engagements as well as another great love: Gaby — Gabrielle Dupont from Normandy: 'Gaby with the green eyes'. They lived together for nine years from the end of the 1880s, though she overlapped with Thérèse Roger, to whom he became engaged for a few weeks in 1894. He ran both mistresses until 1897, when Gaby found out about another affair and attempted suicide.

If gentlemen really prefer blondes, Debussy was obsessed with them, and

Gaby's combination of flaxen hair and green eyes had a devastating effect on him. Number 8 of his First Book of Preludes is called 'The Girl with the Flaxen Hair' (*La fille aux cheveux de lin*) and this miniature tone-poem for piano can be interpreted as a passionate statement of his erotic preferences (a fixation which, sexologists tell us, has something to do with the sparseness or silkiness of natural blondes' pubic hair). Gaby was a simple but forceful girl, not in the least artistic. Her talents, insofar as she had any, were homely, and for a long time they shared a life of poverty in bohemian squalor. Debussy's friend René Peter wrote:

> The most remarkable thing about the appearance of this pretty blonde was the strikingly green colour of her eyes. I don't know where Claude met her — scandalmongers (though we don't listen to them) said it was in some low-class dive. She was certainly the least dizzy blonde I ever came across. Her chin was powerful, she was strongly built and looked at you as resolutely as a cat.

Debussy enjoyed Gaby's company *à deux* — in bed and when he took her to dine, to cafés and public entertainments — but in social engagements with his intellectual equals he was either embarrassed by her inability to hold her own or her way of expressing herself with unladylike vehemence. So he usually left her at home to see to his domestic needs. In 1897, he was enveloped by a domestic storm and wrote to his friend Pierre Louÿs:

> I'm in trouble . . . Gaby with her beady eyes found a letter in my pocket which left no doubt as to the advanced state of a love affair with enough romantic trappings to move the most hardened heart. Whereupon — tears, drama, a real revolver and a story in the *Petit Journal*. Ah, my dear fellow, why aren't you here to get me out of this ghastly mess? It was all barbarous, pointless but will change absolutely nothing. Kisses and caresses can't be rubbed out with an indiarubber. Maybe someone will invent something that can do it and call it the 'Adulterer's Indiarubber'. . . . I am sometimes as sentimental as a seamstress who was Chopin's mistress.

Before long he was dreaming of another flaxen-haired girl. She was the heroine in his opera *Pelléas et Mélisande*, her long flaxen hair so central to Maeterlinck's story that it might almost have been the fantasy of a hair fetishist, with Mélisande letting down her hair, Rapunzel-like. Act III starts with an elaborate hair-grooming song. Into his real life there entered a singer who in the mid-1890s had taken part in the performance of one of his works, Thérèse Roger. Although he was briefly engaged to her and in spite of her evident importance to him, she remains a shadowy figure. Not even his friends knew much about her or their affair: perhaps she, too, was insufficiently intellectual to be paraded before them. But to one friend he wrote, in 1894:

> Cher ami: before leaving for Brussels I wanted to tell you myself that I am engaged to Mademoiselle Thérèse Roger.

To the slightly older composer Ernest Chausson, who had become a close friend and valued colleague, Debussy was a little more forthcoming:

> The Brussels concert was a marvellous occasion for me, chiefly because I owe a large part of its success to Th . . . who sang like a fairy. . . . It was nice for us to be able to whisper sweet nothings to one another in the midst of so many strangers!

At this time Debussy was heavily in debt, and the good news of his engagement to Thérèse was followed by a rather embarrassed request for a loan; together with a few lines of reassurance, because Chausson had been told by mutual friends that he was seeing yet another woman in addition to Thérèse. Debussy wrote:

> Your advice about marriage has touched me deeply, I assure you, and it seems to me (novice that I am in the business) absolutely right. . . . I really feel that I've offered my life once and for all, and that from now on it'll be lived just for one person.

The wedding was fixed for the 16th of April 1894 and an apartment rented for the honeymoon. But the *de facto* honeymoon had taken place long ago — and the ceremony was called off, without apparent explanation. Nothing more is heard about Thérèse. There are no letters, either to or from her. The episode cost Debussy Chausson's friendship — further requests for money doubtless played their part though Chausson was both rich and generous — and other friends also began to desert him. The next beauty was Rosalie Texier, nicknamed Lily, usually described as a *mannequin* but probably little more than a dressmaker who modelled the clothes she helped her employer to make. Their first meeting was disastrous and they took an instant dislike to each other. He found her pretty but peevish and argumentative. Only Gaby liked her — at any rate for a while.

> When I'm not feverish there's a young lady I love with all my heart (a blonde, naturally) with the most beautiful hair in the world and eyes which lend themselves to the most extravagant comparisons . . . in short, she's good enough to marry!

Lily Texier did not last very long either, but long enough to become the first Mme Debussy, on the 19th of October 1899:

> Ma Lily adorée: It's strangely absurd to have you so far away, sleeping like a spoilt child as you do, and me not able to get a glimpse of that pretty spectacle! . . . I'm here . . . trying to kill Time . . . (he's an amazingly healthy old man) as the minutes pass heavily and relentlessly . . . there's no laughter here with Lily gone . . . . I love you. Claude

Letter upon letter follows, in that year of courtship, opening *Ma chère petite Lily; Ma Lily jolie; Petite Lily-Lilo* or *Ma Lily aimeé* — and ending almost in desperation

Mon Dieu, que je t'aime — Claude. The passion — and passionate letters — continued for most of that year, 1899; and on the 19th of October they were married. On the morning of the wedding Debussy had to give a piano lesson so that he could pay for the wedding breakfast at the Brasserie Pousset. To a friend he revealed that, once again, he had fallen for someone who might today be described as slightly 'rough trade'. Like Gaby, Lily could hardly be an intellectual soul-mate, let alone his equal. To his life-long friend, the Swiss journalist Robert Godet, he confided:

> I must tell you at once what happened. Two things: I've moved house and I'm married. Yes, my dear friend, and please remain seated. Mlle Lily Texier has changed her discordant name to Lily Debussy, much more euphonious, as everyone will agree. She is unbelievably fair and pretty, like some character from an old legend. Also, she is not in the least 'modern-style'. She has no taste for music that Willy [the critic Henry Gauthier-Villars] approves but has a taste of her own. Her favourite song is a ditty about a grenadier with a red face who wears his hat on one side like an old campaigner. Not very stimulating, aesthetically. . . .

On the autograph score of his *Nocturnes* Debussy wrote:

> This manuscript belongs to my little Lily-Lilo. All rights reserved. It is proof of the deep and passionate joy I have in being her husband. Claude Debussy. At the very peep of dawn of January 1901.

The first Mrs Debussy proved to be just another amatory episode, and the marriage did not even last as long as his relationship with Gaby. Soon the letters become cold and their content mundane. He complained that they had little to say to each other, and lived 'like two goldfish trapped in a small glass bowl'; but to Robert Godet he confessed that he could no longer stand the sound of her voice: 'It made his blood run cold.' What is perhaps the last letter to her, dated 16th of July 1904, ends, 'Try not to miss any opportunity for laughing, as you like to do so much. Yours passionately, tenderly, Claude.' But the closing words were lies, and she had nothing to laugh about.

If a description of Debussy published at that time by James G. Huneker in the *New York Sun* is to be believed, Debussy's exterior was unprepossessing:

> I met Debussy at the Café Riche the other night and was struck by his unique ugliness. His face is flat, the top of his head is flat, his eyes are prominent — the expression veiled and sombre — and, altogether, with his long hair, unkempt beard, uncouth clothing and soft hat, he looked more like a Bohemian, a Croat, a Hun, than a Gaul. His high, prominent cheekbones lend a Mongolian aspect to his face. The head is brachycephalic, the hair black. . . .

Debussy's personality clearly transcended his ugliness and did not prevent women from falling in love with him. Soon after his marriage to Lily, Debussy had struck up a relationship with Emma Bardac, the wife of one financier and the niece of another, a brilliant conversationalist, a woman of the world — and for good measure also a good singer. In the summer of 1904, he left Lily and eloped with Emma to Jersey and Dieppe, a trip which produced *L'isle joyeuse*. At last, Debussy could combine passion with productivity. But it cost him many friendships, including that of Pierre Louÿs, who later wrote to his brother:

> I never knew a man who was less of a rake than Debussy. In 1896 he was 35, handsome, very masculine, strong and ardent. In fifteen or twenty years of his love life he knew only five women, one of whom (Mme Hochon) ravished him ... but they were all blondes.

In October 1905 he moved with Emma into a house in the Avenue Bois de Boulogne that she had bought with her own money and was to be his home until he died. When he left Lily and told her he was divorcing her, she too made a grand passionate gesture and shot herself, though not fatally. Edward Lockspeiser says she was taken to a nursing home 'wounded near the heart' but according to other reports it was a head wound. At that point most of Debussy's remaining friends deserted him. The satirists declared he had sold himself to a rich woman — and not even a blonde. Whatever they said — whether she was rich or not — Emma Bardac (*née* Moyse) was the intellectual mate he had always longed for. She provided a stimulus which the others had failed to do: the gestation of their daughter Claude-Emma (nicknamed 'Chouchou'), who was born on the 30th of October 1905, was almost concurrent with that of his first set of *Images* for piano, completed in the Grand Hotel, Eastbourne, on the South coast of England. In 1908, they legitimized their union but were obliged to follow a more frugal way of life, as her uncle, disapproving of their immoral life-style, had in 1907 disinherited her.

Almost inevitably marital difficulties arose, as Emma was possessive and resented his trips on conducting engagements. Debussy was to have only ten more years with her and their beloved Chouchou before he died of cancer at the age of 56, on the 25th of March 1918. Emma and Chouchou were with him. In the following year, little Chouchou herself died, of misdiagnosed diphtheria.

For Debussy, love had always been — in the words of the song cliché — an impossible dream. Perhaps he loved love more than he loved women: as soon as he had conquered one he seemed no longer to want her. Or perhaps he was continually searching for another Marie-Blanche. Any account of his love affairs is sure to be incomplete because he was shy, secretive and reticent, committing less to paper than his turbulent life might have suggested. Perhaps it was the blondes who were his downfall (some said that the celebrated singers Maggie Teyte, also blonde, and Mary Garden, who created the role of Mélisande, were among his conquests).

Quoting Paul Dukas, Lockspeiser wrote that Debussy was particularly sensitive to the decorative, aesthetic side of his love affairs: the women had to *look* right. But there must have come a time when he became aware of the lack of deeper emotions in his relationships.

EDWARD WILLIAM ELGAR

Born:	Broadheath, near Worcester, 2nd of June 1857
Died:	Worcester, 23rd of February, 1934
Father:	William Henry Elgar (1821–1906)
Mother:	Anne Greening (1822–1902)
Brothers	Henry John (1850–1864), Lucy Anne (1852–1925),
and Sisters:	Susanna Mary 'Pollie' (1855–1936), Frederick Joseph (1859–1866),
	Francis Thomas 'Frank' (1861–1928), Helen 'Dot' Agnes (1864–1939)
Married:	8th May 1889 Caroline Alice Roberts (b India 9th of October 1848 d.7th of April 1920)
Daughter:	Carice Irene b. 14th of August 1890 d. 1970

Certain kinds of pseudo-biographical films about composers traditionally show the great man tinkling away at the piano, his wife in an armchair nearby, knitting, with a cat in her lap. She looks up and says, 'That's a nice tune, dear!' Then the strumming takes on a more familiar tone, and before long the master is playing his much-loved piano concerto (or whatever), accompanied by an unseen symphony orchestra. This is almost exactly what happened to Elgar in real life (apart from the cat and the orchestra), as he himself reported: 'After a long day's fiddle-teaching at Malvern I came home very tired. Dinner being over, my dear wife said to me, "Edward, you look like a good cigar;" and having lighted it I sat down at the piano. In a little while, soothed and feeling rested, I began to play. Suddenly my wife interrupted, "Edward, that's a nice tune." I awoke from my dream. "Eh? Tune? What tune?" She said "Play it again. I like that tune." I played and strummed and played and then she exclaimed, "*That's* the tune!".'

The whole civilized world now knows and loves that tune — for it turned into the theme of the *Enigma* Variations. Another fragment was based on a familiar call between him and his wife Alice, a kind of signal which either would softly whistle to call the other, or announce their approach — one of many domestic allusions in the work. 'My wife is a wonderful woman. I play phrases and tunes to her because she always likes to see what progress I have been making. Well, she nods her head and says nothing, or just "Oh Edward!" — but I know whether she approves or not, and I always feel that there is something wrong with it if she doesn't.'

Elgar came from a humble background, the son of an itinerant piano tuner from Dover who settled in Worcester in 1841. As a good amateur pianist and violinist — useful accomplishments in a county town which, far from metropolitan musical life had to create its own opportunities — he quickly put down roots and in 1848 married Anne Greening, daughter of a Gloucestershire farmer and his landlord's sister (from whom Edward was to inherit his love for poetry). William, who was also organist at St George's Catholic Church in Worcester (though himself an unbeliever), was joined by his brother Henry, and the two opened a music shop, Elgar Brothers, at 10 High Street. Young Edward Elgar gained much of his early musical education in the shop: 'I saw and learned a great deal from the stream of music that passed through my father's establishment. . . . I read everything, I played everything, and heard everything that I possibly could.' Elgar's parents survived into old age, she until 1902, when the *Enigma* Variations had brought her son fame, and she wrote: 'What can I say to him, the dear one? I feel he is some great historic person — I cannot claim a little bit of him now he belongs to the big world.'

He studied the violin, bassoon and piano and eventually earned his living by serving in the shop and giving private lessons. As late as 1896, when he had already composed the overture *Caractacus* and *Froissart* and was about to embark on *Gerontius*, he was still occasionally to be found serving behind the counter.

He grew up to be rather shy and awkward, and his shyness made him seem aloof, especially with women, though he enjoyed his job as violin teacher at The Mount School for Girls (now a House of the Malvern Girls' College.) Rosa Burley, the Headmistress, recollected that in 1891, 'one day, after ensemble practice, he lingered on over tea, silent and diffident. Suddenly, without knowing how it had begun, I found myself listening to an outpouring of misery. . . . His shyness masked the kind of intense pride with which an unhappy man attempts to console himself for feelings of frustration and disappointment. . . . [He was] one of the most repressed people possible to imagine, enclosed, as it were, by a haunting fear of innumerable disapprovals'. Ostensibly his misery was professional, and Elgar told her that all he wanted was to write great music; but Rosa was young and attractive, and the young and attractive often find themselves used as agony aunts by lonely young men. She liked Edward, decided to take violin lessons from him and also joined his Ladies' Orchestral Class in Worcester.

Some years before his friendship with Rosa, Elgar had suffered a disappointment with a girl called Helen Weaver, the daughter of the owner of Weaver's Shoe Shop at 84 High Street, Worcester. She was studying the violin in Leipzig, and Elgar travelled to Germany to be with her, though his official reason for the trip was to hear the famous Gewandhaus Orchestra. In letters he referred to Helen as 'my *Braut*' — the German for fiancée as well as 'bride.' Even when Helen was with him, and they played music together, he had misgivings about the relationship: 'Miss Weaver is remaining in Worcester and the little music etc. that we get together is the only enjoyment I get and more than I deserve' — but soon he writes even more sadly, that 'Miss W. is going to New Zealand this month — her lungs are affected I hear & there has been a miserable time for me since I came home'. In those days 'affected lungs' usually indicated tuberculosis, usually fatal. She never returned. Some previously unknown letters about Helen did not come to light until 1990, having long been in the possession of a Lake District family, descendants of the recipient, Dr Charles Buck. He was a medical doctor and life-long friend of Elgar's. They suggest that the obstacle to their marrying were religious: she was a Unitarian.

He travelled to Scotland to try to forget her — and, at the Station Hotel, Inverness, in 1884, met another girl. We know nothing about her except that her initials were the same as his, E.E., and that perhaps she, too, was a violinist, as his

Idylle, op.4, for violin and piano, was inspired by her. What little we know is the result of his confiding, some 40 years later, in the object of his most passionate friendship, Alice Stuart Wortley. The two disappointments coming so close together probably set the tone for the musical portraits in the *Enigma* Variations, but these were not to be written until after he was married.

Though he hated teaching ('Like turning a grindstone with a dislocated shoulder,' he told Basil Maine) his practice expanded. When he felt he could cope with more pupils he took a room in Malvern, eight miles distant but likely to produce a better class of family to engage his services. He had a card printed and advertised for pupils in the local paper. As his daughter Carice Elgar Blake recalled later, 'This notice reached a certain lady living in the depths of the country nine miles away on the borders of Worcestershire and Gloucestershire and she decided to apply to Elgar for piano lessons. After the old coachman had driven her to Malvern for two or three months, he was heard to say that he thought there was more in it than music, which turned out to be perfectly true. Miss Roberts and my father were married in 1889, in spite of opposition from her family . . . and she gave up her own ambition to be a writer of repute in order to devote herself entirely to furthering my father's career.'

Alice was nearly a decade older than Edward and rising 41 when they married. Their daughter was born on the 14th of August 1890, and they named her Carice Irene, her first name compounded from her mother's two names, Caroline Alice — two names that before long were to take on an even greater significance for Elgar. (He was fond of such word games: their house at that time was called Craeg Lea, an anagram of E., A.C. ELGAR). Alice was a 'progressive' mother who, unlike other Victorians, neither swaddled her baby nor handed her to a nursemaid for cleansing: Elgar wrote to Charles Buck that Carice was 'a fearful joy & fatal to trousers', and added, 'I wd. as soon nurse an automatic irrigator. But it's a pretty little thing.'

In the summer of 1892, the Elgars took a holiday in Bavaria, visited Bayreuth and walked on the slopes of the Alps. With them came Rosa Burley, the Malvern headmistress, and one of her pupils, Alice Davey, as well as the nineteen-year-old Dora Penny — soon to be immortalized as 'Dorabella,' the girl with the tinkling laugh in Variation X of the *Enigma*. Elgar, as always, loved being the only man among women, and to be fussed over. On their return he wrote *Scenes from the Bavarian Highlands*, part-songs for which Alice provided the words. She was a gifted writer and had already published a novel but, said Carice later, 'She gave up her life-long ambition to be a writer of note because she was so sure that a genius had been given into her charge, and it was her proud responsibility to keep him from every worry and difficulty. . . .' — a feeling she shared with Alma Mahler. In fact most of her verse was feeble and stilted. Carice wrote: 'It was she who made, with very little money, a home of which he could be proud and to which his friends could be invited . . . .' Especially *her* friends, as she came from social circles far above his, and her family considered she had married beneath her. After all, she came from the aristocracy — albeit the recently ennobled — and he from 'trade', but she threw herself, heart and soul, into being her genius's amanuensis. 'It was she who ruled the bar-lines in all his scores and wrote in the choral parts when required, thereby saving him hours of manual labour; it was she who walked nearly two miles in sunshine or pouring rain to post the precious parcels of MSS.' She was tireless in promoting her husband's work, which sometimes meant gaining the ear of influential titled persons. Sir Adrian Boult, who knew Elgar well, said in his delightful reminiscences *My Own Trumpet* (1973) that it was at her suggestion that the Elgar Festival at Covent Garden was organized in 1904. He recollected that she was 'very tiny indeed, and had a quiet, intimate way of speaking . . .' (Boult was very tall), so that it ' . . . caused her to come close to anyone to whom she had anything important to say. As Frank [Schuster] put it, "You know the way dear Alice used to come up to one and confide in one's tummy?" Well, one day she said to my tummy, "Frank, dear, we are always going to Gloucester Festivals or Leeds Festivals and so on. Don't you think we might have an Elgar Festival some time?" My tummy reported what she had said and I went off to see Harry Higgins and that's how it all began.' But if Alice Elgar gave an impression of timidity it was only her social exterior: 'Where Elgar was concerned she was made of iron,' said Boult. She ruled the roost as well as his bar-lines.

As Elgar lost his youthful awkwardness so his love of the company of women became more pronounced. He preferred female pupils to male and liked to go for walks with them, for long bicycle rides, or play tennis: he loved outdoor pursuits. Mary Beatrice Alder, born in 1878, was a violin pupil of his in Malvern from the age of twelve to her late teens, when she went up to Oxford. She recorded her reminiscences for the BBC in the early 1970s, and said that at the end of their class they used to go into the garden and fly kites. Much later, a year or so after Alice Elgar's death, when he was in his mid-sixties, he seems to have been smitten with a 'violent affection' for the 25-year-old violinist Jelly d'Arányi after hearing her play his Violin Sonata, and called her 'My Darling Tenth Muse'. Michael Kennedy, taking his information from the violinist's biography by J. MacLeod, *The Sisters d'Arányi*, says that after he had taken her to lunch at his club in Pall Mall there was a little unseemly occurrence in a London taxi, which left her 'cursing old men'.

It is no coincidence that Elgar's concertos were often played by female soloists, remarkable in an age when women had fewer opportunities than they have now. Of the fourteen musical portraits depicted in the *Enigma* Variations, five are of women, No.1, of course, being Alice Elgar herself; and her Variation grows tenderly, almost imperceptibly, out of the Theme itself. Much has been made of the 'Enigma' of the title, in that it might contain a hidden quotation, or be a counter-subject to another tune. Elgar steadfastly refused to divulge the 'enigma' behind the *Enigma*, and although he teasingly dropped various clues they have led nowhere and he took the secret to his grave. At a dinner given by Frank Schuster on the 20th of November 1902, after the famous Meiningen Orchestra had played the *Enigma* Variations in London, the Elgars met a couple, Charles Beilby Stuart Wortley, a Member of Parliament and barrister, aged 51, and his

40-year-old wife, Alice Sophia Caroline, the daughter of the Pre-Raphaelite painter Sir John Everett Millais and Euphemia Millais ('Effie' Gray, who had been married to Ruskin). A few days after the dinner-party Elgar sent Alice Stuart Wortley a composition of his, a part-song.

Its choice ('this northern-sounding thing') was significant, the clue being the title, 'My Love dwelt in a Northern Land'. Stuart Wortley was MP for Sheffield. However, it is unlikely that any intimacy would have developed between them so quickly. The correspondence between him and Alice Stuart Wortley did not come to light until the late 1980s, when her descendants made it available to that devoted Elgarian, Jerrold Northrop Moore, who published it in 1989 under the title *The Windflower Letters*, followed a year later by *Letters of a Lifetime* — both volumes gratefully acknowledged here. Although the friendship between Edward and Alice was never a secret, the couple's closeness took posterity by surprise when its full extent was revealed.

The correspondence is unfortunately one-sided. Alice Stuart Wortley preserved all, or nearly all, of Elgar's letters, whereas he burnt those he received from her. Even the letters she received from him and kept often had parts either cut out or obliterated — by whom it is not known. Northrop Moore thinks the most likely culprit was Alice Stuart Wortley's daughter Clare, who might have been embarrassed by suggestions of impropriety. Some letters have disappeared altogether. Moore says that Elgar bought a whole box of distinctive, monogrammed stationery in Liverpool on the 1st of March 1915, which he kept exclusively for writing to Alice. Only six survive on this notepaper.

Alice's close friends and family called her Carrie; but Elgar — with old-fashioned English reticence — did not presume the familiarity of a nickname and after they progressed from the more formal address called her by her first given name, Alice — in spite of the possible confusion with Alice Elgar. Thus she was usually referred to in the Elgar household as 'the other Alice'; and Alice Elgar sometimes began letters to her with superscriptions like 'My dearest Namesake'. Alice Elgar knew, and approved, of the friendship, though she cannot have been aware of its extent.

It was not until 1909 that they were officially on first-name terms, when letters became increasingly affectionate. Elgar eventually called her Windflower — a secret name no-one else used. Another occurrence points to a less than innocent relationship. In April 1910 the Elgars had been invited to lunch with friends, but only Alice and Carice went. He stayed behind at their London flat, complaining of a 'dreadful headache' (to which he was genuinely prone). That afternoon he made an assignation with Windflower.

Their correspondence was not one between lovers separated by huge distances and rare meetings, but usually consisted of short, hurried (sometimes cryptic) notes, passed between people physically close who needed the additional comfort of written communication. Sometimes one or the other had gone to the country, but often both were in London. Elgar's London flat was only a short distance from the Stuart Wortleys' house. Elgar was, however, often away, being obliged to accept conducting engagements in the provinces.

The Windflower correspondence continued for more than three decades and proved both rejuvenating and inspirational for the composer. Alice Wortley provided him with the direct impetus, the crucial inspiration, for at least two works: the Violin Concerto (with its two 'Windflower themes') and much of the Symphony No. 2 (*'Your* Symphony,' as he repeatedly wrote to her). Elgar kept sending for her approval extracts or quotations of both works while he was working on them. Although in 1909 he dedicated his *Angelus*, op. 56, to the Windflower, he did not explicitly dedicate the Concerto to her. But at the head of the score he inscribed a Spanish text *'Aqu' está encerrada el alma de. . . .'* 'Here is enshrined the soul of . . . . .' — the five dots standing for Alice Sophia Caroline Stuart Wortley: no asterisks this time.

During the latter part of 1919 Alice Elgar, now over 70, began to be increasingly unwell, causing Edward and Carice much concern. Her condition worsened at the beginning of 1920, and she died on the evening of the 7th of April. At the funeral in Little Malvern, Elgar's violinist friend and favourite orchestral leader W. H. ('Billy') Reed and his string quartet played the slow movement, marked *piacevole*, from Elgar's String Quartet, which had been a favourite of Alice's.

After her death Elgar lost his will to compose and even, for a time, the will to live. He could not bear to return to their house, which he eventually vacated and stayed for a time with his sister Pollie. In a letter to the composer Walford Davies he wrote, on the 1st of May 1920, 'All I have done was owing to her and I am at present a sad and broken man.' He asked his architect friend from Malvern, Arthur Troyte Griffith ('Troyte' of Variation VII), to design Alice's headstone, beautifully cut in the English country churchyard tradition, with something of the elegant style of Eric Gill about it. After Alice's death the tone of his correspondence with the Windflower seemed to become cooler, 'My Dearest' giving way to 'My Dear'; the subscription 'Much love' disappears, to be replaced by the more perfunctory 'Love', and both are increasingly supplanted by 'Yours affectionately', 'Yours ever' or plain 'Yours'. Occasionally he even added his surname: 'Yours ever sincly Edward Elgar.' He seemed tired and old. Even before Alice's death he had written to Windflower, on the 22nd September 1919, 'The world is a changed place & I am awfully tired of it.'

The Windflower theme continued, with references to the real windflowers, which would not grow in his garden; but still none of her letters to him survive, even though there was no longer any need for secrecy. Alice Stuart Wortley had by then become Lady Alice Stuart of Wortley, her husband having been elevated to the peerage in 1917. He died in 1926.

Elgar outlived his wife by nearly 14 lonely years and died in Worcester on the 23rd of February, 1934. The Windflower followed him less than two years later, on the first day of 1936. His daughter Carice (Mrs Samuel Henry Blake) lived until 1970, and in 1954 could be seen, sitting alone in the gallery of Huddersfield Town Hall, listening to Sir Malcolm Sargent recording her father's *Dream of Gerontius* with the Royal Liverpool Philharmonic Orchestra (in which I then played). Dora

Powell ('Dorabella') survived until 1964. Of Helen Weaver nothing more was heard, and she presumably succumbed early in her life to her lung complaint in New Zealand. Rosa Burley never married, and died in 1951. Elgar's favourite sister Pollie (Mrs Susannah Mary Grafton) died in 1936, and his youngest sister, Helen Agnes ('Dot') in 1939. Isabel Fitton ('Ysobel' in the *Enigma* Variations) also remained unmarried, like Rosa, and died in 1936.

GABRIEL URBAIN FAURÉ

Born:	Pamiers, 12th of May 1845
Father:	Honoré Toussaint (1810–1885)
Mother:	Marie-Antoinette-Helène de Lalène-Laprade (1809–1887)
Married:	27th of March 1883 Marie Fremiet (1856–1926)
Sons:	Emmanuel (1883–1971)
	Philippe (1889–1954)
Died:	4th of November 1924

If marriage is a lottery, Fauré's was the result of something more like a prize draw — in which, he felt, fate had conspired to leave him with the booby prize. He had always been attractive to, and attracted by, women and enjoyed a long bachelor-hood full of butterfly affairs: 'the man who loved women' was his nickname in the Paris salons. Life was so pleasant that he delayed marrying until 1883, by which time he was nearly 40.

Everyone kept telling him to take a wife, and he did — often — and always other men's wives, usually for passionate, short-lived affairs. Handsome and unusually self-possessed, he was spoilt for choice, among both single women who saw in him a potential husband and married ones tired of — or neglected by — theirs. But when it came to making a final choice he always drew back, probably because the sheer volume of past experiences had raised his expectations — for, as Kipling said, 'The more you know of the others, the less you settle for one.'

Eventually a disinterested matron took him in hand and decided to act as his matchmaker. She was Mme Marguerite Baugnies, a bored society lady whose chief preoccupation in life was arranging 'suitable' marriages — she later acted as 'fixer' for Debussy's short-lived engagement to Thérèse Roger. At an early point in her matrimonial engineering, in 1870, she tried to 'arrange' Saint-Saëns as a husband for herself, but her parents considered him to be unsuitable.

Fauré had been engaged once: to Marianne, third daughter of Pauline Viardot, the celebrated mezzo-soprano, who was a student of Liszt and the object of Berlioz's admiration. When Fauré's engagement petered out, Mme Baugnies drew up a short list of three: the daughter of the popular author Octave Feuillet, the daughter of Georges Feydeau, the famous writer of French farces, and Marie Fremiet, daughter of the noted animal sculptor Emmanuel Fremiet. Marie Fremiet herself had ambitions to follow in her father's footsteps: she sculpted a little, without notable success, was interested in astronomy and painted flowers on fans. She did, however, possess most of the domestic virtues, which was unusual among Paris bohemians.

Fauré could not decide which of the three he liked best, so Mme Baugnies put their names into a hat. The lucky winner to be drawn was — Marie Fremiet. Only then did Fauré embark on an actual courtship, which involved the formalities customary at the time, the meeting of the families, the flowery request for the daughter's hand — and a discussion of the delicate matter of a dowry.

It had all the signs of an arranged marriage; although the relationship between Gabriel and Marie was not without love, it amounted to little more than an affectionate bond. But unlike many other arranged marriages (and naturally initiated ones) theirs lasted throughout their lives. Close though Gabriel and Marie were to each other, Fauré seemed to get on better with Emmanuel Fremiet than with his Marie: the two men struck up a deep intellectual friendship and became almost bosom pals, in spite of their disparate ages. Fauré was heart-broken when the old man died.

When Gabriel and Marie were separated they wrote many letters to each other, full of friendship and affection; but of passion there is no evidence. Even when they were both in Paris they did not talk much but seemed to prefer to communicate in writing. Only after her husband's death did Marie confide in a friend that their Trappist marriage had given her much hurt: 'He crucified me by his silence.' She confessed that it made her regard herself as 'the zero of the family'.

Gabriel and Marie were married on the 27th of March 1883, and at the end of the year their first son, Emmanuel, was born, followed in 1889 by Philippe. Being left alone with the children for much of the time, she became over-protective and pampered the boys. The elder did not marry until after her death.

The newly-weds spent their summers in a house bought by his in-laws, at Prunay, an area of the Seine valley favoured for holidays by the artistic Paris establishment — Impressionist painters, poets and composers were to be found there during the summer. Nearby lived Emma Moyse and her husband, the banker Sigismond Bardac. Fauré was drawn to Emma, and they had a passionate affair, which started with a 'honeymoon' on the Island of Jersey in 1904. M. Bardac was a tolerant husband — and the tolerance was, no doubt, mutual, leaving him, too, with the freedom he craved. One of their friends reported that after she had finally left her husband to set up home — not with Fauré but with Debussy (whom she eventually married), Bardac said, 'She's just treating herself to the latest fashion in composers; but I'm the one with the money. She'll be back.'

Under her spell, during the summers of 1892 and 1893, Fauré wrote the song-cycle *La bonne chanson* op.61, and also dedicated to her the fifth and sixth *Barcarolles*. As Fauré later told his pupil Jean Roger-Ducasse (quoted in Robert Orledge's Fauré biography): 'I never wrote anything more spontaneously than *La bonne chanson*, and I was aided by the spontaneity of the singer who remained its most moving interpreter. . . . I have never known any pleasure to equal that which I felt as I heard these pages coming to life, one after another, as I brought them to her.' Fauré not only adored Emma and respected her as an interpreter of his songs but allowed her gently to 'correct' parts of them, which he then dutifully rewrote. Their affair continued until he, so to speak, handed her over to Debussy in the same year. Sigismond Bardac gave her her freedom by divorcing her in 1908, by which time she and Debussy had already produced a daughter.

Another biographer, Jean-Michel Nectoux, who wrote the *Grove* article, said that hundreds of women entered Fauré's love life — and left it almost as quickly. To the casual listener the passion in Fauré's music seems understated — in a cool, almost English kind of way, but there is always an undercurrent of eroticism. Debussy likened his *Ballade* to 'a pretty woman adjusting her shoulder-strap'. Yet Fauré managed to paint his love scenes without the help of the orchestra, whose use he avoided for most of his life.

Englishwomen held a life-long attraction for Fauré. 'In London', Fauré wrote in Paris, 'all is dreams and poetry: here, alas, all is work and prose!' The actress Mrs Patrick Campbell was a force in his life, the moving spirit in his providing the music for Maeterlinck's *Pelléas et Mélisande*, in which she appeared. Mrs George Campbell Swinton, a contralto, he found so 'delightful' that he omitted to mention her in one of his usually frank and exhaustive letters home to his wife — a sure sign that there was more to the relationship than he cared to admit. In August 1898, Fauré took a holiday with Mrs Swinton at Llandough Castle near Cowbridge in South Wales, where he wrote the seventh Nocturne and dedicated it to her. But the most significant of Fauré's circle of English female admirers was Adela Maddison (Katherine Mary Adela, née Tindal), the wife of a director of Metzler & Co, the London music publishers founded in 1788 which issued some of Fauré's music. Mrs Maddison, herself a composer, immediately fell under Fauré's spell. The Maddison affair is said to have lasted for seven years. She finally left her husband and children and followed Fauré to Paris — to his embarrassment, for by that time he was pursuing new interests. He also had a long-term relationship with Marguerite Hasselmans, the sister of the cellist and conductor Louis Hasselmans. Although she was officially married to André Tracol, a professional violinist in the Paris Conservatoire Orchestra, the marriage was never consummated. Louis Hasselmans introduced her to Fauré in 1900; and, whilst she was content to be his mistress, their relationship was conducted in a most discreet manner. Everyone knew they were 'artistic companions' — 'an item' — but for once the notorious gossiping society ladies restrained their tongues, partly out of respect for Marie Fauré. No letters seem to have survived. Nor did he, for the sake of discretion, dedicate any of his music to her. Marguerite was the equivalent of the post-Victorian emancipated woman, who smoked cigarettes in public and dressed in an 'advanced' manner — like Chopin's George Sand but more fashionably.

There was probably also a relationship with the pianist Marguerite Long, a young pupil of Fauré, who felt close enough to him to show jealousy of Marguerite Hasselmans. Marie Fauré outlived her husband by eighteen months: she died at the age of 70 in March 1926. Adela Maddison survived him — in Ealing, West London — by four-and-a-half years and died in September 1929. Marguerite Hasselmans, the youngest (and longest-lasting) of his mistresses, endured the privations of the Second World War and died in September 1947 at the age of 71, in her modest Paris apartment, supported by unobtrusive contributions from Fauré's two lawful sons from his marriage to Marie. Here Marguerite would enchant callers with her lively conversation, recalling not only her years with Fauré but also her other friends, Paul Dukas and Isaac Albeniz, bringing to life her reminiscences with short illustrations on an old Erard upright piano.

CARLO GESUALDO, PRINCE OF VENOSA, COUNT OF CONZA, ETC.

Born:	Naples ca. 1561
Father:	Fabrizio Gesualdo (Second Prince of Venosa)
Mother:	Girolama Borromeo ('niece' of Pope Pius IV)
Married:	1st 1586, Donna Maria d'Avalos, Marquesa di Pesquara d.26th of October 1590
Son:	Don Emmanuele
Married:	2nd Leonora d'Este (daughter of Alfonso II) 21st of February 1594
Son:	Don Alfonsino, d. aged five or six in 1600
Died:	Gesualdo, Avellino, 8th September 1613

Skeletons lurk in many a musical cupboard, but Carlo Gesualdo, Prince of Venosa, one of the greatest composers of the Italian Renaissance, provides real corpses. Contemporary court records attest to the murder of his wife, her lover and possibly also their baby, although the *bimbocidio* has never been proved. His homosexual leanings too, can only be presumed circumstantially; but his proclivities for flagellation, disguised as either Christian penance or a cure for chronic constipation, are documented. So is a single, witnessed and premeditated act of transvestism on the part his wife's lover just before they were murdered; and an unsubstantiated report of necrophilia, alleging that a novice monk had 'used' the body of the murdered princess when it was lying unattended before being taken for burial.

From an early age Gesualdo had a passion for music that appeared to displace and supplant all other juvenile pursuits. It was a form of *melomania* almost akin to that of Mozart, who even as a baby was transfixed by the slightest musical sound and forgot all else, his toys and the need for food. All Gesualdo asked was a lute, a harpsichord, and convivial company to play and sing with. His father, Fabrizio Gesualdo, was invested Prince of Venosa by Philip II in 1560 as ruler of his immediate Principality and Lord of half a dozen Dukedoms; his mother was the sister of Cardinal Carlo Borromeo and 'niece' (which usually meant bastard) of Pope Pius IV. Carlo Gesualdo was Fabrizio's second son and thus felt himself absolved from the duty of producing heirs. But in 1585, his elder brother Luigi died, so Carlo found himself as ruling Prince, saddled with the responsibility of continuing the ancestral line. Marriage suddenly became a pressing need.

He was then nearly 30, which by the prevailing life-expectancy made him what today's newspapers call a 'confirmed' bachelor; and the tabloids would mention in the same breath his 'close friendship' with Torquato Tasso (1544–1595), celebrated as a poet and misunderstood as a paranoiac (the subject of poems by Byron and Goethe and posthumous provider of numerous opera libretti) who later poetically chronicled Gesualdo's misfortunes.

Gesualdo set about finding a wife on whom to beget the all-important heir. His choice fell upon his cousin, Donna Maria d'Avalos. For one thing, she was part of his extended family, so that its riches would not be dispersed; and for another — and more important for his purposes — she had already given proof of her fertility, having been married by the time she was fifteen and borne children, but was twice widowed. One gets the impression that Gesualdo wanted to get the tedious business of fathering a son over and done with as quickly as possible so that he could return to making music with his friends.

Not long after Gesualdo and Donna Maria married she gave birth to a son, Emmanuele, the heir to the fortune and titles of Venosa. At such a moment most marriages are cemented into a lasting family bond. Others, however, begin to disintegrate, and for a variety of reasons: the wife is no longer a lover but a mother, with a new focus for her affections; or the husband finds himself threatened by a relationship which appears to exclude him. For the Gesualdos the arrival of a son signalled disaster; and although the marriage remained apparently happy for more than two years, other factors were beginning to take their toll. His preoccupation with the musical *camerata* of young men of his bachelorhood was undiminished. Like all noblemen, he hunted, but nothing delighted him like music. The princess doubtless felt rejected, neglected and excluded, and as a doubly widowed woman known for her sexual appetite she began to cast her eye round for a lover. Her choice fell on the young Don Fabrizio Carafa, Duke of Andria.

Several manuscripts record the terrible events that took place in the year 1590, when Gesualdo caught his unfaithful wife and her lover *in flagrante delicto*. One is a literal transcript of the proceedings at Gesualdo's subsequent trial, entitled *Informatione presa dalla Gran Corte della Vicaria*, another, a contemporary account, in what might be the language of a newspaper reporter and therefore doubtless a little embroidered also. The murder was not merely a momentous news story but, in modern terms, a juicy scandal. Additional reports were sent home by diplomats: for example, the Venetian ambassador to Naples wrote:

> The devil, unable to endure the sight of such love and happiness, such conformity of tastes and desires in two married people, awakened in the bosom of Donna Maria impure desires and a libidinous, unbridled appetite for the sweetness of illicit love; also a longing for the beauty of a certain nobleman. This was Fabrizio Carafa, third Duke of Andria and seventh Count of Ruovo, reputed to be the handsomest and most accomplished prince, in age not yet arrived at the sixth lustre,* in manners so courteous and gracious, in appearance so exquisite, that from his features one would take him for Adonis; while from his manner and bearing he was a Mars. He had already been long married to Donna Maria Carafa, daughter of Don Luigi, Prince of Stigliano, a lady of great beauty and supreme goodness, by whom he had four children. But the

---

Lustrum, a period of five years, so he was under 30.

equality of lovers' ages, the similarity of their tastes, the numerous occasions presented by balls and feasts, the equal desire of both parties to take pleasure in each other, were all tinder to the fire that burnt in their breasts. The first messengers of their mutual flames were their eyes . . . from glances they progressed to words, from words to letters, carried by faithful messengers, in which they challenged each other to sweet combat in the lists of love.

Like many illicit lovers of high standing, the pair lacked privacy for clandestine meetings, being constantly attended and escorted by servants and retainers who had to be taken into their confidence; but they managed to keep their affair from Gesualdo for two years. The Ambassador again:

The first occasion of their coming together was in a convenient place in the garden of the Borgo di Chiaia, in the pavilion whereof the Duke did lie concealed, awaiting his beloved; who, on pretext of diversion and entertainment, was taken there. She, while walking, affected to be overcome by some bodily pain and, separating herself from her escort, entered into the pavilion wherein lay the Duke who, without the loss of one moment, put into execution the work of love. Many and many times did they come together in various and divers secret places according to such opportunities as were afforded by fortune. Most frequently it was in the palace of the Princess, even in her very bedchamber where, with her maidservant keeping watch, they often did dally together in the ultimate delights of love.

The maidservant and others who knew about the affair eventually contributed to the lovers' downfall; and the evidence given by Donna Maria's servants at Gesualdo's trial was crucial for his conviction. Another factor in the tragedy was the jealousy of Gesualdo's uncle, Don Giulio. He had himself hoped to console his nephew's neglected wife, but was rejected:

The lovers' practice, having become frequent and familiar, came to the ears of relations and friends of the Prince, amongst others', to those of Don Giulio Gesualdo, uncle of the Prince Don Carlo. This Don Giulio himself had fiercely lusted after the charms of Donna Maria and had left no stone unturned in order to attain his desire. But, having been several times reproached by her for his foolish frenzy and warned that if he persisted she would report his pestering to her husband the Prince, the unhappy Don Giulio did cease to importune her, believing her to be a chaste Penelope. But when whispers came to his ears concerning the loves and pleasures of Donna Maria and the Duke of Andria, such was the wrath and fury which assailed him on discovering that the strumpet did lie with others, that straightway he revealed all to the Prince. In the meanwhile, the lovers had been warned that their secret had become known, whereupon the Duke of Andria gave pause to his pleasures. But Donna Maria, unable to endure this remission, solicited the Duke that they should resume their dalliance again. He represented to her the dangers to honour and life which would ensue to both of them alike if they did not keep their debauched desires under control. In reply to these prudent reasonings, the Princess taunted him that if his heart was capable of fear he had better become a lackey; and that nature had surely erred in creating a knight with the spirit of a woman while creating in her a woman with the spirit of a valorous knight. If he were capable of sheltering fear in his heart, she said, he had better chase from it his love for her and never enter her presence again.

Donna Maria's barbed taunts about her lover's femininity were well-aimed, if there is any significance in the fact that when the lovers died together, he was found to be wearing her nightshirt — not because he was cold and it happened to be at hand but because she had specially ordered it before his arrival for their tryst in her bedroom. The Duke had forebodings (or else had been warned that he and Maria were under suspicion) and tried to end his relationship, but Maria accused him of cowardice:

To these taunts the unhappy Duke, bowing humbly in token of submission, replied, 'Since you wish to die, I shall die with you. If such is your wish, so be it.' And so did they continue in their delights.

Gesualdo, now alert and on the watch, had all the locks of the doors in the palace secretly changed from iron to wood so they could be broken down, particularly of the room wherein the Princess was wont to dally amorously with her lover. One day he gave out his intention of going to the chase, as was his custom, declaring also that he would not return that night. Accordingly he set out in hunting attire and on horseback, accompanied by a retinue of intimates and followers, and made as if to go to the place known as Gli Astroni, having previously left orders with some of his servants who were privy to the secret, to leave open at night all the necessary doors, but in such wise that they should yet retain the appearance of being closed, and they should keep watch to see if the Duke were to come. Then the Prince took his departure and went to conceal himself in the house of one of his relations.

The Duke, having learnt that the Prince had departed on a hunting expedition and would not return that night, set forth at four hours of the night in search of his usual pleasures and was received by Donna Maria with her wonted affection. Both disrobed and got into bed, where they several times pleasured each other until, overcome by fatigue from their supreme raptures, they fell asleep, both in body and soul. In the meanwhile, the Prince, having returned secretly to the palace at midnight, accompanied by a posse of armed men, made his way rapidly to the bedchamber of the Princess and with one blow broke open the door. Entering furiously he discovered the lovers in bed together, his wife lying naked in the arms of the Duke; at which sight the state of mind of the unhappy Prince can be imagined. But quickly shaking off the dejection into which this miserable spectacle had plunged him, he slew with innumerable dagger thrusts the sleepers before they had time to waken. And after he had ordered that their dead bodies should be dragged from the room and left exposed, he made a statement of his reasons for this butchery and departed with his familiars to his city of Venosa.

This tragedy took place on the night of the 16th of October 1590. The bodies of the wretched lovers remained exposed all the following morning in the midst of the hall, and all the city flocked to see the pitiful sight. The lady's wounds were all in the belly, and more particularly in those parts which she ought to have kept chaste; and the Duke was wounded even more grievously. It is said that while the said corpses were lying on the said staircase a monk of San Dominico ravished the said Donna Maria even though she was dead. At the hour of vespers the Duke's body was removed for burial and that of the Princess the next day, amidst the lamentations of the entire city.

A famous painting shows Gesualdo, the wicked uncle, the corpses of Maria and her lover — as well a representation of Gesualdo's child by Donna Maria, who was said also to have been murdered on that dreadful night because Gesualdo imagined he saw a likeness to his wife's lover. Others have thrown doubt on the story and have even suggested that the child in the painting represents Cupid — in other words, that Gesualdo also murdered Love.

Gesualdo's trial took place on the 27th of October 1590 before the Grand Court of the Vicariate (a Court of Deputies). The Royal Councillors and Criminal Justices of the Grand Court, together with the Magnificent Fiscal Procurator, reported, in the words of the Master of the Grand Court, that on entering into the upper apartments of the palace there had been found:

> . . . in the said house, in the furthest room thereof, stretched out upon the ground, the most illustrious Don Fabrizio Carafa, Duke of Andria. The only clothing upon the body was a woman's nightshirt, worked with lace, with a collar of black silk and with one sleeve red with blood, and the said Duke of Andria was covered with blood and wounded in many places, as follows: an arquebus wound in the left arm passing from one side of the elbow to the other and also through the breast, the sleeve of the said nightshirt being scorched; many and divers wounds in the chest made by sharp steel weapons, also in the arms, in the head and in the face; and another arquebus wound in the temple above the left eye whence there was an abundant flow of blood. And in the selfsame room was found a gilt bed with curtains of green cloth, and within the said bed was found dead Donna Maria d'Avalos clothed in a nightdress, and the bed was filled with blood. On being seen by the aforesaid gentlemen and by me, the aforesaid body was recognized to be that of Donna Maria d'Avalos, lying dead with her throat cut; also with a wound in the head, in the right temple, a dagger thrust in the face, more dagger wounds in the right hand and arm, and in the breast and flank two sword thrusts. . . .

The catalogue of injuries continues in this gruesome manner, and evidence was given of the changed locks, as well as the presence, kind and number, of abandoned torches and bloodstained weapons. Gesualdo was found guilty but, as nobleman and ruler of his particular province, his sentence was no more than temporary banishment to his own estates in the district of Gesualdo — whence he had fled in any case, as his fortified castle offered the best protection against revenge attacks from vendetta-bent relatives of his wife: this threat never materialized, and eventually the inter-family strife was patched up. With two Cardinals in the family — Alfonso Gesualdo, Archbishop of Naples, and Cardinal Borromeo, his mother's brother, he was never in any serious danger from the law:

> The Prince Don Carlo Gesualdo lived to see his crimes punished by God through the infliction of four great misfortunes resulting in the total extermination of his house and race. The first of these was that he did suffer great shame for the space of two years owing to the conduct of Donna Maria d'Avalos, his wife, in lying with Don Fabrizio Carafa, the Duke of Andria, almost every night, practically within sight of her husband. Having slain Donna Maria, by whom he had a son, Don Emmanuele, Don Carlo became deranged and began to treat his vassals not only lasciviously but also tyrannically; and owing to this, the anger of God being aroused against him, he lost a beautiful male child whom he had by Donna Leonora d'Este, and this was his second affliction. The third affliction was that through the agency of God he was assailed and afflicted by a vast horde of demons which gave him no peace for many days on end unless ten or twelve young men, whom he kept specially for the purpose, were to beat him violently three times a day, during which operation he was wont to smile joyfully. And in this state did he die miserably at Gesualdo, but not until he had lived to witness his fourth affliction, the death of his only son Don Emmanuele, who hated his father and had longed for his death and, what was worse, this son died without leaving any children save two daughters, whom he had by Donna Polisena of Fürstemberg, a German princess.

On his banishment to the Gesualdo estates his close friend from bachelor days, the poet Torquato Tasso, deserted him. In spite of his earlier friendship, Tasso now took the side of the lovers, and romanticized their plight. He wrote several sonnets about the tragedy which, in their florid hyperbole, might almost have been texts for Gesualdo's madrigals.

The Duke of Andria's widow remained in shock for the rest of her life. As an act of atonement the Prince founded a monastery in Gesualdo, in whose church, completed two years after the murders, still hangs the famous painting (alluded to above) which bears the only known portrait of the composer and depicts, in metaphorical form, the drama and its main actors. In 1594, Gesualdo married again, a Donna Leonora d'Este of Ferrara, by whom he had a son, Don Alfonsino. She, too, soon complained of neglect and that she was bored by her husband's incessant music-making and the constant presence of poets and composers, whose company he preferred to hers. She was strong-willed, and angered Gesualdo by spending long periods at Modena with her brother, Duke Cesare d'Este. Reports suggest that Gesualdo physically ill-treated Leonora, and at one time divorce proceedings are thought to have been instituted by the d'Este family. Leonora survived him by many years, and it is on her evidence alone, in a letter of the 13th of September 1613 that we have the probable date of Gesualdo's death, earlier in that month. Contemporary sources claimed she was responsible for her husband's death, though it is not known by what means. Gesualdo's heir-presumptive, Don Emmanuele, his son by the murdered Maria d'Avalos, grew to manhood and produced a daughter (possibly two — accounts vary — who being females could not succeed to his title); and Emmanuele himself predeceased Gesualdo by a few months. Thus the curse on the Gesualdos was fulfilled.

Gesualdo himself continued consorting with many of the great composers and performers of his day (he himself played the archlute and guitar) and wrote the most beautiful — almost futuristic — music to come out of Renaissance Italy. His life inspired several plays and novels, including those by Brantôme and Anatole France; and not only Tasso but Giovanni Battista Marino, Capaccio and Cortese produced verse accounts.

CHARLES FRANÇOIS GOUNOD

Born: Paris, 17th of June 1818
Father: François-Louis Gounod (1758–1823)
Mother: Victoire Lemachois (1780–1858)
Married: Anna Zimmermann
Son: Jean Gounod (born 1856)
Daughter: Jeanne (born 1863)
Died: St Cloud, 18th of October 1893

Gounod was torn between opposing forces. His father was a well-known painter who worked and lived in the Louvre, and Charles inherited his artistic gifts. His mother, a pianist, was so impressed by his musical ear that she gave him intensive lessons from infancy. Thus Gounod's career might have gone in either direction. As he began to grow up, he gravitated between his love for religion and the church on the one hand, and opera and the theatre on the other. Soon there were even stronger dichotomies: between his love for his mother and for practically every pretty girl or woman he met; and when he was older the most explosive conflict of all erupted, between his loyalty to his wife and his formidable English mistress, Georgina Weldon. The Catholic religion was always a force in him, and for most of his life the composer of *Faust* was better known as a provider of rather turgid religious music (including some twenty Masses, 30 Motets and Canticles, and half-a-dozen Oratorios) especially among his English admirers, who included Queen Victoria. For a time he took a leaf out of Liszt's book and signed himself 'Abbé Gounod'.

In his *Mémoires d'un artiste* (1896) Gounod said that he owed everything to his mother, a hardworking woman who made sacrifices to feed, clothe and educate her children. She would rise early, receiving her first pupil by 5 a.m. Gounod entered the Paris Conservatoire at the age of eighteen — already proficient as both artist and musician — to study counterpoint under Halévy, composition with Le Sueur, and the piano with Pierre Zimmermann. Such was his aptitude — and so thorough had his upbringing been — that in the following year he won the Second Prix de Rome, and the Grand Prix two years later.

Towards the end of 1839, he left for Rome to take up residence, as required of Rome Prize winners, at the Villa Medici. Its Director was the painter Ingres, who had been a colleague of Gounod's father and was a keen music-lover and amateur violinist — a fact which gave rise to the still-current French expression *le violon d'Ingres*, meaning an artist's artistic hobby drawn from another discipline. Ingres and Gounod got on well: they played music together and each drew portraits of the other. Ingres set him to work making about a hundred copies of his drawings; and, when his musical prize expired, encouraged him (in vain) to enter for the Rome Prize for art. In Rome, Gounod fell under the spell of, and doubtless in love with, Mendelssohn's sister, Fanny, who was a dozen years older than Gounod and by then married to the artist Wilhelm Hensel. Gounod was affected by her masterly playing (she could play Bach's *Forty-Eight* from memory by the time she was thirteen and would probably have been as good a composer as her brother, had she had the same opportunities). It is difficult to tell whether it was love on Gounod's part or simply heroine-worship: at any rate, 'he covered her in kisses.' She in turn wrote in her diary, 'I have seldom known anyone who could enjoy himself so wholeheartedly and completely as he' — but also perceptively noted that he was 'of a weak and impressionable character.' She introduced him to the music of Bach and Beethoven, as well as that of her brother Felix. James Harding says that her 'playing of a Beethoven sonata reduced him to such a state that he ended up screaming absurdities. . . .' and that ' . . . his fellow-students, kindly but firmly, led him off to bed, shouting still'. The Fanny experience seemed slightly to have unhinged Gounod — the first recorded episode of his mental instability, which occurred only occasionally and left no lasting effect.

The young Charles Gounod was next befriended by the celebrated mezzo-soprano Pauline Viardot, about whom Berlioz said, 'Madame Viardot is one of the greatest artists ... in the past and present history of music.' Charles impressed her with his musicality, which she thought close to genius, and she promised to sing the lead role in his first opera, *Sapho* — when he had written it. The new-found friendship inspired him to set to work, but despite her championship and Berlioz's praise, the work proved a failure.

Pauline Viardot was one of the most extraordinary women of the century (Gounod attracted them, as will be seen later). She had made her début at only seventeen as *Desdemona* in Rossini's *Otello* and was Berlioz's favourite singer; but she shone also outside opera: she gave the first performance of Brahms's *Alto Rhapsody*. In 1840, she married the wealthy theatre director, Louis Viardot, 21 years older than herself, and they kept one of the most elegant salons in Paris. She was also, for many years, the reputed mistress of the Russian writer Ivan Turgenev; and indeed the three of them, Pauline, Louis ('Loulou') and Ivan, shared a notorious *ménage à trois*. Young Gounod now made it four. No absolute proof exists that Pauline and the men *were* lovers but circumstances and subsequent events make out a good case. Yet, in spite of much speculation, nothing was proved, and, outwardly at least, proprieties were observed. After the sudden death of Gounod's brother, a young architect, who left a pregnant wife and two-year-old son, Pauline invited Gounod, his parents and relatives, to take up residence in her country house until they had sorted out their affairs. The play which Turgenev was writing at this time, *A Month in the Country*, is thought to reflect some of the gossip concerning the *ménage à quatre*, yet Turgenev and Gounod remained on the best of terms, at least for the time being.

In June 1850, the happy relationship between Pauline and Louis on one hand, and Gounod on the other, came precipitously to an end. Gounod's philandering may have given her cause for jealousy, but the main reason was an act of monstrous, almost inexplicable, tactlessness on his part, which Pauline and Louis rightly regarded as treachery. Gounod unexpectedly announced to Pauline that he was now engaged, so suddenly that at first she had no idea who his betrothed was. His choice had fallen on Anna Zimmermann, the daughter of his former teacher at the Conservatoire. Charles was by this time aged 32, and his social skills had made him a fixture in his professor's domestic entertainments, encouraged by Mme Zimmermann, who immediately saw him as a potential husband for one of her four unmarried daughters. Like Louis Viardot the theatre director, Zimmermann the musical academic was influential, and he too kept a fashionable salon in whose company Gounod thought he would find the key to further success: he did, but apparently the daughter went with the job (a situation both Handel and Bach narrowly escaped when they turned down an apprenticeship with Buxtehude because they did not wish to marry *his* daughter). In addition, the Zimmermanns owned much property, bringing the prospect of an inheritance and, perhaps, eventual retirement to a country seat. Of more immediate importance was a well-paid job.

Gounod was always welcomed at soirées and other social gatherings, as he was able to amuse assemblages of fashionable people by accompanying himself singing at the piano (in a small but charming voice) or to his own guitar. Mme Zimmermann had always been wary of him, calling him behind his back 'the philandering monk' — and indeed he seems to have exuded a strange mixture of piety and simmering eroticism women found irresistible; but she had to find husbands for her four daughters, and Gounod looked like a young genius with prospects. She began to drop hints, suggesting that people had been talking about him and Anna. The hints then turned into an ultimatum: either get engaged or cease your visits to our salon. James Harding, in his biography of Gounod, puts forward the theory that the composer's ill-considered marriage was the result of a tactical error. 'He wrote a letter explaining that under the circumstances he did not think he should aspire to Anna's hand' but made the mistake of delivering it himself, by hand. Mme Zimmermann, misunderstanding his visit, thought he had come to ask for her daughter's in marriage and, '. . . before he could hand over the letter, she exclaimed joyfully, "Ah, my dear child, I was expecting your visit. Come and embrace your betrothed!" Slipping the undelivered letter into his pocket, he dared do nothing else but obey. Later on, he used ruefully to say: "What a subject for a comic opera: *le Fiancé malgré lui*!" ' But then, as Fanny Hensel had said, Gounod did have a weak and impressionable character. The engagement was announced, to the astonishment of the *ménage*, suddenly reduced to three. Gounod this time found the courage to break the news to Pauline, heavily pregnant with her first child. Her breathless account of events survives in a correspondence with her friend George Sand:

> . . . Gounod arrived at the house, looking very strange and, turning purple, told Louis and me, 'My dear friends, I have two great pieces of news to announce to you. I am getting married and I have been chosen Head Supervisor of the Orphéonistes of France.' At the first news I felt as if I had had

a blow in the chest; aware of certain backstage gossip, I trembled at the thought that he was marrying Mlle. Poinsot, which I admit would have distressed me. When he told us it was Mlle. Zimmermann, the relief I felt equalled my surprise, which was not slight. He had never mentioned the family to us except to laugh at them, describing Monsieur Z. as an *old blockhead*, Mme. Z as an *insipid flatterer*, and the girls as *frightful shrimps*. I kept to myself the fresh memory of these epithets, and, upon my word, I complimented him heartily on his choice. Anna, whom I had known since childhood, always seemed to me a good girl, and her family had always shown me an affection which I returned with interest. We were invited to dine there the same day. Upon our arrival, father, mother, daughter, everybody, fell on my neck, kissing me and stifling me with caresses. At my question, 'When is the wedding?' they answered with one voice, 'After your confinement' — 'We will not be married without you' — 'We will select a day of your choice' — and a thousand other affectionate things which moved me to tears. Before parting we settled on a day when we would all dine together at my house.

However, the date was postponed by the Zimmermanns, twice, each time on some contrived pretext. On the third occasion they agreed — the Zimmermanns failed to show up. Pauline reported to George Sand:

> When the chickens were roasted, and the table almost set, Gounod arrived and told me with an embarrassed air that the dinner could not take place because his Anna was indisposed, that she had taken medicine! All this without a word of regret from the Zimmermann family.

Charles and Anna were married in April 1852, but the Viardots were absent. Louis had expected to be a witness at the ceremony, but neither he nor Pauline had been invited. In spite of this snub, Pauline was prepared to be conciliatory, by not withholding the wedding present, as might under the circumstances have been reasonable:

> The next day we sent a handsome inkstand to his home, with an affectionate little note. I added to it a box containing a souvenir for his fiancée, a bracelet with a note for her, which I wrote in bed and which I asked him to give to her from me. . . . The next day I was brought a small package from Gounod. I opened it, and found there — the bracelet! With a word from Gounod, saying that *he* was 'going to give his wife, at the same time as the wedding ring, a bracelet, and *that* one was the only one she wished to wear'; and that consequently, to spare me a refusal which would be as painful for Anna to make as for me to receive, he was taking it upon himself to return this souvenir to me, thanking me nevertheless for my good intentions and desiring me to accept his best wishes for me, my dear husband, and all my family.

In fact, Anna never got to see the bracelet, as Gounod had kept it from her. It

was a monumental insult from the Zimmermann-Gounod families to the Viardot-Turgenev salon, and the clearest indication that Gounod was no longer willing —
or permitted by his in-laws — to be friends with the Viardots. Louis Viardot wrote
an icy letter to his former friend, for whom he and his wife had done so much:

> Paris: 1st of June 1852. Monsieur: It is no longer my wife's duty, but mine, to
> write to you. Since you have had the weakness, I should say the cowardice, to
> make yourself the intermediary and accomplice of an insult addressed to a lady
> whom you should at least respect, you will not be surprised that I am closing to
> you henceforth the door of our home. You will, without doubt, one day be a
> great musician, Sir, and you will have admirers, but I doubt if you will keep any
> friends. Louis Viardot.

The letter brought Gounod to his senses and made him realize how bad his
behaviour had been. He apologized profusely, as verbosely as only he could,
explaining that his in-laws had heard certain rumours about their four-sided
relationships and felt a certain unease, but he expressed the hope that their
friendship might still be mended. Viardot again rebuffed him, and again Gounod
tried to explain, but it was to no avail. One by one his friends deserted him,
including George Sand, who said of him that he was 'a mysterious phenomenon
of a bad heart in conjunction with a beautiful mind'. Pauline summed up
Gounod, and her feelings about him, to Sand:

> Oh, by the way, do you know that Gounod, since the moment when he
> announced his marriage, has behaved to us like an ingrate? With all his
> appearance of feeling, that *heart* of which he talks so much in such eloquent
> language, is nothing but a windbag of egoism, vanity and calculation — in a
> word he is a *Tartuffe*. Dear God, what a disillusionment! If ever a man was
> welcomed into a family like a child of the house it was he. Well, no matter. In
> spite of all the sorrow that his ignoble conduct causes us, especially to me, I
> shall never regret the help I have been able to give him — he is a great
> musician, perhaps the greatest of our time. How is it that such genius can exist
> where there is no *genuine heart*? You, who know men so well, perhaps you can
> explain this mystery to me. All I know about it is that it is horrible.

Even Bizet, whom Gounod had befriended as a boy and employed as assistant,
eventually turned against his master (though that was after he himself had found
success as a composer with *La jolie fille de Perth*, of which, he claimed, Gounod was
jealous). Gounod was, his former friends said, nothing more than an *arriviste* who
had made use of the Viardots when it suited him, but now, under the familial wing
of the rich and influential Zimmermanns, had no further need of them. As
Thérèse Marix-Spire wrote (*Music and Letters*, No.31), 'Gounod was never again to
be a familiar figure of the salon enriched by the free artistic communion of
Berlioz, Rossini, Meyerbeer, Saint-Saëns, Scheffler, Delacroix, George Sand,
Renan, Dickens, Flaubert, Turgenev — the leading musicians, the leading

painters, the leading authors of the century. It is difficult to say what his music lost thereby.' Turgenev continued to live with the Viardots, and Pauline and Louis had several more children (if they were his). Her son became a violinist, later conductor, at the Paris Opera, and the third daughter, Marianne, also found fame as a singer and was for a time engaged to Gabriel Fauré.

Pauline Viardot's *Memories and Adventures* were published in London in 1911 — and what memories she offered! Her voice deteriorated early in her life, but she was well prepared for a second career, having studied the piano with Liszt and composition with Reicha; so she turned to writing and produced a comic opera, *Lindoro*, which was staged in Weimar; and a Cantata *Das Bacchusfest* in Stockholm; also a string quartet and numerous songs. Now that women composers are at last getting the notice many deserve, a revival of interest in Pauline Viardot's works seems overdue.

Gounod's marriage to Anna proved stormy, as she had taken after her domineering mother and tried to manipulate him. Yet she supported him loyally through his disappointments and failures and turned a blind eye when he found consolation in the arms of a procession of other women. Like many a French wife of her class, she took such infidelities her stride. They found joy in their children, although one daughter died soon after her birth; and there is nothing to suggest that Charles Gounod was a bad father. When Pierre Zimmermann died, he left Gounod and Anna a splendid little palace at Saint-Cloud, furnished with fine furniture and containing Pierre's extensive library, the house surrounded by formal gardens. In 1858 Gounod's mother died. She had been ill for a long time but he keenly felt the loss of the woman to whom he owed everything, who had sacrificed herself to set him on the road to success and dominated his life for more than forty years.

The outbreak of the Franco-Prussian War in July 1870 set in train a chain of events which was to change the rest of Gounod's life. To help the war effort he composed a rousing patriotic song, *À la frontière!* — and then hurried in the opposite direction, to the Channel coast, where he had sent his family, as far away as possible from the invading Prussians. Varangeville, near Dieppe, was conveniently situated for escape to England, as the Prussians advanced on Paris, and its citizens were reduced to eating dogs and rats.

The Gounods — he, his wife, mother-in-law and children were installed in a house in Blackheath, near London, belonging to a Mrs Louisa Brown, a family friend. He had always liked England, not least because the country's choral societies loved the grandeur of his religious works, and he hoped for royal patronage. His operas *Faust* and *Roméo et Juliette* had already established his success in England, *Faust* having been first given in June 1863 (in Italian!) at Her Majesty's Theatre.

Once in England Gounod lost no time in composing another patriotic effusion, *Gallia*, in support of his stricken country, and conducted it in the packed Royal Albert Hall on the 1st of May 1871. London brought another bonus in the form of a reconciliation with Louis and Pauline Viardot, fellow-refugees from the war with whom they shared feelings of homesickness. But time had passed, and relations were never the same again. Besides, Gounod was about to meet the woman who was to change his destiny.

On the 26th of February 1871, a dinner-party and *soirée* took place at the home of Sir Julius Benedict, the German-born conductor and composer knighted by Queen Victoria. Among the guests was an Army officer, Captain Harry Weldon, with his outstandingly beautiful wife, Georgina, a society singer. Benedict himself had taken a fancy to her because of her beauty as well as her remarkably pure soprano, a boyish, 'white' type — '*une voix des deux sexes*,' as Gounod described it. He was rising 53 and, as always when there was a beautiful woman in the company, he directed all his attention towards her.

She was born Georgina Thomas, on the 24th of May 1837 in Clapham, South London, the daughter of a barrister. It was none of her doing that she turned into Georgina Traherne: her father had decided it sounded more aristocratic and evoked a putative distant ancestor to justify the change in the family's name. In her late teens she 'came out', which then meant being presented to the Queen among batches of debutantes; a quaint custom that survived beyond the middle of the twentieth century. At some social function, probably one of the Victorian musical evenings the supposedly unmusical English delighted in, she met Captain Harry Weldon, an amiable but bumbling young Hussar, and he asked for her hand. Her parents rejected him, as his fortune less than £2,000 a year — in fact, a quite sizeable income at a time when a schoolmaster might have received one tenth of it. Mr and Mrs Traherne, having an asset on their hands of such rare beauty, had hoped to marry her off to someone worth at least ten thousand. But Georgina had already responded to Weldon's advances and fallen in love with him; and although, as an officer and gentleman, he honourably withdrew his suit, she over-rode her parents' objections and married him. The parents promptly cut her off with the traditional penny. She knew that her future was secure, as she had already been noticed in the highest circles: the Prince of Wales took an interest in her, and she sang in many great houses, Gounod's songs figuring in her repertoire. Her influence secured for Harry, who had retired from the army, a post at the College of Heralds, where he eventually became Rougedragon Pursuivant (the institution still awards these strange titles to its officers, who deal with matters of familial succession and the design of coats of arms for the newly-ennobled).

She later recalled that at the Benedicts' *soirée* Gounod pointedly sang his own song, *À une jeune fille*, while fixing her with his gaze, though she was a not-so-*jeune fille* of 35. Mme Gounod was wearily used to her husband's antics towards girls (even schoolgirls, it was darkly rumoured by Bizet and others) and pretended not to notice. Georgina later gushed, 'He seemed to be specially addressing himself to me. I did not know which way to look. My tears, which had begun to flow at the first line, had become a rivulet, the rivulet had become a stream, the stream a torrent, the torrent sobs, the sobs almost a fit!' Later she claimed that her looks were her misfortune, in that, as she said, 'being beautiful only helps men who are no good to fall in love with one', an inconvenience she apparently bore bravely. Gounod was himself by then no Adonis, having lost the youthful good looks Ingres drew, and become pear-shaped and pinguid. Indeed Georgina in her memoirs recollected that the initial impression he made on her at that first meeting was chiefly one of *roundness.* 'His closed shaped beard *round*, not a hair longer than the other (bristles like a box hedge trimming); his short neck, his *round* stomach, his *round* shoulders, his *round* eyes, with which he glared at me! And then he was fat and old.' If that was how she spoke of the man she was attracted to, one wonders what impression his wife made on her, whom she immediately — and correctly — identified as a shrew, 'a little old brown woman', comparing her to a 'Chinese crockery dog' and reporting that she had met 'the most ill-natured, cross-grained woman'. A relationship quickly developed between Gounod and Georgina (well-placed musicians always have the advantage in such matters by offering to 'discuss the career' of their intended conquests). She called on him to ask if he would let her give a benefit concert for the French wounded, to which he happily agreed; and she also offered to look after his interests *vis-à-vis* English music publishers and concert promoters. He got out a copy of his *Faust* and, standing close to and behind him as he sat at the piano (another sure-fire way of generating amorous electrical sparks), she sang through the opera with him, the two taking all the parts between them. By the middle of May he decided that he would leave Mme Gounod — taking a priest with him to help break the news to Georgina (Mme Gounod was used to it, as she had heard it many times before, and wearily said, 'He'll be back'). Mme Gounod flounced back to Paris. The war was over and the city was returning to normal. Gounod stayed in London to be near Georgina.

When, a little while later, the Paris Conservatoire reopened, Georgina and Gounod crossed the Channel, and she sang the solo part of *Gallia*. He had a brief reunion with Mme Gounod, during which he slapped her face and tore her gown, and she called Georgina a prostitute. Georgina and Gounod returned to London and lived together for almost three tempestuous years. Or rather, Gounod joined her and Harry in Tavistock House (which had recently been vacated by Charles Dickens) — these *ménages* seem to have become a habit. Georgina had persuaded — probably ordered — Harry to take a lease on this great mansion in West Central London with the help of a family inheritance. When Gounod moved in, Harry realized that his role was now to play second fiddle and faded into the background; though he stayed with Georgina and loyally supported her musical enterprises and her efforts to teach music to the poor. She idolized and hero-worshipped Gounod, calling him 'my dear old papa-mamma', and he nicknamed her 'Mousie', 'Raton', or '*ma chère Mimi*'. Harry was 'Poomps', and Gounod was 'Old Man'. In spite of the scandalized comments of London society, Georgina denied that there was anything improper in their relationship, yet she and the composer had indubitably become a couple. She energetically fought law suits — against publishers, concert promoters, etc. (and, eventually, against Gounod *and* her husband) — all closely described in books which Georgina wrote with compulsive energy in her late-middle and old age, continuing almost to her death in 1914 — tomes with strangely catchy titles, like *The Quarrel of the Royal Albert Hall Company with Ch. Gounod* (1873), *How I Escaped the Mad Doctors* (1882), and *The Ghastly Consequences of Living in Charles Dickens' House* (1882) — and six volumes of memoirs.

Gounod was enthusiastic about her project to set up singing schools for orphans, though less keen when it meant organizing concerts of other men's music in support of them. She filled Tavistock House with orphans, servants, music teachers, monkeys, parrots and dogs (one of them called 'Whiddles'), but Gounod was too preoccupied with himself to be of much use to her. In the first flush of his wooing, he had promised Georgina to give to her schools all his English earnings left after ensuring a dowry for his daughter. When his love cooled, he reneged on the promise. Besides, his health was giving him concern: accounts of his ailments, real or imagined, read like one of those Victorian Home Doctors — piles, eczema, glandular fever, rheumatism, 'cerebral attacks' (i.e. headaches) and doubtless chronic hypochondria. Georgina cooked for him, acted as his secretary and even managed to stop his smoking and snuff-taking (largely to curb his French habit of spitting everywhere, on the floor as well as into spittoons). She bathed him and rubbed him down with Turkish towels, Harry never far away as enthusiastic and solicitous helper — what *was* going on? Meanwhile Mme Gounod made every effort to get her husband back, sending his *Faust* librettist Jules Barbier as an emissary. Georgina dismissed him as 'Madame Gounod's parrot'.

The Gounod-Weldon domestic set-up was too good to last. He took her services for granted and offered little in exchange. They began to quarrel, and things came to a head on 27th of May 1874 in ludicrous circumstances. He and Georgina were driving to Blackheath to visit Mrs Brown, when Whiddles had a fit in the coach. Georgina's solicitude for the dog made it clear to Charles that she now cared more for her pet than for him and all his own ailments. They had a row, and Georgina returned to Tavistock House alone with Whiddles, leaving Gounod in the care of Mrs Brown. It was the last straw for Gounod. He succumbed to the pull of France and his family and, without bothering to pick up his belongings from the Weldons' house, took a boat for France. He even left some of his manuscripts, including the opera *Polyeucte*, which he had composed in London, with Georgina in mind for the leading role — a character named Pauline.

Back in Paris, the Gounods lived out their days in the mutual coolness they had long been accustomed to — the domestic barricades never dismantled, but no actual conflict. Their son Jean lived at home, on a separate floor of their house, and their daughter Jeanne moved out only when she got married: to a Baron — to the strains of his (and Bach's) *Ave Maria.*

Gounod also returned to salon society. Joseph Primoli wrote in his Journal on the 22nd of June 1893, a few months before Gounod's death:

'Gounod came to spend the day at Saint-Gratien with his old consort. He had come back to her one day, after all his escapades in England with Mrs Weldon.

I put Gounod among the four greatest charmers in Paris. They are for me: Alexandre Dumas, *fils*, Sardou, Alfonse Daudet and Gounod. Dumas has the most wit and depth, Sardou most erudition and vitality, Daudet the most verve and poetry, Gounod the most eloquence and youth. The composer of *Mireille* is astonishingly young. With his blue eyes and white beard he looks like Faust in person. You feel his false beard is about to fall off and he'll be twenty. He says things which seem to be engraved on some oriental talisman and they fall, perfectly chiselled, from his lips: 'One is attached to people according to what one gives them. Debtors are often ungrateful, but benefactors can never be.'

Relations with Georgina continued by letter only and deteriorated fast. She wrote to Gounod, pointing out, not unreasonably, that she had devoted years to his care in more capacities than any wife, that he had made use of her and then discarded her. He replied with sarcasm, 'Send me an invoice.' She took him at his word and submitted a closely written account for services rendered, which occupies sixteen pages of her memoirs. It added up to £9,787, 5s. 9d., including sums for board and lodgings at Tavistock House, to which Gounod had never contributed; and she started court proceedings. She also sued him for libel — but had meanwhile herself libelled another Frenchman, the conductor Jules Rivière, for which she was sent to Holloway Prison for six months. Gounod never paid, in spite of a further judgement for £11,640, including interest. However, she still held hostage his clothes, drawings and a gold snuff-box — and most important of all, his manuscripts. Gounod tried to persuade her to return them and, before she finally relented, was obliged to orchestrate *Polyeucte* from memory (the differences might make a rewarding study). When she did send the score, she retained the title page. This turned up in 1988, when it was sold by Lisa Cox to the Pierpont Morgan Library. It features the significant dedication '*à Georgina Weldon (Pauline)*'. He never paid the money, yet it cost him dear. He was never able to set foot in England again, obliged even to refuse a Royal Command Performance ordered by Queen Victoria: Georgina said she would have had him arrested on the rostrum of the Royal Albert Hall, right in the middle of the performance of his *Mors e Vita* which the Queen had asked for.

On the 17th of October 1893, his wife discovered him in a coma, dying, clutching a crucifix. He was given a state funeral. Georgina did not attend, although she now lived in France. She crammed much more into her life than a few years' devotion to a composer. She was a determined and enterprising person far ahead of her time. She featured in a Pears Soap advertisement to show how beautiful her complexion still was at the age of 50; studied law so that she could better represent herself in her many law suits; became a table-moving spiritualist (yes, she conjured up the spirit of Gounod and, from the other side, he called her Mimi); supported the case for the wronged Colonel Dreyfus and even joined the Land Reform Union — her energy seems to have been boundless. The Bow Cemetery Grievance Committee needed a spokeswoman? Georgina was ready to speak up for it. She also supported the firebrand MP Charles Bradlaugh in his court battle for press freedom, after he had defied a ban on the publication of a work advocating contraception; so she even struck a blow for what would only much later be called feminism. James Harding was so fortunate as to be able to interview a Miss Marjory Pegram, who remembered 'Grannie Weldon' and passed on to him her recollections of some of Georgina's exploits. What a woman she must have been. She insisted on her rights but bore no grudges. 'Grannie,' incidentally, was an honorary title: she never had any children, nor therefore grandchildren. Shortly before she died in 1914 she wrote in her Diary, 'Poor old man — how I did love him, and how hard all hope died;' and later, 'Old man gone and I fast going. His music is thought nothing of now.'

GEORGE PERCY ALDRIDGE GRAINGER

Born: Brighton, Melbourne, Australia, 8th of July 1882
Father: John Grainger, born on a train near London, 30th of November 1855
Mother: Rosa Annie Aldridge, born Adelaide, 3rd of July 1861
Married: Ella Viola Ström-Bandelius, born Stockholm, 1889
Best Friend: Mother
Died: White Plains, New York, 20th of February 1961

In an Aldeburgh Festival programme, Benjamin Britten described Percy Aldridge Grainger as 'a Flawed Genius'. Britten was well qualified to pronounce on the subject, as he was himself a genius with a major flaw — his almost pathological hatred of those with whom he had fallen out and thenceforth tried to destroy. But Grainger's personality — of his genius there can be no doubt — was more than flawed. He was unhinged: a flagellant, sado-masochist and abuser of children. About these perversions — the word is now unfashionable but here inescapable — he was perfectly frank. Homosexuality was still illegal, but as Grainger was not a homosexual he freely confessed to what he called his 'mad side', for example fantasizing about flogging his own offspring and having sex with the daughters he planned to have (but fortunately never did — nor sons); and he described all those fantasies in a letter to, of all people, a woman he was hoping to marry in order to produce them. He exulted in pain, self-flagellation and probably self-mutilation, and conducted tests on himself to find out how much pain he could endure. If that were not enough, his proto-Nazi theories propounded the creation of a 'pure', blue-eyed, blond-haired race. As the Nazis were to do later to German, he proposed establishing a reformed English language from which all foreign words were banned. None of his aberrations troubled him: on the contrary, he enjoyed and gloried in them — and furthermore documented them for posterity, in letters, artefacts and, where he could, photographs. Yet he was a warm, sunny and apparently humane person who charmed his friends with 'a saintlike gentleness, sweetness and kindliness of nature', as John Bird says in his startling biography of Grainger, which in 1976 revealed for the first time the full extent of Grainger's iniquity (the quotations from the composer's letters below are Bird's transcripts). As Britten and Pears, who shared Grainger's interest in beautiful, blond boys, wrote in the preface to the biography — again delicately understating, 'It was hardly to be expected that the depths beneath the dazzling surface could be without some turbulence.'

Perhaps one should not read too much into a schoolboy's preoccupation with war and violence, but Grainger revealed how he came to be enthralled by it. Analysts take note:

Between seven & ten I read a lot of Homer & phrases like 'The javelin crashed through the shield' were always on my lips. Later on when I was ten or twelve when I read the Icelandic Sagas the thought of the battleaxe hewing from the shoulder to the waist gave me the greatest mental delights. In the meantime, I had read in Dickens passages such as the one where Nicholas [Nickleby] strikes the schoolmaster on the cheek leaving a livid streak — & all sorts of stories — one about a boy leaving home to join the circus & being whipped by the circus manager. . . . These passions were quite unconscious & I had no idea what caused me to shake with delight when I read such descriptions. . . . Each person must have some subject that fires him to madness, whatever it is. To put up with less seems crazy. . . . Out of this world of violence, war, cruelhood & tragedy, my longing to compose arose. Many children are cruel to animals & many little boys harsh to little girls, but this fierceness wanes as they grow up. But I never grew up in this respect & fierceness is the keynote of my music. . . . The object of my music is not to entertain, but to agonize — to make mankind think of the agony of young men forced to kill each other against their will & all the other thwartments & torturings of the young.

Grainger's music is in fact not at all fierce: discordant occasionally, and sometimes 'experimental', but often also gentle and full of affectionate humour. If one were to analyze musical works in terms of how brutal they sounded, many perfectly harmless composers, from Holst to Vaughan Williams and Mahler, would have been locked up on the strength of their scoring.

Grainger's story really belongs not under the heading of Wives but Mothers of the Great Composers. Other musicians, and many composers, have had domineering mothers and most of them, as the obituaries put it, 'never married' (or else tried and failed at being husbands). Grainger's mother always 'auditioned' his girl friends, and if they met with her approval gave him permission to 'take them out' (as the quaint phrase delicately puts it in English). But when his relationships looked like becoming more intense, she did everything in her power to prevent him from marrying. She frightened away every girl friend by any means at her disposal, fair or foul. Only after her violent death (the indirect result of his 'mad side') — and after a careful search for someone with the appropriate qualifications — did he find a bride. Mother called the infant Percy 'Bubbles', after the Pears Soap advertisement, because of his bright blond hair. Later it grew darker, and some of the curls straightened. She refused to accept this and regularly bleached it white-blond with hydrogen peroxide. He continued dyeing it long after her death, perhaps as a kind of tribute; but he also hoped that the exaggerated blondness would make him look more Nordic. None of his friends were deceived by the artifice — such attempts at cheating time seldom work. All he achieved was to be taken for a homosexual — which annoyed him because he was not: so unremarkable a divergence as homosexuality was for him too close to the norm.

Grainger is said also to have shared his mother's bed longer than most boys, some said until he was 36, and it was as a direct result of incest rumours that she committed suicide. When he and his mother were separated they exchanged hundreds of deeply affectionate love letters, postcards and telegrams (of the 'longing to hold you in my arms again . . .' kind) which to postmen, telegraph boys and anyone else who encountered them could have spelt only one thing—a love affair. None reveals unequivocally that there *was* a sexual relationship between them. But then, if homosexuality was in those times a love that dared not speak its name, incest would hardly have shouted from the roof tops.

Like many mother-dominated men, Grainger tried all his life to remain studiedly, almost absurdly, boyish—full of exhibitionist, attention-seeking pranks and crazy ideas; a Peter Pan who did not want to grow up in case Mother disowned him. One of his (adult) show-off tricks was to throw a tennis ball over the roof-ridge of a house, then race round to the other side of the building to catch it again as it rolled down the slope. When he gave piano recitals or played concertos he would anchor a handkerchief to the inside of his breast pocket with a piece of elastic, so that he could speedily wipe his brow, or protect his thumbs from *glissandi*, and then let go of the hankie to make it disappear back into its pouch (it takes an Australian to think of that). He loved railways and retained a life-long interest in mechanical toys, which he ingeniously adapted into semi-automatic musical instruments.

The outer shell of me (the part that faces the world) has learned to go thru the motions of acting the part of a grown man; I can earn money, I can build concert programs, I can force my concert-hearers, I can think out money matters, with a worldly eye & a seemingly grown-up, manlike air. But the core of me, my inner self, my senses, have stayed those of a child — a child that knows he is naughty & looks to be punished for it. I always feel 'the world' to be a cruel monster whose avenging ill-will I am just about to bitterly taste. War & sport & wild country & race pride pick me up & carry me away & drunken me, & don't leave me half-filled & questioning & cold, & therefore I worship them & serve them & sing them & shall till I drop. . . . That's why I say I hate love, that love is the cruelest thing in human affairs. I like only those things that leave men & women perfectly free. The only kind of love I like is platonic love. But there was heaps of that between Mother & me. The reason I say I worship lust but hate love is because lust, like platonic love, leaves people perfectly free. . . . Almost all the stirs I am moved by are considered evil by most people & that most people, if they knew my thoughts, habits & feelings would disgrace me & put me in prison if they could. It is not a matter of being weak & unable to 'resist temptation'. I am quite strong in being able to control myself in all sorts of ways & I do not do deeds that I disapprove of. But the fact is that I really worship evil & find everything else un-worth while. But it may (nay, must) be said that all my worship of cruelty cruises only round sex-instincts. Apart from sex I am not such a bad fellow. But as I am really not interested in anything but sex it just boils down to this: that I hardly think of anything but sex & that all my sex thoughts are full of evil & cruelty. And one of the greatest & most continual worries is that I may die without the full evilness of my sex feelings being known to the world or recorded. If I knew of a country where I could publish an unabridged account of my sex-life & sex-feelings I would be a happy man indeed.

When, at the age of eighteen, Grainger visited Amsterdam he found much in that city — even then — to 'drunken' (as he put it in Grainger-speak) his libido and widen the horizons of his sexuality. It reassured him, that however strange his predilections were, others shared them. His wish to publish everything he did in the privacy of his bedroom was — fortunately — not fulfilled.

Grainger was a mother's boy but not a softie. When he heard that German soldiers (his favourite personification of Teutonic heroism) were obliged to go on route marches, each carrying a 50-lb load, he filled a knapsack with 60 lb — and yomped through the heat of the Australian desert. In New Zealand, he thought nothing of marching 56 miles between concerts, carrying his own music (though not his piano). As a student in Frankfurt, he would brave the coldest winter weather by taking off all his clothes and, pretending to be a statue, stand in the snow for hours on end. Taking a taxi meant throwing his luggage into the back and running alongside it. When he made a sea voyage he was not content with jogging round the decks: he persuaded the captain to allow him into the boiler room and shovel coal for an hour each day, stripped naked. He wanted men for friendship and Australian mateyness, women for sex. This had to be of the sado-masochistic kind, involving consenting, mutual violence (he called his imagined lovers 'sweethearts', thereby defiling a good old English word). When searching for a bride he had a fixed idea of what he wanted her to look like: Mother. Blonde, slim and stately — in short, 'a Nordic Princess':

> There are those who say that a man gets more perfect happiness with a man than with a woman sweetheart . . . With me it is the race, not the sex, that matters. . . . If the race is right I'm in heaven. A Nordic type of womanhood, half-boyish yet wholely [sic] womanly. . . . To meet her [would be] to have all one's boyhood fairy-dreams come true.

Not surprisingly, his courtships always turned into disasters. If his physical demands or lurid fantasies failed to frighten the women away, his mother did. When he went to study in Germany, Mother came too, of course. There she chose a fiancée for him; a young woman called Mimi Kwast (who later married the odious German composer Hans Pfitzner — more about him in Mahler's chapter). When Grainger's relationship with Mimi appeared to be getting too intimate, Mrs Grainger quickly intervened. And Percy always obeyed Mother. His brutal frankness in telling every young women exactly what he wanted of them might be just about imaginable in the climate of explicit, end-of-century sexual openness; but at the beginning of the twentieth century such demands would have terrified even the most worldly-wise woman. To another possible Nordic-beauty candidate, Karen Holten, a Dane, he wrote on the 6th of November 1908:

I wish to procreate independent children. . . . I long for no slave children of my own, thanks. I propose this: Never to whip them till they are old enough to grasp the meaning of lots of things, and say to them: Look here! I want to ask a favour from you kids. I want to whip you, because it gives me extraordinary pleasure. I don't know why it does, but it does. It gladdens me more than eating even. I know it's rotten for you, but then: I am particularly kind to you kids. I've worked hard to make you free in life, so that your childhood not only may be jollier now than ordinary children's, but may last ever so long, if you're pure-minded like I am, & don't grow worldly out of pure cussedness. . . . I don't *deserve* any reward for this, or for the freedom I allow & encourage, for that is every grown up's duty to the young, but I say this to you: I'm kind & a good old thing, & polite & obliging. Now why not do me a great favour, as one equal to another, let me whip you; because, it gives me such unexplainable delight. . . . I have hopes. Then encourage them to whip each other as a form of athletic fight. (They have a game like that in Japan, I've just read.) I believe one could easily get decent, plucky, blue-eyed children to do it. . . . You know that I long to flog children. It must be wonderful to hurt this soft unspoiled skin . . . & when my girls begin to awaken sexually I would gradually like to have carnal knowledge with them. . . . I would love to explain things to them & open to their eyes in this area the whole way of the world without shame or shyness or cowardice. . . . Why should a man not be sensual with his own children? . . . All these mixed father — and lover — instincts I have had since I was 14/15. I have always dreamed about having children & whipping them, & to have a sensual life with my own daughters.

Needless to say, Karen fled in horror, and, mercifully, Grainger never did father any known children. Before her, he had a relationship with Alfhild de Luce, fiancée of the cellist Herman Sandby (1881–1965), who later became the Princi-pal Cellist of the Philadelphia Orchestra and a composer and conductor. Grainger fell in love with her, kissed her and gave his reason for doing so: 'Really, Alfhild, mother must have looked something like you when she was young.' When he and Sandby went on an Australian recital tour, he insisted that Alfhild came too, and they lived in some sort of a threesome until Alfhild realized the extent of his mother-domination (and probably other traits of his character) and married Sandby. Grainger was an extraordinarily handsome man, with fine features and a winsome manner; and, not surprisingly, many of his women students fell in love with him. One of these, an Englishwoman, was indirectly responsible for Rose Grainger's death. John Bird calls her E— in his Grainger biography, so perhaps she was still alive in 1976, when the book was published; and if she was it would have been interesting to hear her side of the story. She had been a piano pupil of Grainger's when he lived in London, and they carried on a relationship of sorts, or at least came to enough of an understanding to contemplate marriage. As he did nothing without his mother's consent, she was invited to America to stay at Mrs Grainger's house in White Plains, on a vetting and inspection visit. With a

European war looming the Graingers had moved to America in 1914, as Britten was to do in 1939 — both were subjected to abuse: Grainger was sent an anonymous postcard addressing him as 'Herr Percy Grainger' and calling him a 'white-livered pro-German'). E— got on well with his mother and remained with her and Percy for some time, helping to nurse Rose when she was ill. During the course of her stay, she saw one of the intimate letters from Percy to his mother and not unreasonably interpreted it as incestuous sex. Sensing it might come in useful, she stole it. John Bird, writing of this extraordinary correspondence, commented:

> The relationship between Percy and his mother had been, in every sense of the word, unusual. The thousands of letters, notes and telegrams they exchanged present us with a fascinating, if frightening, picture which is almost impossible to grasp in its enormity and complexity. There is material enough for a dozen dissertations on the psychological aspects of Mother Love. Before her death she was Percy's biggest single influence, and even after her death her memory served as the most sacred altar at which he worshipped. The umbilical cord was never severed.

Percy's father was an architect, a stereotypical, hard-drinking Australian, although born in England — on a train as it approached London, in November 1855. As Rose was in labour with Percy, John Grainger boasted to the doctor — who, incidentally, was in love with Rose and hoped to elope with her — that this was not the first child he, John, had fathered; also that in the course of one night in Paris he had eighteen whores. As soon as Rose knew she was pregnant, she refused to have anything more to do with him, slept in a separate bedroom and constantly gazed at a Greek statue of a boy, hoping that she could make her fetus absorb its beauty. In his alcoholic stupors, John Grainger lurched between violence and remorse. Often he would be driven out of the house by his wife, who kept a horse whip which she used also to chastize Percy if he neglected his piano practice. Each time she whipped him, he loved her all the more. She refused to send him to school but educated him herself, at home, away from the contaminating influence of other children. He was her life's work and sole preoccupation, and in return she demanded his total devotion and gratitude. His father had infected Rose with syphilis, and she was terrified that their child would be born with the disease, which probably accounts for her cosseting of Percy on finding that he was born healthy. But she lived in constant dread of developing symptoms of insanity. Percy's affair with E—, and the woman's subsequent moral blackmail, probably helped to unhinge Rose's mind. She had always been unstable: sometimes when Percy came home he would find her lying on the floor, feigning death. When he took her in his arms she sat bolt upright and said, 'That's all right. I only wanted to see if you still loved me.'

After the affair between Percy and E— came to an end following the intervention of his mother (he in effect jilted her), E— brought out the stolen letter, her evidential trophy, and told anyone who would listen that the reason for his jilting her had not been her fault, but that Percy and his mother had had an incestuous love affair, which put an end to the chances of the marriage. Friends (friends?) lost no time in bringing the rumours to Mrs Grainger's ears. She cabled Percy, 'The unmentionable has been laid at my door.' If that is how she mentioned it, without having to explain, there may well have been grounds for E—'s suspicions. It devastated Rose, by then a very sick woman. In her last letter, hastily written in pencil, she wrote:

> My dear Son, I am out of my mind and cannot think properly. I asked E— over the phone whether you told her if I had any improper love for you . . . ? You must tell the truth, that in spite of everything I said — I have never for one moment loved you wrongly — or you me — not for one moment nor the thought of doing so. The whole thing has driven me insane — and I have accused myself of something I have never thought of. You and I never loved one another anything but purely and right. No one will believe me but it is the real truth, as you know. It is quite unbelievable what I have said to E—, but I am insane — not on all points, but I cannot do any more — and only feel like lying in bed and thinking not sleeping — but just unable to do anything. I am insane. I am oh so sorry and want to do something to help you but I cannot. I doubt whether I will be able to dress myself in a day or so. Every day gets worse — I am an idiot, and no one seems to realize it. I am so sorry — I have loved you and so many others so dearly.

> Your poor insane mother.

> PS You have tried too hard to be all that is noble — but your mad side has ruined us — dear God knows the truth — man will not believe the truth I am writing.

Having written that distraught letter, Rose Grainger tore it up and put it in a drawer with other letters she never sent, pushed a chair to a window on the eighteenth floor of the Aeolian Building in New York and leapt to her death. She was found, still conscious, on the roof of the adjacent Central Building but died from a fractured skull and internal injuries before she could be moved. Percy was meanwhile giving a concert before a rapturous audience in the Los Angeles Philharmonic Hall. As he left the platform, a telegram was handed to him, which stated simply that his mother had died in New York. He embarked on the long cross-continental railroad journey back to New York. Only when he bought a newspaper did he learn the manner of his mother's death, though not the reason for her suicide; nor did he suspect it until he found and pieced together her torn-up last letter.

From that day onwards and for the rest of his life he carried the letter in a capsule round his neck, an amulet to mark his mother's constant presence. To the English composer Roger Quilter (another troubled mind) he wrote:

She was a brave soldier always, fighting for 30 years a cruel disease (not of her Aldridge blood), & if, at the last, she felt her mind giving way, was she not a brave soldier to leap from the eighteenth floor?

He confided greater detail of his mother's death to Alfhild Sandby.

I returned to New York, and heard the truth about E— from friends who told me that she had slandered me and my Mother in this disgusting way. Mother had been ill: her nerves were worn out; she hadn't long to live; the shock was too much for her; I firmly believe her mind gave way. She wanted peace; she took it. . . . I faced E— and told her she was a despicable liar; I told her that I never loved her and could never love her; and that I never again wanted to see her. What people believe now I do not know; but in case I die before you, and you hear anyone accusing me and my Mother of having lived in incest, I want you to come forward & tell them what I tell you now. This is the sacred truth; & I want you to know it.

Another letter to Alfhild criticizes a libretto she had proposed writing for him: more evidence of his mother-dominated make-up:

To me as an Australian . . . it seems unbelievable that 2 young people should behave as your Leon and Varenka do: live for love (or passion) in defiance of a mother's expressed wish. That any young man or woman should be disobedient to a parent seems to me incredibly low . . . I blush at the mere thought that two young people could dare to wish to live together against the will of a parent! I (in my life) have taken love action only when advised to do by my Mother. Any other thought is sickeningly repugnant to me.

Grainger only freed himself from his mother when he met Ella Ström-Bandelius, the very 'Nordic princess' he had always dreamed of:

Every romantic thought of my life seemed to rise out of dim memories & rush towards her for fulfilment. . . . It may be she said to me 'Hello, little boy' or some other playful greeting, her bright eyes sparkling . . . she left the thought in me that she sensed the boy in me — which is the only way I want to be thought of. . . . Likewise it was the girl in her — the playmate, the sister, the skittish-one (not the woman) — that I loved and worshipped.

That was in 1926, when the 'little boy' was 44 and Ella 37, on a liner bound for Vancouver. He had just completed an exhausting Australian tour and was feeling a little depressed ('mood-slumped', as he preferred to say). He had first noticed Ella at Auckland, standing in a passport queue, when an official called out a Swedish name — Ström: anything or anybody Scandinavian immediately fascinated him. He turned round, and responding to the call was a radiantly beautiful, blonde, fair-skinned, blue-eyed woman.

Ella Viola Ström-Bandelius was born in Stockholm in 1889 but moved to London to study at the Slade School of Art, where she met Augustus John, who made several drawings of her. After their inauspicious first meeting on the liner, it was Ella who made the first approach: the attraction was clearly mutual. Fortunately the leisurely pace of a 1920s sea voyage permitted their relationship to develop. According to John Bird's account it was not without farce. Hearing Percy practise in the saloon, Ella mistook him for the leader of the ship's band and asked him to show her some chords on the banjolele. Several days later she discovered that her 'bandmaster' friend was in fact Percy Grainger, then already a famous pianist — though he had not yet found fame as a composer — and she apologized for her gaffe. It was not an immediate union of soulmates, and there were certain obstacles. For one thing, he talked unceasingly of his mother, and told Ella frankly that he was attracted to her because she looked so very like early photographs of Mrs Grainger. For another, she kept asking him to play Chopin to her — and he could not stand Chopin. She told him about her lover in London, while he talked about Mother — showing Ella his locket containing her last, tragic letter. It is not clear how much of his 'mad side' he revealed at that time, but whenever Percy felt mood-slumped, Ella would get out her banjolele and serenade him with *I wanna be happy*. One day Grainger found Ella weeping in the writing room. She had just received a cable from London announcing that her lover had suddenly died. Grainger comforted her — presumably not with Chopin — and they realized they were made for each other. On disembarking, they spent further time together on a train to the East coast of America, where they parted temporarily. She took a boat to Southampton while he stayed in the USA. He overwhelmed her with gifts, including a $5,000 life settlement and all the books he felt she should read, including Macfadden's *Keeping Fit* and *The Rose Grainger Book*.

They were married on the 9th of August 1928 before an immense audience in the Hollywood Bowl auditorium. The groom conducted an orchestra of 126 players, in a piece of music he had composed for the occasion, *To a Nordic Princess*. The marriage continued without apparent upsets until Percy's death in 1961. For many years they worked happily together on his folk-song collecting and other musical projects. When John Bird wrote his biography, Ella was still alive, so a measure of tact was required. But husbands can seldom keep their 'mad side', whatever it may be, from their wives, so Ella must have known and tolerated his strange proclivities. Where other caring wives of touring musicians pack a tail-suit, black shoes and socks, collars and cufflinks, Ella was obliged to put in Percy's luggage sado-masochistic implements, as well as his camera, fitted with a self-timer so that he could capture self-inflicted injuries for posterity, meticulously noting film speed, exposure-time and camera aperture. He bequeathed the evidence, together with his manuscripts and other property, to the Grainger Museum and Grainger Library, White Plains, New York, which he founded and endowed from his considerable royalties; though understandably not all his effects are on display. He endowed another shrine to himself in Melbourne, also called the Grainger Museum, which he helped to construct with his own hands, joining the labourers and bricklayers at 6.00 a.m. each morning. Many documents are held in the Library of Congress, Washington, D.C. Grainger wanted everything about himself to be known, revealed and, if possible, displayed — even his corpse or, if that proved unpractical, his skeleton. His motto, which he wrote down on the 13th of November 1936, was:

Destroy nothing, forget nothing.
Remember all, say all.
Trust life, trust mankind.
As long as the picture of truth is placed
in the right form (art, science, history)
it will offend no-one.

Franz Joseph Haydn

Born:	Rohrau, 31st of March 1732
Father:	Mathias Haydn (1699–1763)
Mother:	Anna Maria Keller (1707–1754)
Married:	Maria Anna Aloysia Apollonia Keller
Died:	Vienna, 31st of May 1809

During his lifetime 'The Father of the Symphony' was affectionately known in London as 'Papa Haydn', yet he and his wife had no children of their own. For most of their long marriage they lived under the same roof, but not as man and wife, though he may have fathered a son by his long-term mistress. Like Mozart and Dvorak, he had the misfortune of loving the 'wrong' sister. His first sweetheart was Therese Keller, daughter of a Bohemian-born wig-maker and hairdresser. The Kellers lived in the Ungargasse, now in the third district of Vienna (the street where Beethoven wrote part of his Ninth — the house still stands). Young Joseph became almost a son to the Keller family, gave music lessons to the attractive Therese and fell in love with her. Unfortunately for him, she decided she had no vocation for marriage and became a nun in the Order of Poor Clares, leaving Haydn heartbroken. She took her vows on the 12th of May 1756, and, although it must have been a poignant occasion for him, Haydn provided and directed the music for the induction. He preserved the scores as mementos for the rest of his life; almost half a century. The Double Concerto in F for Organ, Violin and Orchestra is said to be one of these works, according to the Haydn scholar, H. C. Robbins Landon, to whose Haydn biography I am indebted for many of the facts in this chapter (though most of the translations are my own).

The Kellers having had one daughter take the veil, suggested that Haydn should marry the other, who was rather plain. According to Haydn's own account, given to his biographer Dies, Herr Keller later said to him, 'Haydn, you ought to marry my elder daughter.' And being an amenable fellow, he married Maria Anna Keller in 1760, at the age of 28, only to repent at leisure. He did not know that she, too, had been touched by an excess of religion. The marriage proved a disaster. Griesinger reported that Haydn was perfectly frank about it and said to his friend Griesinger: 'We became fond of each other, but nevertheless I soon found that my wife was empty-headed and irresponsible by nature.' The word Haydn used was *leichtsinnig*, a combination of impetuosity and spendthrift profligacy; other contemporaries wrote of her 'stubborn nature'. In fairness to her, she has had a bad press, much of it probably undeserved. She was a simple woman who spoke in broad Viennese dialect, was fond of cats and dogs — and priests, whom she was constantly entertaining. She was totally unmusical and puzzled by the success of her husband's music. A visiting Swedish musician called Berwald (father of Franz Berwald) once asked her what she thought about her husband's Oratorio, *The*

Creation, and she replied: 'People say it's *supposed* to be good, but I wouldn't know.' But the story that she used her husband's manuscripts for lighting the fire, or for making paper curlers, is probably a romantic fiction best left to factitious films. Haydn was easy-going, and they lived together, even shared rooms, for forty years: 'their Forty Years' War', biographers said. Giuseppe Carpani's recollections about Haydn's marriage to Maria Anna include the passage (as translated by Landon), 'For a time all went well, but later the relationship was one of Socrates and Xantippe*. Signora Anna was neither beautiful nor ugly but was exceedingly stubborn and given to excesses of religious fervour, which manifested itself in luncheons, dinners and teas to the clergy. Haydn, frugal by nature, began to view with alarm this drain on his modest income; nor did the noise of these gatherings encourage a man of his scholarly pursuits . . . The monks expected Haydn to provide, *gratis*, church music of all kinds, and if he refused there were great scenes — tears and recriminations, and Haydn could pay the doctors' and apothecaries' bills, too. . . .' Haydn remained on good terms with his in-laws, and when his brother-in-law Joseph Keller in 1797 was confined to a lunatic-asylum, Haydn wrote a touching letter to the authorities asking to be allowed to remove him from the institution so that he could be 'watched over day and night by an attendant' at his (Haydn's) apartment and expense.

Haydn blamed the fact that he kept a mistress on his wife who, he said, turned him into a womanizer; and he gave as a rather strange reason that she ' . . . was unable to have children, and so I was more susceptible to the charms of other women'. She may have been infertile, but he probably meant she hated sex. In May 1769, when Haydn had been married for seven years, he and his orchestra accompanied Prince Eszterházy to Bratislava. There he met a young woman, her name — Catherine Csech — is all we know, and that she was someone's lady-in-waiting, and that he could not bear to tear himself away from her. He overstayed, delaying his return for several days, and giving as an excuse that, 'The weather was too bad to travel.' The rest we have to imagine, as no letters between them have survived. But he never forgot Catherine — and remembered her in his will. He was less generous to his wife. Although he never kept her short of housekeeping money, he was rather mean in the matter of presents or other tokens of appreciation. 'Once, when Haydn had done someone a favour and would take no payment (Griesinger wrote) it was suggested that something should be given to his wife. He replied: "She doesn't deserve anything, because it's a matter of indifference to her whether her husband is a cobbler or an artist." ' She had reason to complain about Haydn's infidelities long before her alleged barrenness provided him with his feeble excuse. Prince Eszterházy kept a large artistic establishment and the court at Eszterháza appears to have been a den of promiscuity. Frau Haydn was the mistress of the Court Painter, Ludwig Guttenbrunn. Unlike his harpist, Krumpholz, who committed suicide after *his*

---

* Xantippe: The name of the wife of Socrates, hence, allusively, an ill-tempered woman or wife, a shrew or scold. Shakespeare: 'As cust and shrew'd as Socrates' Xantippe.'

unfaithful wife left him, Haydn cheerfully told anyone who cared to listen what his wife was up to. And when they did finally part, and she insisted on keeping a portrait Guttenbrunn had painted of Haydn, he said, 'She only wants it because *he* painted it.' (It is said to have been burnt in 1945 by Russian soldiers on the lawns of Eszterháza, along with many other treasures including furniture).

Haydn's mistress was an Italian singer, Luigia Polzelli, who entered his life on the 26th of March 1779, when her much older husband, Antonio, became one of his violinists in the Eszterháza orchestra. When they fell in love, Haydn was 47, Luigia 29, dark-haired and olive-skinned. There was doubtless a bit of the old *droit du seigneur* about the affair. A relationship with the Kapellmeister would have done her career no harm. He blatantly favoured her above other and better singers at the palace, although the talents that pleased Haydn most lay neither in her acting nor her singing: he constantly had to scale down arias to suit her limited abilities. When Luigia's husband was dismissed by the palace authorities, Haydn intervened to get him reinstated rather than have the Polzellis go back to Italy and lose her. That affair lasted for most of Haydn's life, but brought him little happiness. If his wife was careless with money, his mistress was a veritable gold-digger. When they were apart, almost every letter she wrote to him contained requests for money, as well as references to 'the two living obstacles' to their getting married. Luigia's husband died before Frau Haydn, but the liaison ended in sadness.

Haydn also carried on an affectionate correspondence with a Frau von Genzinger, and while there is no proof that it was more than a friendship, the tone of the correspondence is intimate enough to suggest it. Haydn had numerous female admirers in London. One of these, Rebecca Schroeter, was the widow of a pianist and minor composer, and, in spite of the German name, an Englishwoman. In 1806, Haydn's biographer, Dies, was shown one of the composer's London notebooks and reported that they stirred fond memories in him:

> 'I opened it up and found a couple of dozen letters from an English widow in London, who loved me; but she was, although already sixty years old, still a beautiful and charming woman, and I easily would have married her if I had been free at the time.' This woman is a widow, still living, of the famous pianist Schröter, whose melodious songs Haydn emphatically praised . . . he usually dined with her. He freely admitted that he loved pretty women, but he couldn't understand how it happened that in his life he had been loved by many a pretty woman. 'They can't have been led to it by my beauty,' said he. 'You have,' said I, 'something of genius in your face and in your whole bearing, and one likes to see that and knows it's good.' 'One can see [Haydn replied to Dies] that I mean well with everyone.' [Dies:] 'That will have laid you open to attacks.' Haydn: 'Oh yes, sometimes, but I was clever.'

Rebecca was useful to Haydn when he was in England, helping him in practical matters and acting for him in the matter of a publisher's contract. He, in turn, gave her lessons.

Mrs Schroeter presents her compliments to Mr Haydn, and informs him she is just returned to town, and will be very happy to see him whenever it is convenient for him to give her a lesson.

That formal note, without superscription, is dated June the 29th, 1791. The next dated letter, on the 8th of February 1792, opens with 'M[y] D[ear]':

M:D: I wish much to know, HOW DO YOU DO to day, I am very sorry to lose the pleasure of seeing you this morning, but I hope you will have time to come to morrow. I beg my D[ear]: you will take great care of your health, and do not fatigue yourself with too much application to business. My thoughts and best wishes are always with you, and I ever am with the utmost Sincerity M[y] D[ear] your F[aithful]: etc.

Within a short time a remarkable intimacy developed, though only her letters have survived.

My Dear: I was extremely sorry to part with you so suddenly last night. Our conversation was particularly interesting and I had [a] thousand affectionate things to say to you, my heart WAS and is full of TENDERNESS for you, but no language can express HALF the LOVE and AFFECTION I feel for you, you are DEARER to me EVERY DAY of my life. I am very sorry I was so dull and stupid yesterday, indeed my DEAREST it was nothing but my being indisposed with a cold occasion'd my stupidity. I thank you a thousand times for your concern for me, I am truly sensible of your goodness, and I assure you my D[ear] if anything had happened to trouble me I wou'd have opened my heart, & told you with the most perfect confidence. Oh, how earnes[t]ly [I] wish to see you, I hope you will come to me to morrow. I shall be happy to see you both in the Morning and the Evening. God Bless you my love, my thoughts and best wishes ever accompany you, and I always am with the most sincere and invariable Regard my D[ear]:

My Dearest I cannot be happy
till I see you if you know
do, tell me, when you will come.

Soon 'My Dear' and 'My Dearest' becomes 'My Dearest Love,' and the tone increasingly intimate. Was Haydn already feigning headaches?

My Dear. I beg to know HOW YOU DO? Hope to hear your head-ache is ENTIRELY GONE and that you have slept well. I hope to see you my Dear Love on Tuesday as usual to Dinner — and all night with me?

The last few words are crossed out, but still visible. The gushing Rebecca may have become a bit of a nuisance. Another of the twenty-odd letters ends:

I am TRULY ANXIOUs and IMPATIENT TO SEE YOU, and I wish to have as much of

YOUR COMPANY as possible; indeed my Dearest Haydn I FEEL for YOU the FONDEST and TENDEREST AFFECTION the HUMAN HEART is capable of, and ever am with the FIRMEST attachment, my Dearest Love, most Sincerely, Faithfully and most Affectionately yours.

Rebecca Schroeter was not his only female London admirer. Other women sent him verses they had written for him to set and wore head-dresses and badges with 'Haydn' embroidered on them. One lady gave him a song, 'When from thy Sight', which he took back to Vienna and annotated, 'This Song is by Mrs Hodges, the most beautiful woman I ever saw in my life, a great piano player. Text and Music by Her.' When he heard of her death, he added, in a shaky hand, 'Reqiescat in pace J. Haydn.'

Meanwhile he was still sending money to Luigia at home, though never quite enough for her. In August 1791, in addition to the usual requests for money, she told him that her husband had died. His reply was brief:

> Dear Polzelli, I hope you received the last letter from Count Fries, and with it the 100 guilders I sent you. I would like to have sent more, but at the moment I cannot. In respect of your husband, I tell you that fate was kind to you in freeing you of this grave burden. It is better for him, too, to be in the hereafter than useless in this world. The poor man has suffered enough. Dear Polzelli! Perhaps the time we have so often longed for will still come, when *four* eyes close. Two have now closed, but the other two. . . . Enough of this, it shall be as God decrees. . . .

Frau Haydn's eyes did not close for another nine years, in 1800. Polzelli was still waiting for him, but he had tired of her. He had known too many other, kinder, and less rapacious, women. But still she persisted in her monetary demands and asked him to sign a declaration:

> I, the undersigned, promise the Signora Luigia Polzelli, that, in the event of my considering remarrying, I shall take no woman to be my wife other than the aforementioned Luigia Polzelli. Further, I promise to bequeathe to the said Polzelli a pension for life of 300 guilders . . . signed and sealed by Joseph Haydn, Kapellmeister of the Prince Eszterházy.

At this, Haydn's good nature deserted him. When he died, on the 31st of May 1809, there was no pension for Luigia Polzelli. But the mysterious Catherine Csech, whom he met in Bratislava all those years earlier, received the enormous sum of 1,000 guilders. Polzelli eventually married again and lived to the age of 82. There were two sons from her first marriage, Pietro and Antonio. Haydn was devoted to both and had them educated at his expense. He was heartbroken when Pietro, a violinist, died at only nineteen. Antonio was born on the 22nd of April 1783, at the height of Haydn's affair with Luigia, and may have been his son. Was there, after all, a real Papa Haydn?

AUGUSTA MARY ANNE HOLMÈS

Born: Paris, 16th of December 1847
Father: Charles William Scott Dalkeith Holmes
Mother: Tryphina Anna Constance Augusta Shearer
Died: Paris, 28th of January 1903

Augusta Holmès lived all her life in Paris, the daughter of an Irish military officer, of Youghall, County Cork, who fought at Waterloo and settled in France; and a Scottish-Irish mother, Tryphina Shearer. However, persistent rumours circulated in Paris that Augusta Holmès was in reality the daughter of the poet Alfred de Vigny, who had a close and unusually romantic friendship with Tryphina. Officially he was Augusta's godfather, but showed a greater interest in her well-being than might have been expected even of the most conscientious godparent (she was orphaned when still a child: her mother had died while living in de Vigny's house). A visitor to Augusta's house noticed de Vigny's portrait, and asked whether she had known him. She replied, 'Indeed I did. Don't you think I'm very like him?' Although the Holmeses moved in the grander Paris *salons*, they were determined to keep their Emerald Isle roots showing. Augusta considered herself French, yet she never lost her devotion to everything Irish. Among her 'Irish' works is a tone poem called *Irlande* (1882) and an *Orange Song*: her family was Protestant.

The fact that Augusta wanted to be accepted as a Frenchwoman accounts for the *grave* accent on the final *e* of Holmès — which was as bogus an accent as the acute one which Karl (the future Sir Charles) Halle added to *his* surname when he moved to England. But Hallé's 'French' spelling served only to persuade Englishmen to sound the last letter of his name according to its original German pronunciation (that is, not to call him 'Hall'), whereas Augusta Holmès wished to be — and still is — pronounced 'ol-mez'.

She was a musical child and was keen to learn the piano, but her mother not only prevented her from studying music but denied her access to an instrument. Augusta is said to have attempted to stab herself with a dagger in protest, and only after Mrs Holmes's death was she allowed to take music lessons, first from the organist of Versailles Cathedral and then from the German-Swiss composer Friedrich Klosé. (Herr Klose's accent, too, was bogus!) By all accounts Augusta grew up into a remarkable woman as well as an outstanding composer, with a work list of four operas, a dozen symphonies, all conceived on a grand scale (several in the form of symphonic poems with voices). She also wrote military band music; solo pieces for flute and piano; for clarinet and piano, and about 100 songs. Hardly any of her works are nowadays played — though at the time these words are being written the compact disc revolution (combined with a growing interest in women composers) is throwing up unsuspected rarities.

Men pursued Augusta all her life. Adolphe Louis Jullien, the prototype of abominable-showman conductors, wrote poetry to her in which he compared her to Astarte ('who had her beauty but not her brains') and to Sappho ('who had her brains but not her beauty'). The poet Stéphane Mallarmé addressed letters to her in verse. Vincent d'Indy confessed to being *'complètement toqué'* (absolutely crazy) about her. She studied composition with César Franck — and soon he, too, was besotted and wanted to leave his wife to set up home with her. His impassioned F minor Piano Quintet was written under her spell. This did not please Mme Franck, who for ever after said she could not *abide* the work. Franck also dedicated to his young pupil the last of his *Trois chorals*, into which he worked her best-known song, *Trois anges sont venues ce soir*.

Even Camille Saint-Saëns — whose mysterious love-life is recounted (with all its gaps) in another chapter — was also smitten. He declared later, 'We were all in love with her — literary lions, painters, musicians — any one of us would have been proud to make her his wife.' He did indeed propose, but she turned him down as she had turned down all the others. She also rejected the attentions of Vincent d'Indy — as well as those of the poet Villiers de l'Isle-Adam, who described her as '. . . very pretty, with a wealth of golden hair [and] a being possessed of genius . . . not one of those infant prodigies destined to become worthy and excellent houswives, but a genuine artist whose future is assured.' Debussy, who was obsessed by *all* blondes, cryptically quoted to her some lines from one of her own songs, 'Yes, I have captured your heart in my golden claws and your golden hair has fettered my life.' All the same, when her back was turned he liked to amuse his friends by parodying her style, both as composer and poetess, which suggests that he was either not serious in his pursuit or was piqued that he, too, failed.

Fearing she might not be accepted as a female composer, Augusta at first published her music under the pseudonym Hermann Zenta, but all that changed when, in 1875, under the tutelage of César Franck, she began an opera, *Héro et Léandre*, and also — presumably on his recommendation — had part of her first Symphony played by Pasdeloup, who followed this with her Symphonic Poem *Les argonautes* (classical subjects held a special fascination for her). Although César Franck loved Augusta as a person, he was able to remain objective about her music. When he reviewed a performance of *Les argonautes* he declared that it was '. . . a score that is not that of a master, but of its importance and artistic value there can be no doubt at all. . . .' Nor did he take kindly to her Wagnerian inclinations, because he thought these brought in their wake 'excessive virility — a frequent fault with women composers.'

After successfully withstanding all amorous sieges, Augusta Holmès eventually bestowed her favours not on a musician but on one of the many *litterateurs* of her circle: ultimately she was more partial to poets than musicians. She bore three daughters to the poet, journalist and novelist Catulle Mendès but never married him.

LEO EUGEN (LEOS) JANACEK

Born:	Hukvaldy, Moravia, 3rd of July 1854
Father:	Jiri Janacek, music teacher
Mother:	Amalie Grulichova, housewife
Married:	On 13th of July 1881 Zdenka Schulzova (1865–1938)
Daughter:	Olga (1882–1903)
Son:	Vladimir (1888–1890)
Greatest Love:	Kamila Stösslova, i.e. Mrs David Stössel (1891–1935)
Died:	Morava Ostrava, 12th of August 1928

In Ernest Hemingway's novel *For whom the Bell Tolls*, the heroine, Pilar, reports that after a particularly energetic bout of *al fresco* love-making, 'the earth moved'. The novel, written in 1940, when the Spanish Civil War had just finished, would now be forgotten, had that eroto-seismic disturbance not entered the language. However, for Leos Janacek and his mistress Kamila Stösslova the earth 'shook' or 'trembled' — even 'burst open' — under amorous circumstances, considerably earlier, most notably on the 21st of April 1927; and the occasions were immortalized in the third movement of his String Quartet No.2. On the 18th of February 1928 he wrote to her:

> Today I was successful with that movement 'When the earth trembled'. It will be the best. Ah, that was an amazingly beautiful time! And it was true. Only the most beautiful melodies can find a place in it. I hope I can still bring off the last movement . . . .

The quartet is subtitled 'Intimate Letters'; and for the benefit of those unfamiliar with the work, the movement in question is marked *Con moto — Vivace — Andante* and its average duration about three-and-a-half minutes. Long enough for the earth to move.

Hundreds of intimate letters, possibly more than a thousand, passed between Leos Janacek and Kamila Stösslova. In those that survive, his letters to her often had words, passages or whole pages removed, with consequent loss of 'innocent' material on the reverse. She did not wish to preserve anything improper for posterity, yet she could not bear to destroy the letters, except one or two that proved too strong which she destroyed in their entirety, but kept the empty envelopes. Even in their censored form the letters were suppressed by the Czech Communist governments, who thought nothing of murdering thousands but balked at an extramarital affair and a few unremarkable expressions of sexual attraction. (But then, as will be seen in Tchaikovsky's story, the even more prudish Soviets covered up and tried to straighten out *his* sex life). Janacek wrote love letters to Kamila almost openly, ignoring the presence of her husband. David Stössel was either amazingly good-natured or, more likely, complaisant because he was ploughing his own furrows. He certainly felt flattered that his wife had been taken up by the most famous Czech composer since Dvorak. Janacek, although wishing to preserve Kamila's letters for sentimental reasons, kept them from his wife, Zdenka. Mr and Mrs Janacek were effectively no longer married: they lived apart under the same roof; and she had acknowledged the existence of a mistress previous to Kamila. Nevertheless, after she read one of Kamila's letters and found it was cast in intimate terms she threw a tantrum. As a result, he took to burning them, which is why comparatively few exist. The surviving Janacek-Stösslova correspondence was not published in Czechoslovakia until 1990, and English readers had to wait till 1994, when most of the letters were translated, edited and annotated by John Tyrrell, who has also written three other books about the composer as well as the comprehensive Janacek article in *Grove*. The correspondence reveals a strange relationship — between, on the one hand, an elderly, besotted, rather humourless man, self-important and preoccupied with his own success; and, on the other, a not very articulate, under-educated woman 38 years younger, a seamstress in her youth. She was totally unmusical, uninterested in either music or musicians. He tried, gently, to persuade her to read more books, so that she might become a little more sophisticated. At the same time he himself was unsophisticated enough to allow her respectfully to address him as 'Maestro' in her letter superscriptions (though to his dismay she was curiously reluctant to address him with the Czech 'Ty', the intimate equivalent of 'you'). He mostly signed himself with variations on the standard eternal-love protestations 'Yours for ever', etc., with 'L' or 'L. J.' — but occasionally added his abbreviated doctorate, 'Dr.phil.' — Doctor of Philosophy.

Janacek was born at Hukvaldy, the tenth of fourteen children of a poor Moravian couple. His father was a musician, a teacher and Catholic precentor (or *Kantor*, as the Czech-Austro-German tradition named the office), who in 1838 married Amalie Grulichova. There was no more room in their small house, as children were arriving almost every year, so some had to be farmed out, and Leos was sent away to the town of Brno when he was only eleven. There he entered a *Konvikt*, a boarding-school run by priests in a monastery. He became, first, a chorister, receiving his early musical education from the priests; and then (like Bruckner) was put to work teaching the juniors. The choirmaster took him under his wing and widened his musical horizons. From Brno he went on to study music in Prague, then Leipzig and Vienna. He supported himself by taking private pupils, to one of whom he became unoffically engaged in 1879, when he was 25. She was a fourteen-year-old piano pupil, Zdenka Schulzova. Further musical studies followed, and while he was away at college he carried on a rather one-sided correspondence with her, largely to unburden himself of his unhappiness and general discontent. The last student work he wrote at Leipzig was a piano piece, the *Zdenka Variations* dedicated to her. It was perhaps — one cannot be certain of a starting point for his eroto-musical impulses — the first of his many effusions inspired by his love for women. Leos and Zdenka were married on the 13th of July 1881, before she was sixteen — and both realized almost from the honeymoon that marriage had been a mistake.

In August 1882, their daughter Olga was born; after which Zdenka went back to her mother: she had been an only a child and was homesick. She and Leos had a brief reconciliation in 1884, which did not last long, but a son, Vladimir, was born. He died of scarlet fever in 1890, by which time the marriage had foundered again. Leos and Zdenka decided they would stay together but effectively live separate lives.

Janacek was a compulsive musical autobiographer, and most of his compositions seem to have some kind of root in, or reference to, his love-life. After a chance holiday encounter in the summer of 1903, in Luhacovice, Janacek had a brief affair with Kamila Urvalkova, who was around for long enough to be the inspiration of his autobiographical opera *Osud* ('Fate').

In 1903, the Prague National Theatre engaged the soprano Gabriela Horvatova, whom Janacek auditioned for the Kostelnicka role in *Jenufa*. Janacek declared his love and wrote many passionate letters to her, complaining, as usual, about his unhappiness, but their affair was brief. In the same year, and while he was working on *Jenufa*, the Janaceks' daughter Olga died just before her 21st birthday, and the opera is dedicated to her memory. John Tyrrell says that the Janacek-Horvatova affair was conducted openly and ostentatiously (unlike most casting-couch adventures between singers and operatic power-brokers which are usually confined to the vicinity of the dressing room). It led Mrs Janacek to obtain an out-of-court separation from her husband (Gabriela died in 1967 at the age of 90). When Kamila entered Janacek's life he dropped Gabriela and later disloyally wrote some uncomplimentary things about her: ' . . . that Horvatova witch' and, 'You saved me from that terrible perverted woman Horvatova . . . one day Zdenka will see that you protect me and that she was unable to do so.'

In all his correspondences with young women Janacek whinged on and on about how his wife did not understand him, how she could not fulfil the needs of a great composer. In fact, she understood him only too well, as she revealed in her memoirs (translated and extracted in Tyrrell's 'Intimate Letters'). In 1917, Janacek was on one of his regular summer holidays: he set great store by his summer breaks and sometimes planned them as early as January. Most were spent in Luhacovice, and he always went alone, or so he told his wife. During his 1917 holiday he sent a verbal message to Mrs Janacek that he was investigating a source of provisions and had found someone 'in flour' (it was late in World War I, and food was short); and he also revealed that he was there alone. Her reactions were sardonic, but not without a kind of hands-on-hips, housewifely sense of sarcasm. 'From the same messenger I also learnt that that Mrs Horvatova was not in Luhacovice. That was news! My husband in Luhacovice alone and taking care of provisions for our household!' (a household, we must remember, which the Janaceks shared separately: he upstairs, she downstairs — and remember also that his affair with Mrs Horvatova was known to his wife, and practically everybody else). When Janacek returned home, the reason became clear why Mrs Horvatova had not been in Luhacovice:

As early as ten in the morning a carriage clattered up in front of the gardens, Leos leapt out of it, beaming, and at once began telling me merrily that he'd travelled first thing by the early morning express, and that in Luhacovice he'd met a young married couple. 'They really love one another.' He pulled out a photograph and gave it to me. A young woman, evidently a second edition of Mrs Horvatova, except much younger, about twenty-five years old, in a *dirndl**or something peculiar. . . . My instinct clearly told me: 'Mrs Horvatova has fallen off his shovel, now this one takes over.' But my reason objected that I was wrong, that this lady was surely too young. And furthermore, my husband continually related how much the couple loved one another, how delightful they were, until suddenly he blurted out: 'You know, I've invited them, they're coming on Saturday.' I was surprised by Leos's liveliness, his kindliness to me, and because he was again inviting guests to visit us. 'But I'd wanted to go away. . . .' — 'Oh no you can't, you must be here, I've told her about you, she wants to meet you.' How could I go when such things were happening? I thought hard how I would entertain these two: at this time there was everywhere a terrible shortage of provisions. I had my work cut out, but on Saturday, when my husband went to meet the guests at the station, I was decently prepared. I received them on the veranda. I was surprised to see two decidedly Jewish types, especially Mr Stössel, although he was in soldier's uniform, looked very much like a red-haired Polish Jew. Of course I didn't let on at all myself, but I was most surprised at Leos. The wife apologized profusely that she was putting me out, but my husband apparently wouldn't have it otherwise and definitely wanted the two of us to get to know one another. I thought she was quite nice: young, cheerful, one could have a really good talk with her, she was always laughing. She was of medium height, dark, curly-haired like Gypsy woman, with great black, seemingly bulgy eyes, an 'ox-eyed Hera' like Mrs Horvatova — with heavy eyebrows, a sensuous mouth. The voice was unpleasant, shrill, strident. Her husband was sturdy, much taller than Leos, with reddish blond hair, but with a pleasing appearance and very nice manners. She was called Kamila, he David . . . . One thing was certain; that they brought action and laughter into our sad quietness. We had tea in the garden, Leos beamed, and busily waited on her, Mr Stössel was overjoyed at his wife's success. She began to pick apricots. She stood on the ladder, Leos looked at her enthusiastically from below, not caring that people from the opposite windows were looking on curiously to see what was going on at our place. They slept the night downstairs with me, in the morning they went to see friends and arrived back only at tea-time. She again saw to it that there was lots of commotion and fuss until, late in the evening, someone from the military

---

Dirndl: The apparently perennial imitation peasant dress, with a tight bodice and full skirt, much worn in Austria and surrounding countries. The fashion for it among bourgeois women started as a form of nationalism and even today, in Austria and Bavaria, green loden suits with horn buttons, surmounted by a shaving-brush hat, may be worn as a political statement.

hospital next door told her off for carrying on like that at night. Only then did she quieten down. . . . When in the evening my husband went upstairs to sleep, the three of us remained sitting around and chatting. She soon turned the conversation to Mrs Horvatova. She knew about everything; Leos, she said, had confided everything in her, and apparently also complained about my not having understood his friendship. In reply Mrs Stösslova had told him it was difficult for her to make a judgement when she didn't know me. That was the reason why he invited her to see me. So this was it, then: my husband made this young person, whom he'd just met, the judge in our affairs. Fine, I went along with that, too. I told her how I saw it. She readily felt sorry for me, she showed friendly concern, she was full of understanding, so much so that Mara [the Janaceks' maid] and I later said to one another that it was probably good that my husband brought her to us, because she understands me and could have a good effect on him. That she really did have a big influence on Leos was something I found out very soon.

The Stössls stayed with the Janaceks for a few days, and on the Monday Zdenka saw Kamila looking at a photograph of her husband's mistress Mrs Horvatova which hung in his study (the man was hardly a paragon of tact) and told her how she felt every time she saw it. Kamila told her she knew what to do, went into the garden and spoke to Leos. This is Zdenka's account:

[She] rushed back and laughed, 'He gave me that picture, because it's not important to him any more.' Together we took down the picture of Mrs Horvatova and Mrs Stösslova took it back with her to Prerov. What I, our friends and lawyers, couldn't manage, was achieved in a trice by this clever, cheerful little Jewess. In this way she very much won me over. After that I rather liked her.

At this point Janacek's plans could easily have gone wrong. As every philandering husband knows, there is always a risk in introducing women-friends to the wife. They may hate each other at first sight, in which case the new friendship starts off on the wrong foot, is thwarted, or driven underground; or they may take a liking to each other — they may well have much in common, and be of a type that attracts the husband — and form a bond that excludes him.

In June 1924, the Janaceks made their first visit to the Stössels' home in Pisek, and it was not until April 1927 that Janacek confessed to Kamila what she knew for years, that he loved her. But in general they seldom met unless one or the other's spouse was present: much of their love affair was carried on by correspondence, which explains his relentless expressions of frustration.

Often the most unsuitable persons fall in love with each other, and Janacek's love for Kamila was about as unsuitable as could be. At their first holiday encounter in 1917, Janacek was 63, Kamila 23, her husband David 25, and they had with them their two small sons, Rudolf (born in 1913) and Otto (in 1916). Janacek later recalled that he had spotted her sitting on the grass 'like an exhausted little bird who doesn't yet know how to fly'. He was so taken by the sight that he embarked on a chatting-up process from cold, without preliminary introduction — anyway, there was no-one to introduce them — or a polite pretext, like 'Lovely weather we're having', or 'Do you come here often?' As he reminded her in a letter dated 6th of June 1925 he blurted out: 'You must be a Jewess!' and she replied 'How do you know?' — hardly a tactful opening gambit in a country where Jews were subjected to discrimination and abuse. She wrote, on the 20th of January 1925: 'For me you will always remain that old friend from Luhacovice. I have to smile to myself when I remember it all; how I didn't want to speak to you.'

Janacek found out the address of the pension in the spa where the Stössels were staying, and sent her a bouquet:

Dear Madam,
Accept these roses as a token of my unbounded esteem for you. You are so lovely in character and appearance that in your company one's spirits are lifted; you breathe warmheartedness, you look on the world with such kindness that one wants to do only good and pleasant things for you in return. You will not believe how glad I am that I have met you. Happy you! All the more painfully I feel my own desolation and bitter fate. Always think well of me — just as you will always stay in my memory. Heartily devoted to you:

Leos Janacek.

John Tyrrell supposes that David Stössel, being on army service, may have had to rejoin his unit, leaving Kamila and the children behind, and giving her and Janacek the chance to get to know each other; though it must be stressed that — chatting up apart — Janacek was not a fast worker. It was years before anything remotely improper took place. However, there must have been an occasion during those first few days when, as they sat on a bench, Janacek tried to edge closer: six years later he reminded her that, ' . . . each of us told the other from the heart our worries and desires — there in Luhacovice on that path, on that bench, where you split off a branch of a shrub. . . .' And again, four years later still, recalled, ' . . . that bench, where you used to put a twig between you and me to divide us.'

When Janacek left the spa to return home, he extended an invitation to her and her husband for the visit already described. Her acceptance letter, sent by return, is signed 'Kamila and Dori' (her nickname for David), suggesting that she and Janacek had already achieved what was for the formal manners of the time a fairly close friendship.

During the time of his love for Kamila (and for about 25 years before) Janacek was short and fat — fatter even than the 'all round' Charles Gounod described by Georgina Weldon. He was obsessed by her breasts — which, judging from her photographs, wearing Czech folk-dresses as well as formal clothes, must have been quite remarkable. He constantly refers to them, wants to cover them with sheets of his music (having presumably first uncovered them); and, more surprisingly, 'into your womb I'd put the most beautiful things that would ever occur to me'. He likened Kamila's breasts to 'the waves of the Vltava' — an estimate he revises upwards during a trip to London, when they become like 'the waves in the English Channel' (though he reassures her he was not seasick). During the summer she sunbathed a lot: her descriptions of her 'black' body always got him excited and he invented a nickname for her, 'my negress'.

Kamila often appears in Janaceks' works, sometimes recognisably, sometimes cryptically. About *Katya Kabanova* he wrote to Kamila (24th July 1924): ' . . . Katya, you know, that was *you* beside me.' The plot concerns a woman whose husband — like David — is often absent on business. She takes a lover but he does not make her happy, and she commits suicide by throwing herself into a river. *The Cunning Little Vixen* is meant as a portrait of Kamila; he saw the *Glagolitic Mass* as a nuptial mass for himself and Kamila (he was constantly writing about how she was his wife, and weaving fantasies about their children). 'And that black Gypsy girl in my *Diary of One Who Disappeared* — that was especially you even more. That's why there's such emotional heat in these works.' The chief character of *The Makropulos Affair*, Elina Makropulos, is in her youth given a longevity potion, as a result of which she is already 300 years old when the curtain rises. In his letters to Kamila, Janacek sometimes refers to his wife in Makropulos terms as 'the cold one', or 'the icy one', or 'the 300-year-old one', suggesting that the ancient character in the opera was a portrait of Zdenka. In May 1927, he writes: 'You're in my new opera [*From the House of the Dead*] under the name *Aljelja*: such a tender, dear person.'

Janacek died at the age of 74 on Sunday morning, the 12th of August 1928, eleven years and one month after his first meeting with Kamila at Luhacovice, when she had long removed that symbolic twig she had placed between them. Contributory causes of his final illness were given variously as a chill caught when he helped to search for one of Kamila's sons (an unconfirmed story), a discharge from the ears, breathing difficulties after a steep climb up a forest path — but the final diagnosis was pneumonia. Kamila was at his bedside, still in mourning for her mother, Jetty Neumannova, who had died three weeks earlier. Only after his death did Kamila send a telegram to Zdenka, telling her that her husband was 'seriously ill' — heeding his instructions not to ask his wife to come while he was alive. Kamila remained on good terms with Zdenka and returned to her such articles as were more appropriately a wife's, including a gold ring.

Leos and Kamila kept an album of love, into which both wrote thoughts, messages and he some music. The entries made during his final illness are particularly poignant. Yet in spite of all the erotic undertones of the relationship — eroticism which she never reciprocated in her letters — there is no conclusive proof that their love was ever consummated. Two days before he died, he recorded in their album a restless night and his gratitude to Kamila. It ends with an unsteadily-written entry in his hand:

And I kissed you.

And you were sitting beside me and I am happy and at peace.

In such a way do the days pass for the angels.

Janacek's last musical work remained a fragment, written for Kamila in the final days of his life, *I'm waiting for you.*

FRANZ KOTZWARA

Born:	Prague ca. 1750
Wife:	Unknown, if any
Worst friend:	Susan Hill
Hanged:	London, 2nd of September 1791

Kotzwara's exact year of birth has not yet been established, but the circumstances of his death in London, on the 2nd of September 1791, are more closely chronicled and documented than any other event in his life. He worked abroad for much of his life; first, following the well-trodden paths of most Bohemian musicians, in Austria; then in France, Italy, the Netherlands, and finally Dublin and London. In England he was always described as 'a German master of music' and his name was usually given in the German manner, Kotzwara, or Kotzwarra.

In his short life, he gained much notoriety. Although his work list is extensive, containing some 40 opus numbers, he was known chiefly for *The Battle of Prague,* a 'descriptive' trifle of eigthteenth-century programme music which went through nearly 50 editions and was published all over the world.

Kotzwara's other claim to notoriety rests on two things: first, his chameleon-like facility in imitating other composers, which made him much in demand by unscrupulous publishers of fake symphonies. The London oboist and chronicler of musical gossip William Thomas Parke (1762–1847), who knew Kotzwara, says in his *Musical Memoirs* (1830):

> His productions displayed so accurately the taste and science of his prototypes, that, like the admirable copies of the pictures of the old masters by Renigale [Philip Reinagle] the best judges considered them to be originals . . . .

Parke also mentions, secondly, the manner of Kotzwara's death:

> He [was] found hanging in a house of ill fame, in a low court leading into Chandos Street, Covent Garden [actually it was Vine Street, St Martin's]. The case, as it afterwards appeared on [sic] the trial, was a very singular one; but, as it was proved that he was suspended by his own desire, and that neither he nor the other parties implicated in the transaction ever contemplated death, they were acquitted.

Most musical reference works describe Kotzwara's death either as suicide or, like Parke, delicately hint at erotic strangulation. It entered the annals of forensic medicine on the subject of sado-masochistic practices. Today such fatal accidents often figure in the news, especially when famous people succumb to them. The deaths are usually described as the result of 'experiments gone wrong' in which boys and young men take their own lives without meaning to — though they are hardly *experiments*, as if they were playing with a chemistry set. A German traveller, J. W. von Archenholtz, whose *British Annals of the Year 1791* were translated in that year by Joseph Trapp, absurdly suggests it was 'an English vice' — and tells us rather more than we probably want to know about Kotzwara's final curtain and exit.

A most curious incident occurred in London resulting in a criminal prosecution. There was a musician there, Kotzwarra of Prague, a man possessing extraordinary musical gifts, who played thirteen different instruments, some of them with considerable virtuosity. I knew him personally and frequently admired his talent. The famous musicians Bach and Abel, who achieved such fame in England, regarded him as unique in Europe as a performer on the contra-bass; he had also beaten all his rivals in the playing of this instrument in London, Paris and Venice. The above-mentioned musicians in the years 1769 and 1770 frequently invited him to participate in their great concerts at Hanover Square, paying him princely fees. However, Kotzwarra soon began to neglect his talents and lived a life of dissipation. He became a voluptuary of the worst kind, and thought of nothing but the artificial intensification of his sensual pleasures. He was told that a hanged person, owing to the more rapid circulation of the blood and the distension of certain vessels, enjoys a very pleasant sensation for several minutes. According to the evidence of witnesses, he had frequently tried the experiment, always in the presence of prostitutes, whom he rewarded for their assistance. In order to repeat the experiment once more he visited, one day in September, a prostitute living in the neighbourhood of Covent Garden and requested her to hang him, but to release the rope after five minutes. The poor girl at first refused to participate in this strange performance, but Kotzwarra finally succeeded in overcoming her objections by means of persuasion and gifts of money. She hanged Kotzwarra, fixing the rope to the door, and released it at the end of five minutes. But the man gave no sign of life and, although every effort was made to revive him, he remained dead. The girl, Susan Hill, was arrested for murder, and a verdict of 'wilful murder' was returned against her at the preliminary proceedings by the jury, who deliberated from five o'clock in the afternoon till two the next morning. They debated the question for nine hours and finally thought that by their severe verdict they would prevent the co-operation of such girls in abnormal sexual practices. The poor girl had to stand her trial at the Old Bailey [on the 16th of September] on a charge involving life or death [i.e. her own execution by hanging] but the judge regarded her act not as murder but as unpremeditated manslaughter, which was, of course, the logical view to take. She was therefore liberated immediately, with the exhortation to lead a better life. The facts that came to light in the course of the trial were so subversive of modesty, and dangerous to public morality, that the judge not only requested all the women present to leave the court, but also ordered all the documents relating to the case to be destroyed.

However, the writer of a contemporary publication, *Modern Propensities, or An Essay on the Art of Strangling*— who showed the persistence of any sensationalizing tabloid reporter — managed to get hold of part of Susan Hill's police evidence:

> ... on the afternoon of the 2nd September, between the hours of one and two, a man whom she had never seen, and who was identical with the deceased, had come to the house where she was residing, the street door having been open. He asked her whether she would like to have a drink with him. She asked for port, he for brandy and water, and he gave her some money for both, also two shillings for ham and beef, which she also purchased. A little later they went to a back room, where a number of the most indecent acts took place. In particular he asked her to tear his genital organ in two, which she refused. Then he said he would like to be hanged for five minutes and observed, while giving her the money to buy the rope, that this would increase his pleasure and produce the desired effect. She brought two thin cords and placed them round his neck. He then drew himself up on the door of the back room, where he was hanging very low, and drew up his legs. After five minutes she cut him down and he fell to the floor. She thought he had only fainted and called a neighbour woman living opposite to her assistance . . . .

It also emerged at the trial that the Vine Street *filles de joie*, having suspended their client by the door, were distracted from their efforts by a circus procession in the street. They rushed to the window to watch — and by the time they remembered Kotzwara, it was too late.

JEAN-MARIE LECLAIR

Born: Lyons,10th of May 1697
Married: Marie-Rose Casthagnié and Louise Roussel
Murdered: Paris, 22nd or 23rd of October 1764

Jean-Marie Leclair was a member of a notable family of French musicians, mostly violinists and composers, who included a remarkable woman violinist and teacher, Jeanne Leclair, an almost exact contemporary, perhaps a sister. He composed numerous works for violin and one opera, several divertissements and much ballet music, for which there was in France an insatiable demand. Leclair was one of those many-sided, multi-talented French musicians: Dalayrac the lawyer, Jean-Jacques Rousseau the philosopher and Phildor the chess champion, to name only three others. Leclair was not only a composer and fiddler, the founder of the post-Lully eighteenth-century French school of playing and pioneer of remarkable technical demands on performers, but also a lace maker, dancer and dancing master — the last-named profession carried on with the help of a small violin, or kit, which the ballet teacher played as he demonstrated his steps and pirouettes. At the age of nineteen (or perhaps even a little earlier) he joined a Lyons opera company as a dancer, not a player.

On the 9th of November 1716, still in his teens, he married Marie-Rose Casthagnié, who died childless. Leclair was appointed *Ordinaire de la musique du Roi* to Louis XV. His second wife, Louise Roussel, was so devoted to him that she trained as an engraver of music, enabling them to publish all his works subsequent to opus 2 from their home, without the expensive need for a publishing house. Their publications bore the proud inscription *Graveé par Madame son Épouse* — 'Engraved by Madame, his Wife.' The Leclairs produced a daughter, also named Louise, who followed in her mother's footsteps, for she, too, became a skilled engraver and worked for her father. She eventually married the famous painter Louis Quenet. After about 28 years of marriage, Jean-Marie and Louise Leclair parted company — amicably, for presumably he did not want to lose his engraver. They set up separate homes, Leclair moving away to a smaller house in the suburbs, in a rough area of Paris. An attempt by his patron, the Duke of Gramont, to persuade him to live in a more salubrious quarter failed, and one night, as he returned home, he was waylaid on his doorstep, mugged and murdered — a fate not unlike that which befell the entertainer John Lennon in New York two hundred years later (though there the comparison ends). As the eighteenth-century musical historian Sir John Hawkins recorded in his *History of the Science and Practice of Music* (London, 1776):

The character and demeanour of Le Clair were such as attracted the esteem of all that knew him; he had little reason to fear the shafts of envy; nevertheless it seems that he fell a sacrifice to his own fame, for, without having given offence to any one, being abroad in the streets of Paris, in the evening of the 22nd day of October, 1764, and returning to his own home, he was assassinated.

Few personal details of his life and character are known, but contrary to Hawkins's bland description he was also described as 'taciturn and misanthropic, a quality which worsened with age'. According to contemporary police reports the immediate suspicion fell on the gardener who discovered Leclair's body; then on Madame Leclair (for the simple reason that they had announced they parted company, in those times a rare event); and on his nephew Guillaume-Francois Vial, a rising and ambitious violinist with whom Leclair had quarrelled. Paris detectives of the mid-eigthteenth century were no Poirots; but even without recourse to modern forensic methods the surviving crime archives strongly incriminate the nephew. Neal Zaslaw, who wrote the Leclairs' biographies in *Grove*, says, 'The only remaining mystery is that he was never brought to trial.'

FRANZ (FERENCZ) LISZT

Born:	Raiding, Hungary, 22nd of October 1811
Father:	Adam Liszt (1776–1827) Estates Manager to the Princes Eszterházy
Mother:	Anna Laager (1788–1866)
Mistresses:	Marie Duplessis; Lola Montez (1818–1861); Amy Fay; Caroline de Saint-Cricq; Countess Marie d'Agoult (1805–1876); 'Countess' Olga Janina; Princess Caroline Sayn-Wittgenstein (1819 1887) etc. etc.
Children:	(all by Marie d'Agoult): Blandine Rachel, b. 18th of December 1835 (d. 1862) Cosima, b. 25th of December 1837, Daniel b. 9th of May 1839
Died:	Bayreuth, 31st July 1886.

Franz Liszt and his son-in-law Richard Wagner were the most important musicians of the second half of the nineteenth century, yet both are known today more for their influence on others than their own appearances on concert programmes. The two, as men, were also the most obnoxious. Although not as blatantly egotistical as Wagner, Liszt was second only to him in selfishness, self-aggrandisement and sheer, shining chutzpah. His numerous piano arrangements of other men's music perfectly illustrate the man and his philosophy. Just as no female was safe from his attentions, so was no Adagio by Mozart, no song by Schubert — whose genius expressed itself in economy and simplicity — considered anything but a vehicle for his self-pleasuring exhibitionism. He could not abide simple compositions, but had to burden them with squashy harmonies and aren't-I-clever, show-off embellishments — yet his reinterpretations stand as works of art of their own. The saintly Mendelssohn had the measure of him:

> Liszt has lost much of my esteem because of the silly pranks he plays, not only with the public — when they are of no consequence — but with *music*. He played works by Beethoven, Bach and Handel in such a pitifully imperfect manner, so uncleanly [German *unrein*], so ignorantly, that I would have listened to many a mediocre pianist with more pleasure. Here six bars were added, there seven bars were omitted; here wrong harmonies, there a horrible fortissimo was employed in the softest passages, and there were all sorts of other lamentable misdemeanours.

There were many women in Liszt's life, most of them either accomplished, noble or famous; or all three. They included the poet Bettina von Arnim, now ageing but useful to the young Liszt as the archetypal 'older woman' ('An imp of magnetic intelligence,' he wrote of her, who in her youth had bewitched both Goethe and Beethoven), princesses, countesses, actresses, writers and bluestockings. There was Caroline Unger, the flighty singer with whom Beethoven had also been in love and who created the contralto part in the Ninth Symphony. Also Princess Cristina Belgiojoso; the high-class courtesan Marie Duplessis (the original '*dame aux camélias*' upon whom Dumas based his story); the notorious adventuress Lola Montez (of whom more later); and the *nymphomane pianiste* Mme Camille Pleyel, whose accommodating thighs were open to all comers. There was also a beautiful actress, Charlotte Hagn, whom he (somewhat proudly, one feels) described as 'the mistress of two kings': moving in the right circles was important to him. As he was the most sought-after teacher of his age there was a constant succession of young piano pupils who moved between his music room and his bedroom but failed to enter the record books. But Liszt himself was a trophy to be boasted about, and at least two of his mistresses afterwards wrote kiss-and-tell reminiscences.

In 1827, at only sixteen, having been taken to Paris to study, he earned a living by teaching, and fell in love with a sixteen-year-old pupil, Caroline Saint-Cricq, the dark-haired, blue-eyed daughter of a wealthy French count and Minister of Commerce. Their lessons became more and more frequent and prolonged, until her father's suspicions were roused and he barred him from his house. Her romantically inclined mother, however, approved of the relationship, but she died, and her father immediately arranged a 'good' marriage for Caroline, with another French nobleman. Liszt was mortified, though his claim that Caroline's loss made him 'ill for two years' was no doubt an exaggeration. It did, however, strengthen his resolve to enter the priesthood, aware, no doubt that the cloth combined maximum trust with non-stop opportunity for sexual adventures. He continued to teach in Paris, where in 1832 he heard Chopin and was introduced to his mistress George Sand. With her, and the writer Alfred de Musset, Liszt met Countess Marie d'Agoult. It was at a party whose roll-call sounds like a small *Who's Who in Paris*: Frédéric Chopin, Heinrich Heine, Eugene Delacroix, Gioacchino Rossini, Giacomo Meyerbeer and George Sand herself. Marie was born in Frankfurt-am-Main, on the 31st of December 1805, of a French father, the Vicomte de Flavigny, and a German mother from the Bethmann banking family. She was not christened Marie (her family nickname) but Catherine Sophie. In 1827 she entered into an arranged marriage to Comte Charles d'Agoult, equerry to the Dauphin, twenty years older than his bride. She was slim and blonde, with classical features, and Liszt fell in love with her — at first sight, he said; but then he always said it. She wrote (and this translation is taken from Ronald Taylor's 1987 biography of Liszt):

Suddenly there appeared the most extraordinary person I had ever seen. Tall, extremely thin, pale, with large, sea-green eyes flashing with sudden brilliance like waves glinting in the sun, strong features shot through with suffering, hesitant in his movements, and seeming to glide rather than walk, seemingly preoccupied yet at the same time restless, like a ghost waiting for the clock to strike and summon him back to the shades . . . . Franz talked emotionally, breathlessly; with passion he uttered thoughts and opinions totally strange to ears like mine, accustomed as they were to hearing only banal, conventional views. I recall his shining eyes, his gestures and the way he smiled — sometimes earnestly and with profound gentleness, sometimes ironically, caustically.

Liszt was her social inferior, a hired musician, paid to entertain at her society gatherings. She was 28, he 22, a significant age gap, especially as she was far more highly educated than Liszt, who had read little except music. Nevertheless, Liszt's first letter to Marie began:

> My heart overflows with affection and happiness! I cannot tell you what heavenly longing, what inexpressible desire permeates my soul and totally consumes me. It is as if I had never been in love before, had never been loved!!! Tell me, from where comes this mysterious disquiet, these unutterable forebodings, these god-like vibrations of love? Ah, it can come only from you, Sister, Angel, Woman, Marie! My God, my God, have mercy on us, let us never be parted . . .

. . . and, as long again, an extended prayer of thanksgiving to God for the blessings 'He has poured on both our flesh and our soul'. He ends with six words in English:

> Marie! Marie! Ah, let me repeat this name a hundred, a thousand times; it is now three days that it dwells within me, burns and threatens to consume me. I am not writing to you, no, I am with you. I see you, I hear you. Oh the eternity in your arms . . . heaven, hell, everything dwells within you, yes, within you . . . ah, let me be crazy, demented . . . I'm beyond help . . .
> [In English] This is to be! to be!!

Marie decided to leave her husband and elope with Liszt. She fled to Basle, in Switzerland, where Liszt was waiting for her. She wrote to him:

> Let me know immediately the name of your hotel and your room number. Don't leave the room. My mother is here; my brother-in-law has left. By the time you read this I will have spoken, but so far I have not had the courage to say anything. It is a last and hardest test, but I believe in my love and thirst after martyrdom.

On the 18th of December Blandine, the first of their three children, was born. Liszt described Marie as '. . . straight as a candle, white as a communion wafer. . . .' The inept religious simile may have been tasteless, but religion was always important in his life — probably the third most important thing, the second being music. Unfortunately, Liszt's self-esteem was as justified as Wagner's, except that Liszt's genius is probably still underestimated, as many of his works remain unplayed. Here is one of his love letters (a *love* letter!) written in December 1839 to Marie d'Agoult when he was away on tour:

> My Dearest. I have given my third concert, yesterday; Thursday, my fourth.

Ever growing success. My new Fantasies . . . made an explosive impression. In every concert I had to give two encores. The day after tomorrow, Sunday, I give my fifth concert, and . . . next Saturday my sixth. I enclose a letter from Count Festetics. . . . You will see from it the degree of enthusiasm. But I must take six days' rest, or all these feasts and dinners being held in my honour will kill me. That's why I must make a break between my fifth and sixth concerts. When I return from Prague and Pest I'll probably give another two concerts — or perhaps only one, which will bring in at least 7 to 8,000 francs. The net receipts of my concerts are usually . . . rather more than 4,000. . . . Last week there was a concert at Court. I played . . . the Duo from *Somnambula* with Beriot, and then, on my own, the Andante from *Lucia*, with great success. At the end the Empress requested me to play a song of Schubert's. I chose the *Ave Maria*, but at the second bar the Princess of Saxony started to cough, and didn't stop for about twenty bars. I was furious. The Princess of Vasa noticed my anger and broke into laughter in an almost almost scandalous way. Farewell, my love. By the same post you should receive a whole heap of newspapers — as printed matter: that's the most economical way of sending them.

Then Liszt has the good grace to call himself to order:

This is almost a business letter, but so far I've done nothing in Vienna except give concerts, practise, take medicine and keep to my room. Kiss Mouche and Cosima for me. . . . In closing this letter I must tell you — yesterday, after my concert, I learnt Beethoven's C major Concerto, which I did not know, in 24 hours, and played it in a *concert spirituel* (together with an improvised pedal-point cadenza) to utterly unprecedented applause.

Then follow a dozen or more lines of name-dropping, listing all the important personages who had expressed a desire to meet him. At last he finishes this love letter to himself with what he doubtless intended to be a reassurance to his mistress:

So far as women are concerned, their raptures for me are universal. I need hardly tell you that I pay little attention to them. I can think of no woman here whom I find physically attractive, even in the smallest degree. And you know that in moments of exhaustion or utter boredom, that is my only weak point.

'Mouche', mentioned above, was their first daughter Blandine, who married Emile Ollivier (later Prime Minister of France); and Cosima, their second illegitimate daughter, was born on Christmas Day 1837 in the house Liszt and Marie d'Agoult shared by Lake Como, and became, first, the wife of the conductor and pianist Hans von Bülow, then Wagner's mistress and subsequently his wife. She seems to have inherited more than her share of her father's unpleasant traits, which Wagner honed to a fine pitch of nastiness. A son, Daniel, was born in May 1839 (he died aged only twenty). As relations between Liszt and Marie became more strained she wrote to him:

Take care of my love, if you can. It is yours as completely now as it ever was in the old days. I fear that trouble will come from the way in which you can no longer bear to hear the truth, and that you are unwilling to submit to any restraint. The only language you have been willing to listen to is the language of flattery. I cannot believe that a man ought to surrender himself so blindly to all his instincts.

The year 1845 brought another liaison attended by scandal: a brutally sexual relationship with the notorious high-class tart Lola Montez (real name Marie Gilbert). She was famous for her outrageous behaviour — and for having served under both Tsar Nicholas I and the 'Mad' King Ludwig I of Bavaria. Ludwig was mad enough to have himself rowed across the Lake Starnberg for assignations with her on an island — for what purpose is unclear as he was supposed to be a homosexual: perhaps he thought that if anyone could get him going, the notorious Lola might. If the contemporary French caricature is to be believed she seduced the King by flaunting herself to him naked (another picture shows her being caned on her naked bottom). Lola soon got on Liszt's nerves, but he found it difficult to get rid of her. In 1845, when he was staying at the *Gasthof zum Stern* in Bonn during the Beethoven celebrations, she persuaded the hotel manager to admit her to Liszt's rooms, claiming that the composer had invited her. Liszt bribed a porter to lock her in the room while he made his escape. She chose the most public occasion possible to exact her revenge. During the Grand Dinner after the unveiling of The Beethoven Memorial (at which not only Liszt was guest of honour but also King Friedrich Wilhelm IV and his Queen, Berlioz, Spohr, Hallé, Meyerbeer and Moscheles) Lola gate-crashed the banqueting hall and did an erotic dance on the table — 'baring all', as the papers in those days would not have said. It must have been a hilarious occasion, for instead of the naked Lola being ejected it was the horrified guests who fled out of the room and from the building. The situation was further enlivened by the fact that as soon as they got outside, a violent thunderstorm broke. I doubt whether Liszt was in the least discountenanced; but Marie was not amused:

I have no objection to being your mistress, but I will not be one of your mistresses. Try at least to spare me the public vulgarities. This persistent moral drunkenness will lead to a decay of the soul, a disgust for all natural affection.

He replied in apparent contrition:

When I first left you — that was my crime, and is my profound sorrow. . . . I have developed a disgust for my piano; I wish I could play for you alone. I do not know why the crowd listens to me and pays me. The acclamations of the crowd, the intoxications and excesses of my life, and the banal and lying embraces of my mistresses in Vienna, in Hungary, in Trieste, indeed everywhere, have sounded the pitiless funeral bell of that fatal hour when I left you.

They patched up a reunion for a while, but she finally brought their relationship to an end with a brutally frank letter:

> What was I doing with a charming, good-for-nothing, upstart Don Juan, half
> mountebank, half juggler, who makes ideas and sentiments disappear up his
> sleeve and looks in a self-satisfied manner at the bewildered public that
> applauds him? Ten years of illusion! Is that not the very height of folly? Adieu.
> My heart is bursting with bitterness.

Two years later, under the pseudonym Daniel Stern, she published a novel entitled *Nelida* (an anagram of 'Daniel') in which she made her affair with Liszt public, in all its embarrassing detail, exposing his self-awarded 'greatness' as a sham. She announced that Liszt's physical presence may have been impressive, but his character was small and mean. The French took such revelations in their stride, as a natural outcome of love gone sour, and shrugged their Gallic shoulders. But the Germans' sense of propriety was offended, and for a while Liszt's stock was low; especially as he had always professed such strong religious feelings.

That his constant pursuit of women left him enough time for producing more than 1,000 compositions, in addition to all the travelling necessary to give at least as many concerts (both playing and conducting) proves that he must have had extraordinary reserves of emotional energy and physical stamina. But then, Liszt needed to expend little energy on his courtships. He never had to chase after women: they pursued him — sometimes across Europe — with the near-hysteria of any pop-singer's groupie. A young American pianist, Amy Fay (described by Vincent d'Indy as '*une blonde et piquante Américaine*') arrived in Weimar to study with Liszt — and immediately came under his spell, recounting her impressions with girlish breathlessness:

> Liszt is the most interesting and striking-looking man imaginable, tall and
> slight, with deep-set eyes, shaggy eye brows and long, iron-grey hair, which he
> wears parted in the middle. His mouth turns up at the corners, which gives him
> a most crafty and Mephistophelean expression when he smiles, and his whole
> appearance has a sort of Jesuitical elegance and ease.... But the most
> extraordinary thing about him is his wonderful variety of expression and play
> of his features. One moment his face will look dreamy, shadowy, tragic. The
> next he will be insinuating, amiable, ironic, sardonic .... People say that
> women still go perfectly crazy over him ....

Amy was clearly one of them though Liszt was by then sixty-two.

> He made me think of an old-time magician more than anything else, and I felt
> that at a touch of his wand he could transform us all.

Although Liszt entered the priesthood and finished up as an Abbé he took only minor orders, four of the seven degrees, being first doorkeeper, then reader, acolyte and exorcist. He had much to exorcise, for underneath the clerical robes nothing ever changed. There was also an adventure, beginning in Rome in 1869, with another pupil, Olga Janina, a beautiful Cossack Countess (by which time he was a fully-fledged Abbé, which made the affair all the more piquant). She was not really a Countess but plain Olga Zielinska, a Polish boot-polish manufacturer's daughter from Lvov, who had been married off to an older husband whom she horse-whipped on their wedding night (whether in anger or by request is not revealed) and then left. She was a gifted pianist — and sought out Liszt as a genuine pupil, not an amorous adventuress. As a member of his piano class she had offended him by not kissing his hand, which his pupils were expected to do. He studiedly ignored her. Afterwards he visited her in her apartment, 'Just to apologize for my rudeness,' he said. She later reported: 'He was no longer the same man. He took my head between his hands and kissed it.' She declared her love for him and later described the affair in two scandalous books; *Les amours d'une cosaque, par une amie de l'Abbé X*, and *Le roman du pianiste et de la cosaque*. Twice, she says, she nearly killed him and reported (much of the story is hers, though the essence was never denied by Liszt) that he said to her:

> I ought not to love. But I do love and cannot conceal it. I beg you — here his voice became so caressing that I trembled from head to foot — to have pity on me now that you have torn this confession from me. Let your love be sweet to me. Do not let it make me perjure myself.

Liszt replied in what must be one of the most bathos-laden statements in the history of seduction:

> 'Call me Franz. *Tu-toie* me.' And he covered me with passionate kisses.

In fact nothing much happened on that occasion, and Liszt, perhaps feeling a little peeved that he was not the hunter but the quarry, went into retreat again, in the Villa d'Este (the home of all those French *Prix de Rome* winners alluded to elsewhere). She gained access by disguising herself as a gardener's boy delivering a basket of flowers, and there was an immediate reunion in his room, after which he fell asleep in her arms. She took this as an insult.

> He showed such joy that I could see how dreadfully his solitude had weighed on his mind. He said to me: 'I can no longer deny myself to you.' He was mine. But when he wakes, I thought he would perhaps recoil from me, and, weeping, take refuge at the feet of a crucifix . . . . Yes, I am bound to lose him. He will grovel in the dust, to some priest or other, and implore God's pardon for the sin of love . . . he will sully me with the most hateful names.

'Countess' Janina was a woman of experience. And, as a Cossack lady who never knew what beastly persons she might encounter, she always carried a poisoned dagger which, according to her own account, could have seriously harmed the prospects of nineteenth-century music:

> One tiny puncture — and he would be mine for all eternity. I held the dagger in my hand and waited for his first word . . . but when he awoke, it was one of love. He was radiant. He was *saved*. He carried his head proudly. His eyes were ardent, passionate. He embraced me. Never did any Christian celebrate better the resurrection of his Saviour.

But what about those priestly vows? No problem. According to Olga:

> Every six months he consecrates a week to the salvation of his soul. You see, my dear, there's nothing like putting one's conscience in order.

Liszt had a taste for Russian noblewomen, for in 1847 — just after Marie had published her revelatory novel — he embarked on his last big affair, with the Princess Caroline von Sayn-Wittgenstein, born to a rich land-owning family in the Kiev region, on the 8th of February 1819 and therefore eight years younger than Liszt. Her family had married her off when she was only seventeen, and (as Marie had been) Caroline was bored with her husband, and with life in the country. In 1847, Liszt was on tour in Kiev, and she fell in love with him when she watched him give a concert. She sent him a note for 100 roubles, enclosed in an envelope with a note, 'For your favourite charity. . . .' Her feelings were heightened even more when, in church, she heard his setting for male voices and organ of *The Lord's Prayer*, which he had written the year before. Just like Marie, Caroline was fascinated by Liszt's heady mixture of religious fervour and sexual excess. She invited Liszt to stay with her at one of her husband's country seats, ostensibly to plan charity concerts, and their affair quickly ripened. In the following summer they arranged to meet in Odessa, when she decided to leave her husband. Before she did so she sold one of his estates to finance her trip and raise money for her subsistence abroad (he was immensely rich and owned many properties, so presumably she thought he would not miss one). But Russian vengeance can be fierce, and her action made both her and her daughter into fugitives. Caroline had chosen the wrong moment, for they were overtaken by the 1848 rebellions that broke out all over Europe. They managed to get to Austria, where Liszt's friend Prince Lichnovsky (a name familiar for the family's support of Beethoven) took care of them at one of his estates in Silesia. The Caroline liaison was happy while it lasted, and artistically fruitful: under her inspiration Liszt produced no fewer than twelve symphonic poems, the Dante and Faust symphonies, the piano concertos and numerous other works. Hundreds of letters passed between them, full of tenderness, even the occasional flash of poetry — but never the slightest hint of laughter (neither Liszt nor Wagner were strong on jokes) — unless one interprets as salacious an allusion to his early-morning thoughts of love:

You ask me in your letter today, 'What is your first thought on waking, what's the first thing you think of, the first thing you want?' Oh, but don't you know about these things, don't you feel it yourself? It's just as if you were touching it with your hand . . . .

Slowly the relationship faded out. After thirteen years of cohabitation Caroline wanted to regularize the union, and petitioned the Pope for an annulment of her marriage (unaware that her husband had quietly divorced her, years earlier, without telling her). Perhaps she reminded his Holiness that he had already met her lover. Liszt had previously received Pius IX in audience: yes, it was the *Pope* who came to see *Liszt*, not the usual way round. Liszt, after all, was no ordinary Catholic. Princess Caroline and Liszt were to be married on the 22nd of October 1861, his 50th birthday. The night before the wedding he was suddenly beset by doubts, and to Caroline's distress called it off without warning. His love for her had waned, while hers was stronger than ever. She refused to accept his decision, but he escaped into a religious retreat, an asylum-seeker from his amorous creditors, resolving to devote himself to the church. Needless to say, this faltered when further opportunities presented themselves. The story of Liszt's countless remaining affairs, as he took advantage of one wide-eyed pupil after another or was sought out by amorous headhuntresses, eventually becomes as monotonous as Don Giovanni's catalogue and lacks the wit. One mistress nearly shot him, another framed the chair cover that had been sanctified by his bottom; and one was in later life shunned by everyone because of her evil smell — until it was discovered that for 25 years she had carried the stump of one of Liszt's cigars in her corset.

Liszt died in Bayreuth on the 31st of July 1886, and is buried near Wagner and the Wagners' dog Russ, where he was later joined by his daughter Cosima Wagner. Princess Wittgenstein followed him eight months later, on the 8th of March 1887, far away, in Rome. She was buried in that city to the strains of her lover's Requiem.

GUSTAV MAHLER

Born:	Kalischt, Bohemia, 7th July 1860
Married to:	Alma Maria Schindler (1879-1964)
Children:	Maria Anna (1902–1907) Anna Justine (1904–1988)
Died:	Vienna, 18th May, 1911.

Alma Mahler's *Reminiscences* were published in 1939, soon after she escaped from German-occupied Austria, and they form the basis of much of what has been written about her marriage to Gustav Mahler. He had been dead nearly 30 years, and her recollection was becoming dimmer. Only her bitchiness, her determination to pay off old scores (of the non-musical kind) were as fresh as ever. She also made sure to portray herself in the best light possible. Towards the end of her life, she mellowed: a sad old lady, sometimes receiving Mahler pilgrims, but essentially ill-at-ease in the brash new America, so different from the *fin de siècle* Vienna in which she grew up.

It almost became a cliché that Alma Schindler was 'the most beautiful girl in Vienna' — though by present-day standards her photographs reveal nothing particularly remarkable: perhaps because a certain kind of radiance resists capture on a portrait photograph — and ideas of female beauty have changed. She was tall, light-haired (some said blonde, but photographs suggest a light brunette), had a good bearing and could hold her own, somewhat aggressively, in philosophical and political arguments.

In 1897, she was a music student, taking composition lessons with Alexander von Zemlinsky (1871–1942), a protegé of Brahms and teacher (later brother-in-law) of Arnold Schoenberg. She composed numerous songs, which for many years were assumed to be little more than the effusions of a clever music student. Mahler did his utmost to smother her talents: one composer in the family was enough, he told her, and ordered her to put her fluent music hand to better use, copying out the performance material of his compositions. Early in their brief courtship she ended a letter to him, 'Must stop now, got to do my harmony exercises' (or words to that effect). The outburst occasioned by this innocent explanation gave her a foretaste of his overweening selfishness. She wrote:

> He was outraged that there might be anything in the world that could have been more important to me than to write to him. He sent me a long letter in which he forbade me from any further composition. If only he knew what that did to me! I cried the whole night long. In the morning I went to mother and she was so horrified by this ban that, much as she loved Mahler, she seriously advised me to break off the relationship. Her support brought me to my senses. I calmed down, became more confident and finally wrote him a letter in which I explained things to him and promised to do what he wanted me to do — and I have kept that promise.

Only when more of Alma's songs became known in the last two decades of the twentieth century were their musicality and technical confidence appreciated. They are now firmly in the repertoire: performed and recorded. By an ironic twist of fate and fashion, Zemlinsky's neo-Brahmsian romanticism, like Alma's music, is also gaining a belated foothold; and by a further irony this increase is in inverse proportion to the fading of interest in the strict Twelve-Note music of Schoenberg and his disciples. Zemlinsky was the most influential teacher of his day, and is often called the Father of the Second Viennese School. He took her to operas, concerts, parties and musical evenings, and raised her intellectual horizons. Alma fell in love with him, and he taught her rather more than double counterpoint and musical form. In one of the social gatherings of the Viennese intelligentsia she found herself attracted to an even older man, the by then nearly middle-aged Gustav Mahler, whom she knew as the renowned conductor of the Vienna State Opera. She did not have the courage to speak to him, but a meeting came about through a chance encounter with mutual friends:

> It was an autumn afternoon in 1901 when some friends and I, walking along the Ringstraße, bumped into the Zuckerkandls. Dr Zuckerkandl was a noted anatomist of great and wide-ranging intellect, full of humour. He said at once, 'Mahler is coming to see us soon. Won't you come too?' I answered 'no,' because I didn't want to. That was because of all the lies that had been told about him. I recollected a small, nervous little man with a magnificent head, but at the same time restless and absent-minded. Then I remembered the rumours about his many casting-couch love affairs. Not least I recalled a recent concert at which his first symphony was played, a work which had filled me with anger and protest. He was important to me as a conductor, and I could not deny that I had always secretly felt a great attraction for him. But I disguised it. My 'no' had hardly been uttered than Frau Zuckerkandl said, 'It's no use anyway. I promised Mahler's sister Justine that it would be a private occasion. Mahler can't stand strangers.' But Zukerkandl interjected, 'Nonsense. I'd like her to be there.'

In the event, Mahler himself cried off, and the evening was postponed until the following Sunday, when the guests included the painter Gustav Klimt and the poet, writer and theatre director Max Burkhard.

> Mahler curiously enough took notice of me immediately. Not because of my face but my nervously loud and forward manner. He peered at me long and searchingly through his spectacles. The last guests arrived and we went to the table. Klimt and Burkhard sat on either side of me, and we were a merry trio, laughing a lot. I saw Mahler looking at us from the other end of the table, at first furtively, then brazenly; and finally he called across to us, with undisguised envy, 'Is anyone else allowed to share the joke?' He paid little attention to the poor woman who sat at his side. Then a late-comer arrived for the meal who had just been to a concert by the violinist Kubelik and was full of enthusiasm

for him. He asked me if I'd heard Kubelik and I replied, 'I'm not interested in concerts with soloists.' This seemed to please Mahler, who again called out from the other end of the table, 'Nor me, either!' After we had risen from the meal and small groups formed, separately conversing, the talk turned to the relative perception of beauty. Mahler said he found the head of Socrates beautiful. I agreed and said I thought the musician Alexander von Zemlinksy beautiful. Mahler shrugged his shoulders and said surely that was going a bit far. This fired me and made me even more argumentative, and I turned the conversation back to Zemlinsky. 'Now that we've mentioned him, why don't you perform his Hofmannsthal ballet *Das goldene Herz*? After all, you promised him.' He said, 'Because I don't understand it.' I had been told about the somewhat muddled symbolism of the story in great detail by Zemlinsky himself, and said, 'Then I'll bring you the book and explain it to you.' Mahler smiled, 'I can't wait.' To which I replied, 'But not before you've explained to me the "Bride from Korea," ' — a ballet that was then constantly in the Viennese repertoire though it had a stupid plot. Now Mahler laughed out loud and flashed his teeth at me. Afterwards he showed interest only in my studies, having learnt that I was a composition pupil of Zemlinsky. He asked me to bring some of my work to him . . . .

So far it was a classic party chatting-up scenario. But an extraordinary rapport had already developed between Mahler and Alma. Outwardly Mahler was a prude and a tyrant. He lived with his sister Justine after the death of their parents and guarded her like a jealous husband. Time and again he called female opera singers into his office if he suspected there had been the slightest hint of impropriety on their part. Yet he did not live by the rules he prescribed for others. In Cassel he had a passionate liaison with the singer Jehanne Richter — a love affair which ended unhappily for him. She felt that he had no future and would be unable to support her, so she abandoned him. His unhappiness resulted in the cycle of orchestral songs, *Lieder eines fahrenden Gesellen*. When he was at Hamburg he did resist the advances of a soprano who tried to seduce him and have an uncomplicated affair with him. Presumably he found her insufficiently attractive, for at the same opera house he succumbed to the charms of a 23-year-old singer, Anna Bahr-Mildenburg, who joined Hamburg Opera in 1895. Meanwhile the rejected temptress (according to Alma) spread the 'nastiest gossip' about him. He was so much in love with Mildenburg that he acted as her personal repetiteur (a task usually allotted to a junior member of the music staff) and indeed made her into one of the great dramatic sopranos of the time. According to some sources they were briefly engaged. After he had moved to Vienna (following a spell at the Budapest Opera) to take up the Directorship of the State Opera, he wrote to her many intimate — though not passionate — letters. They show a closeness that survived long after the affair had come to an end, apparently by mutual agreement. Within a year of his taking up the *Staatsoper* post she followed him to join the Vienna company, and they remained close friends right up to and during his marriage. Alma, for her part, was ungenerous to her and claimed — falsely — that she was trying to cling to him. Anna lived until 1947. In Vienna he had his longest-running love affair with the violinist Natalie Bauer-Lechner, two years his senior, whom he had known since they were fellow-students at the Conservatoire, and she was among the first to recognize his genius. She knew about the Mildenburg affair and was glad for them both; only when she heard of his engagement to Alma, some 21 years younger than herself, did she abandon hope of marrying him.

The most dramatic of Mahler's affairs took place when he was working at the Leipzig opera. There he met and fell in love with an older woman, the wife of a Captain von Weber, grandson of Carl Maria von Weber. In 1888 the English composer and militant feminist Ethel Smyth was studying in Leipzig, and in her book, *Impressions that Remained* (1919) wrote:

> Gustav Mahler, who was one of the conductors at the Leipzig Opera, fell in love with her [Frau Weber] and his passion was reciprocated — as well it might be, for in spite of his ugliness he had demoniacal charm. A scandal would mean his [her husband's] leaving the Army, and Weber shut his eyes for as long as possible, but Mahler, a tyrannical lover, never hesitated to compromise his mistresses. Things were getting critical, when, one day, travelling to Dresden in the company of strangers, Weber suddenly burst out laughing, drew a revolver, and began taking William Tell-like shots at the head-rests between the seats. He was overpowered, the train brought to a standstill, and they took him to a police station raving mad — thence to an asylum. Always considered rather queer in the Army, the Mahler business had broken down his brain. I afterwards heard that he had lucid intervals, that his wife in an agony of remorse refused to see her lover again . . . and the rest is silence.

Not total silence, as the Weber affair provided Mahler with at least some of the inspiration for his tone poem 'Titan,' later reworked as Symphony No.1. As a signed love token, Mahler wrote for Alma one of his most beautiful songs, *Liebst Du um Schönheit*: 'If you love me, love me not for Beauty but for Love . . . .' Alma again:

> On the 9th of March 1902 Mahler and I were married. Mahler came to the wedding on foot, wearing galoshes as it was raining heavily. My mother, Mahler's sister Justine and I, drove. We were quite alone in the Karlskirche, just us and the witnesses, [Karl] Moll [Alma's stepfather] and Rosé. It was early in the morning. When it came to kneeling down, Mahler overlooked the hassock and got to his knees on the stone flags. He was quite small, so he had to get up again and get down a second time. We all smiled, even the priest. Afterwards the six of us had a rather silent lunch and immediately afterwards we made our farewells to our guests, packed and drove to the station. Our wedding had been announced for the evening, when the church was crowded with inquisitive spectators. Once we were in the train for St Petersburg we could breathe

again. Mahler's depressions disappeared in a flash. . . . He had been invited to conduct three concerts in St Petersburg and we had decided to make the trip our honeymoon. . . . In the first years of marriage I felt very unsure of myself in Mahler's company. Having captured him by means of sheer, unthinking cheek I found my self-confidence drained away by my becoming prematurely pregnant. And how strange that as soon as Mahler had mentally declared himself victorious over me he looked down on me, only starting to love me again when I had freed myself from his tyrannical influence.

Alma did not mention in her *Reminiscences* that when they got married, she was two-and-a-half months pregnant. Nor does she reveal whether she had accepted Mahler's terms and conditions. He had set out clearly enough what he expected of a wife, and any woman less blinded than Alma by hero-worship would have read the danger signs and fled.

You must understand that I could not bear the sight of an untidy woman with unkempt hair and neglected appearance. Solitude is essential to me when I am composing. As an artist I demand this, unconditionally. My wife would have to agree to my living separately from her, perhaps several rooms apart, and to my having a separate entrance. She would have to be content with sharing my company only at certain times, to be determined in advance, and then I would expect her to be perfectly groomed and well dressed. Finally, she should not feel offended, or interpret it as lack of interest, as coldness or even disdain on my part, if at times I do not wish to see her. In a word she would need to have qualities that even the best and most devoted women do not possess.

On the 3rd of November 1902 their first child, Maria Anna, was born. It was a difficult breech birth and she emerged buttocks first. Mahler said, 'That's my child all right, showing the world exactly what it deserves — her bottom.' Anna Justine (her second Christian name after Mahler's sister) followed on the 15th of June 1904.

In 1905 Mahler conducted the Viennese première of *Die Rose vom Liebesgarten* by Hans Pfitzner (1869–1949) at the State Opera, in the composer's presence. Pfitzner's reputation was then in the ascendant but later dropped sharply, partly because of his rabid right-wing views, which ran counter to the liberalism of the Viennese intelligentsia, and partly because he found the process of composition an intolerable effort. Mahler had at first refused Pfitzner's entreaties for a production, but Alma took a liking to him and persuaded her husband to conduct it.

During the rehearsals for the '*Rose*' Pfitzner pretended to take an interest in Alma's songs, but it was a ruse. His enthusiasm was for her, and although Mahler was jealous of their friendship, she sensed he was fostering it, going out of his way to leave the two alone and almost encouraging an affair.

Whether Pfitzner ever seduced Alma was not revealed, as he was still alive when she published her *Reminiscences*. Pfitzner was by then already married to Mimi

Kwast, one of Percy Grainger's mistresses, mentioned elsewhere in this book. In 1907, in Paris, the famous pianist Ossip Gabrilovich (1878–1936) declared his love for her (the scene is reported by Alma in her *Reminiscences*) but at the same time assured her that he did not wish to hurt Mahler, who on switching the light in a room had discovered them holding hands — but 'was nice about it'.

Selfishness, and a belief that his genius deserved everyone's devoted attention, were central to Mahler's actions. Nothing was permitted to disturb him. Alma had strict instructions to shield him from the slightest unpleasantness. She was ordered to keep from him any uncongenial news, even tradesmen's bills, until he had done his morning's work and had his lunch, followed by an afternoon nap. Then she could break it to him, gently, that the grocer needed paying.

In 1908, the Mahlers, with Alma's mother, went for their summer stay in Styria. That holiday proved a fateful one in the Mahlers' relationship. Alma had deposited Mahler in Toblach and left him there 'in the care of reliable servants' to work on his Symphony No. 10. She then went off on a spa cure to Tobelbad, also in Styria. She declared herself 'totally worn out and very ill owing to constant heart trouble'. It was not her own heart that was troubling her but her husband's, that 'giant motor which drove his spirit', as she described it, and which was giving him and his doctors cause for serious concern — and was eventually to kill him. In the spa, said Alma, she was:

> so lonely and sad that the director of the sanatorium, worried for my well-being, introduced me to young people who were asked to accompany me on my walks. I found artist X particularly *sympathisch* and soon I was left in no doubt that he was in love with me and hoped for his love to be returned. So I left.

There was more to it than that. 'Artist X' was 27, blond and handsome — the already famous architect Walter Gropius. Never one to resist fame and talent, she did indeed return his love. In fact after Mahler's death in 1911 he became her second husband, so why did she need to disguise his identity in her 1939 *Reminiscences*?

> Back in Toblach Mahler met me at the station and was suddenly more in love with me than before. It might have been that the love of that strange man X had restored my self-confidence — in short, I was happier and more optimistic. But I wished for no change. About eight days later there arrived a letter from this young man in which he told me he could not live without me and that if I had the slightest feelings for him I would leave everything and come to him. This letter was written to me, but the envelope was clearly addressed 'To Herr Direktor Mahler', so of course Mahler had opened it. It has never been explained whether this youth was writing in the heat of his love fever or whether he really wanted to make his feelings for me known to Mahler direct.

Mahler demanded a meeting with Gropius, which was conducted quietly and

with dignity. Afterwards he said to Alma, 'You must decide. Whatever choice you
make will be the right choice.' Alma decided to stay. Mahler even had second
thoughts about her songs. She used to keep them in a folder she called their
'coffin' as he had peremptorily forbidden her to work at composition. Now there
was a sudden change of heart. One day, as she neared the house on returning
from a walk, she

> stood rooted to the spot. I heard my songs being played and sung. My poor
> forgotten songs. Chastened and a little angry, I went into the room. As Mahler
> met me he was so full of joy that I was lost for words. 'What have I done?' he
> said. 'These songs are *good*. Simply excellent! I demand that you revise them
> and we shall publish them. I won't rest until you start working again. God, was
> I mean in those days!' And he played them again and again. I had to sit down
> at once and start working at any flaws in them. After a ten-year gap. Yes, he was
> almost beside himself with exclamations of praise, which I will not write down
> in case I appear to overvalue my own talent.

On the 26th of August 1910 Mahler, clutching at straws, decided to undergo
psychoanalysis with Sigmund Freud. There are accounts of this from Alma, from
Freud's English disciple Ernest Jones and (long after Mahler's death and in
general terms, not in confidence-breaking detail) from Freud himself. Not
surprisingly, Freud established that Gustav and Alma had been playing at mothers
and fathers: Mahler was seeking in Alma his late mother, 'his Maria-complex',
Freud called it, while Alma found in him a father-replacement figure. After the
sessions Mahler sent his wife a cheerful telegram reporting success:

> Am cheerful again. Consultation interesting. Straws have turned into planks.

But Alma was still in turmoil about her holiday lover. Less than two weeks later,
she and Gropius made a secret assignment — in a Munich hotel room. Perhaps
it was Alma who should have had the therapy. She loved attention from famous
men, finding the very idea of genius erotic. In the following year, the year of
Mahler's death, Gropius founded the Bauhaus school, which changed the face of
architecture throughout the world, setting in train concrete blight and the
'House is a Machine for Living In' myth of Le Corbusier. In 1915, Gropius and
Alma were married, and had a daughter, Manon, who died tragically early, aged
eighteen. On her death Alban Berg dedicated his Violin Concerto *To the Memory
of an Angel*. When that marriage ended (Gropius lived until 1969), Alma met, fell
in love with and married the novelist Franz Werfel, celebrated author of *The Song
of Bernadette*, twelve years her junior. He predeceased her by nearly twenty. During
Mahler's lifetime she had also had an affair with the celebrated painter Oskar
Kokoschka, seven years younger. He was at first a disciple of Gustav Klimt but later
turned expressionist — and incidentally, when the Mahlers' friend Arnold
Schoenberg was not knitting his tone-rows for the Second Viennese School he,
too, painted expressionist paintings, a member of the Blue Rider School. Alma

did not mention Kokoschka in her *Reminiscences*— but he effectively 'outed' their affair in his famous *Windsbraut* painting — Bride of the Wind — which shows them both in bed together. Many years later, long World War II, they both regretted not having married. Kokoschka suggested a reunion but she refused to see him: she wanted him to remember her as she was in 1914. Kokoschka died in 1980, having lived some years in London, where he was often seen at concerts. Alma's liking for famous men ran in the family, her daughter Anna (1904–1988) by turn married the composer Ernst Krenek and then the conductor Anatole Fistoulari (1907–1995). Alma lived out her life in America. When she was an old lady she was asked by a reporter if she had any opinions as to who were the geniuses of today, she replied, 'Geniuses? There aren't any. Only perhaps Leonard Bernstein or Thornton Wilder.' She died in America in 1964 at the age of 85, when the great surge in the popularity of her husband's music was about to start in Britain and the USA (on the continent it had never stopped, apart from the Nazi years). Marriage had three times changed her surname and many Americans were unaware that in their midst there lived the widow of the greatest composer since Beethoven. In one of the obituaries her name was misprinted Alma Mater; and her burial rites, at the Frank E. Campbell Funeral Home, were performed not to the glorious Adagietto of her first husband's fifth symphony (which he dedicated to her and their love) but to non-stop muzak.

JOHANNES WOLFGANGUS AMADEUS CHRYSOSTOMUS SIGISMUNDUS MOZART

Born:	Salzburg, 27th of January 1756
Father:	Johann Georg Leopold Mozart (1719–1787)
Mother:	Anna Maria Pertl (1720-
Sister:	Maria Anna ('Nannerl') (1751–1829)
Married:	Maria Constanze Caecilia Josepha Johanna Aloysia Weber.
Died:	Vienna, 5th of December 1791

Mozart's first serious girl friend was his *Bäsle,* his 'little girl cousin' Maria Anna Thekla, two and a half years younger. She was in her late teens, a naughty tomboy. Wolfgang had just passed his 21st birthday and was, as he confessed to his father just before his marriage, a virgin: in those days hardly surprising for a son of a God-fearing family. The first surviving reference to his cousin occurs in a letter home to his father. Wolfgang was on his way to Paris with his mother and conveniently began his tour in Augsburg, where they were able to save the cost of inn lodgings by staying with Leopold's brother, the father of Maria Anna Thekla.

> If it were not for my dear little girl cousin I'd be sorry to be here in Augsburg. . . . She is beautiful, sensible, amiable, clever and merry . . . the two of us get on well together; like me she's a bit naughty — we tease people no end and it's very comic.

Leopold Mozart was worried by his niece's naughtiness and warned Wolfgang, 'She knocks around with priests rather too much . . . .' Wolfgang already knew this, and it probably added to his excitement. He had no close friends of his own age: after all, he was a full-time composer and performer from infancy. Now, suddenly, here he was in close contact with a girl who must have seemed to him an experienced young woman. In another letter, written towards the end of October 1777, he told his family how provocative she could be:

> Yesterday, my dear little Bäsle, who sends her love to you both, dressed up in the French manner just to please me, and it made her five per cent more beautiful. She is nothing less than a Pfaffenschnitzl.

Pfaff is Austrian dialect for a Catholic priest, and *Schnitzl,* familiar from culinary use, is literally a small offcut; so Mozart called his cousin 'a little bit-on-the-side for priests' ('Parsons' Pleasure'?), doubtless in a light-hearted manner. And he told her so, at which she 'solemnly protested'. Priests played a large role in the education of the young, and a teenager to whom a priest showed more than ordinary friendliness would have been considered no more than a 'teachers' pet'. However, seven years later, the *Bäsle* produced practical evidence that these family jokes had contained an element of truth. In February 1784, she gave birth to an illegitimate daughter — and the man who admitted fathering the child was Canon Berbier of Augsburg Cathedral. She was christened Josepha and later legitimized: in the Catholic Church everything is possible. Leopold was furious; angry not only with her but with his brother for the way he and his wife had brought her up. 'As soon as I have the time I shall send a hell of a letter from here to Augsburg. And to think of all the presents her Uncle sent her. What an "honour" for me!' A small but significant footnote to this clerical error is provided by a traveller, J. K. Riesbeck, who reported in 1784 that the Augsburg Cathedral canon operated a sort of *droit du seigneur* in procuring 'the maidenheads of free-and-easy citizens by the dozen. . . .'

Mozart was obviously much taken with his *Bäsle*. He left Augsburg after a fortnight's stay at her home and continued his concert tour, writing to her assiduously. The first letter (31st of October 1777) was brief and 'clean'. The second, written four days later begins 'Darlingest little Cousin, little Rabbit' (in German *Allerliebstes Bäsle Häsle* — rhyming slang) which is full of obscenities — chiefly excretory, repetitive and boring: her replies have not survived but doubtless they were in the same vein. His letter ends with what Mozart described as

> a sad story which happened this very instant. Just as I was in full flow writing this letter and it was going really well, I hear something in the street. I stop writing — I get up, I go to the window — but I hear nothing. — I sit down again, start to write again — I hardly write ten words when I hear something again — I get up again — and as I rise I hear something, but faintly — and I get a sort of burnt taste in my mouth — wherever I go there's a stink. When I look out of the window the smell disappears — I go back into the room and the smell starts up again — then at last Mama says to me: what shall I bet you that you let one rip? — I don't believe so Mama. Mama: Yes, I'm sure. So I make this test. I stick my forefinger up my arse, put it to my nose, and — *ecce provatum est*; Mama was right. Now farewell. I kiss you 10,000 times and am, as always, the old young pig's tail Wolfgang Amadé Rosenkranz . . . ♥ 333 till the grave, if I live.

Rosenkranz means rosary but here has no religious significance. It is an example of the facetious and often obscene rhyming slang with which Mozart loved to pepper his letters. *Kranz* rhymes with *Schwanz*, which literally means a tail but is also a dysphemism for the penis (*penis* being Latin for tail). So when Mozart signs himself *Dein alter junger Sauschwanz* he means, 'Your old young pig's prick'. The figure 333, in German *drei, drei, drei*, represents the dialect pronunciation of *treu, treu, treu*, 'faithful, faithful, faithful unto the grave, so long as I live'. In another letter (10th of May 1780) he extols her 'enchanting beauty, both the bits you can see and those you can't', for which parts he lapses into Latin, *visibilia and invisibilia*, a reference to the Credo of the Catholic Mass, *Credo in unum Deum. Patrem ominipotentem, factorem coeli et terrae, visibilium et invisibilium*. Just the thing for a *Pfaffenschnitzl!*

No doubt the *Bäsle* enjoyed Mozart's letters. She kept them in a ribboned bundle but later, perhaps after his marriage, returned them to him — whether in delayed disapproval, sorrow at losing him or retrospective regrets, we do not know. The *Bäsle* letters were suppressed or bowdlerized until the mid-twentieth century. They were bought — and published in full — by the Austrian novelist Stefan Zweig — who sent copies to Sigmund Freud, as possibly relevant to Freudian theories of anal-sexual fixation. . . .

The *Bäsle* relationship continued — mostly by letter — until Mozart moved to Vienna and became engaged. The last letter to his cousin, written from Vienna on the 23rd of October 1781, starts in a formal manner *Ma très chère Cousine!*, and contains neither obscenities nor nonsense and ends with a significant sentence, 'Now fare well, dearest, best cousin! and preserve for me your so estimable friendship. I can quite certainly assure you of mine. I remain, Eternally, *Ma très chère Cousine*, your sincere Cousin and Friend, Wolfgang Amadé Mozart.' In a postscript (which ends '*Adieu ma chère,* write to me soon') he sends greetings from 'Madame Weber and her 3 Daughters' — without mentioning that one of the three was about to become his wife.

But first he had to overcome his father's objections to his marriage. During his bachelor days Mozart held cynical views on marriage. In February 1778, aged 22, he wrote a minuet for the wedding of a rich acquaintance who, he said, had merely married for money. In a letter to his father he commented:

> Rich and noble people have to marry for convenience and self-interest, just to do their duty and produce a plum little heir. We poor common folk, who are of low class, can marry whom we wish. Good luck to them from all my heart, but it's nothing but a money-wedding. When I get married I want to make my wife happy, not gain a fortune by marrying her. That's why I want to leave matrimony alone and enjoy my golden liberty, at least until I'm so well off that I can support a wife and children.

Mozart's first reference to his future in-laws occurs in a letter of the 17th of January 1778, when he wrote to his father that 'a certain Herr Weber' had done some copying for him. He was Fridolin Weber, a kind of operatic dogsbody: bass, prompter and copyist, and related to Carl Maria von Weber.

> I don't know if I've already mentioned his daughter — she sings really excellently and has a lovely, pure voice. The only thing she lacks is dramatic interpretation. Once she has acquired it she can make a prima donna on any stage. She is only sixteen years old. Her father is a basically honest German who has brought up his children well; and that's why she is being showered with attention. He has six children, five girls and one son . . . .

The sixteen-year-old he raved about was Aloysia Weber, the younger sister, not his wife-to-be Constanze. Aloysia was the first to attract Wolfgang's attention, not least because her beauty was combined with a rare musical talent. He spent much time with her, taught her the art of vocal ornamentation, gave her piano lessons, admired her sight-reading and wrote some glorious songs for her. Almost every letter at that time contains some laudatory reference to Aloysia. He was clearly in love. But she rejected him and married the painter Joseph Lange (who left a fine portrait of Mozart). Wolfgang later turned rather sour:

> As far as the Lange woman is concerned I was a fool, but who isn't when in love? I did love her, though; and still can't feel indifferent to her. It's lucky for me that her husband is a jealous fool and doesn't allow her out anywhere, so I seldom get the opportunity of seeing her.

Aloysia lived until 1839; Josepha (who created the coloratura role of the Queen of the Night in *Die Zauberflöte*) until 1819; and the youngest Weber sister, Sophie, who was only a child at the time of Mozart's courtship, until 1846. He seems to have tried all the grown-up sisters, and Constanze was his third choice; or rather, the choice made for him by her mother, who disliked her and wanted her married off. In a letter from Vienna (15th of December 1781) to his father — his mother had recently died while they were in Paris together — he broke the news of his intentions as gently as he could, knowing that Leopold disapproved of the Weber *ménage*:

> The urges of nature speak as loudly in me as in any man, and perhaps louder than in many a big, strong lout. I cannot possibly live the way most young people do. First, I have too much religion; secondly, too much love for my fellow-humans and I'm too honourable to seduce an innocent girl; and thirdly, too much horror and revulsion, too much shyness and fear of disease; I care too much for my health to mess about with whores. In this respect I can swear to you that I have never had anything to do with a woman of that kind . . . . My temperament is more inclined towards quiet domestic life than revelry. From my youth I was never able to look after my own clothes, washing, etc., so I can't think of anything more necessary to me than a wife . . . . A bachelor is, in my opinion, only half alive. This is my view and I can't help it. I've thought it over and considered it deeply — and my mind is made up. So who is the object of my love? Don't get a fright, I pray you. Surely not one of the Weber girls, you ask? Yes, one of the Weber girls. But not Josepha, not Sophie — but Constanze, the middle one. I have never come across a family with such differences in character. The eldest [Josepha, for whom he later wrote the song *Nun lacht der holde Frühling*, K580] is a lazy, coarse, false person and cunning with it. The Lange Woman [Aloysia, with whom he had also been in love] is a false, malicious person, and a coquette. The youngest, well, is still too young to come into consideration — she is just a good-natured, empty-headed creature: may God preserve her from seduction. But the middle one, my good, dear Constanze, she's the martyr of the family. Perhaps that's why she is the most kind-hearted, the cleverest — in short, the best of them all. She runs the whole household — and yet can't do a thing right. Oh my dearest father, I could fill reams with

stories of what goes on in that house. . . . But before I end my chattering I must tell you something more about the character of my beloved Constanze. She's not ugly, but at the same time nothing less than beautiful. Her whole beauty lies in two little black eyes and a good figure.

Constanze's portrait, painted rather perfunctorily by her brother-in-law Lange, in fact shows remarkably big eyes and sensual, asymmetrical lips: a homely young woman aged twenty.

She's not very witty but has plenty of common sense — enough to do her duty as wife and mother. She is not inclined towards extravagance: on the contrary, she is used to being badly dressed. What little their mother could do for her children she did for the other two, never for her. True, she would like to dress neatly and daintily, if not smartly, and most of the things a woman needs she can make herself; she even dresses her own hair every day. She understands housekeeping and is the kindest-hearted person in the world. I love her and she loves me with all her heart. Tell me, could I wish for a better wife?

Leopold had hoped his son would make a better match than the impoverished Weber family could offer (there was no mention of dowry). Nor was he happy with the circumstances of Wolfgang's commitment to Constanze. He had, it turned out, been tricked into marriage. In May 1781, he took lodgings with Frau Weber, by then widowed, and he must have got himself into some compromising situation with Constanze — a small intimacy perhaps, or a stolen kiss. With the help of an accomplice, Johann von Thorwardt, the finance director of the Vienna National Theatre and the Weber girls' guardian (probably their mother's lover), a contract was drawn up which Mozart was forced to sign. He agreed to marry Constanze or, should he change his mind, pay her the huge, annual sum of 300 florins as compensation. In another letter to his father he tries to make light of the whole affair and tries to explain why he signed the document:

As for the marriage contract, or rather, the written assurances as to my honourable intentions towards the girl . . . as the father is unfortunately no longer living there is a guardian, who doesn't know me at all. And certain busybodies and nosey-parkers have spread certain stories about me — put fleas in certain ears . . . to the effect that people should beware of me, that I had no secure income, that I had been too intimate with her and would probably leave her in the lurch and make her unhappy. All that made this Mister Guardian smell a rat — though the mother, who knows me and my honesty, never said a word. My entire association with the girl consisted in the fact that I lodged under the same roof. Outside the house not a soul ever saw me with her. But this man kept bending the mother's ear until she mentioned the matter to me and asked me to speak to him myself. As I couldn't express myself as well as I might have wished, the upshot was that he told the mother to forbid me all association with her daughter until I had signed a written agreement. What could I do? I could either sign the written declaration or lose the girl. So I [!] drew up a document to the effect that I undertook to marry Mlle Constanze Weber within a period of three years but if the impossible happened, and I changed my mind, that she would be entitled to claim from me the sum of 300 guilders a year. I knew it would never come to that, as I'd never leave her . . . and in any case Constanze would be too proud to let herself be sold. What man who loves sincerely and honestly could desert his love? Indeed it was the easiest thing in the world, for after all, it's no hardship to promise to marry Mlle Weber. But as soon as the guardian was out of sight, what did this heavenly girl do? She asked her mother to give her the contract, said to me, 'Dear Mozart, I don't need a written agreement from you. I believe every word you say.'

Without waiting for his father's approval he married Constanze on the 4th of August 1782 in St Stephen's Cathedral. The marriage lines survive and are preserved in the British Library. Two letters written by his father on the day before the wedding have disappeared, but their content can be guessed: Leopold was furious. The marriage was happy enough and lasted until Mozart's death in 1791, but it was not unclouded. Only a few weeks after their honeymoon Mozart had to reprimand her for some — probably innocent — horseplay with a man, during the course of which she allowed him to take her calf-measurements. She shared Wolfgang's fecklessness with money, but kept house as well as she could in their straitened circumstances. Her chronic untidiness reflected and probably exacerbated his. Although Mozart once or twice mentioned his 'strong appetite' he seems to have been a small eater, though he liked junk food like ice-cream and chocolate: his father described the meals in their household in 1785 as 'frugal', Constanze as *leichtsinnig* — literally 'of easy spirit', but in practice meaning frivolously reckless and with an easy-come, easy-go attitude to money. It was not until the summer of 1783 that he introduced her to his father and sister Nannerl. Both were cool towards her. When, during their unofficial betrothal, Constanze fell ill, and they were waiting for his father's consent (which they eventually ignored anyway), Mozart 'made a promise in his heart' that if he could marry her he would write a special work of thanksgiving. It was the glorious Mass in C minor (K.427/417a); and although a fragmentary form was performed on the 26th of October 1783 with Constanze singing the soprano part he seemed to lose interest and never completed it (it is now heard in a number of speculative completions). Those who search for secret musical ciphers and subconscious quotations may like to compare the soprano line in the *Kyrie* of Constanze's Mass with a sheet of exercises in vocal ornamentation he had earlier written for Aloysia: the same theme but rapturously embellished.

Although Constanze's letters confirm Wolfgang's early judgement that she had 'no sense of humour', they are affectionate and devoted. Nor was she as good a singer as the Weber sisters who rejected him. She could, however, sing at sight and play the piano. When Mozart was introduced to the music of Bach and Handel, she shared his enthusiasm for fugues and fugal writing. He declared that her need for fugues (and 'English beer'!) was 'like the craving of a pregnant woman'. Mozart was happy to provide the fugues for her — and doubtless also the beer — although it must be said that nearly all remained unfinished, petering out soon after subject and answer had been established — conjugally interrupted cadences if ever there were. One of these fragments has words, about '*Bimperl und Stanzerl*' — Bimperl being the family dog — see Pets of the Great Composers — and *Stanzerl* the familiar diminutive of Constanze. They produced children in rapid succession — six altogether; but apart from two sons none survived infancy and some died within days. Compared with their father's and siblings' sickliness, the two surviving children managed to live to a good age: Carl Thomas died in 1858 aged 74, while the younger, Franz Xaver Amadeus, died in 1844 at 53. Both remained bachelors, as if to ensure that their father's genius was not to re-emerge, as the Bachs' had done.

Mozart's letters to Constanze, written between April and June 1789, when he was on tour in Berlin, Leipzig and Dresden, contain many references to their sex life. Although she treasured the letters, her second husband later tried to deface the more intimate sections. Most have recently been restored with the aid of modern X-ray techniques, apart from one or two obscene words he scratched out with such force as to damage the paper. One that Nissen missed was the repeated exclamation 'Stu! — Stu! — Stu!', which he must have failed to understand, for it was part of Wolfgang and Constanze's sex talk*. Mozart told his wife from Dresden on 13, April 1789 that he often took her portrait out of its little slip-case, looked at it lovingly to assuage his frustration, and replaced it — only to repeat the process again and again:

> If I told you what I did with your protrait you'd laugh. For example, when I take it out of its cover I say, 'Hello, Stanzerl, good day, little pussy, you mischief-maker, you little pointy-nose, you little nothing . . .' and when I put it in again, and let it slide in by and by, I always say 'Stu! Stu! Stu!' — but with a certain extra pressure, which this word demands . . . then faster — and at last — it's 'good night little mouse: sleep well'. I think I've written down some rather silly things for posterity but for us, who love each other so dearly, they're certainly not silly. Today is the sixth day I've been away from you and by God it already seems like a year.

On the 19th of May 1789, in a short letter from Berlin, he promised Constanze that by the 27th he would be on his way home and

> . . . the first thing I'll do is take you by the arse-feathers . . . and give you a sound spanking on your lovable-kissable little arselet. That you can count on. Adieu.

Recalling perhaps her earlier escapade with a strange man, to whom she offered her calves for 'measurement', Mozart felt obliged to issue a warning as to

---

* In Italian opera houses, when a singer sings flat, or pitches a final 'high' note below its true intonation, audiences cry — as they doubtless did in Mozart's time — 'Su! Su! Su!' — higher, higher, higher!

her conduct in his absence, referring to one of her letters she had written to him but which was either lost or destroyed, so we can only guess at its contents. But it reveals him as a jealous and worried husband:

Dearest little Wife, I have a lot to ask you.
1st: That you aren't sad.
2nd: That you *look after your health* and *don't trust to the spring breezes.*
3rd: That you don't go out walking — or better still, *not to go out on foot at all.*
4th: *That you feel absolutely assured of my love. . . .*
5th: I beg you to be aware, in your conduct, not only of *your honour and mine* but also to consider *appearances.* Don't be angry with me for asking this of you. You ought to love me all the more because I value our honour . . . .

As the tour approached its end his letters became increasingly fervent.

My dearest, best, darlingest little wife. On Thursday 28th I'm in Dresden; on the 1st of June I'll be sleeping in Prague; and on the 4th — the 5th? *With my dearest little wife.* Make your little nest nice and clean and tidy, because willie has been a good little boy and deserves nothing better than to come to your beautiful [obliterated]. And just imagine what he's up to. Even as I write this he's trying to creep up on the table to see what's going on. I gave him a good whack on the nose but the rogue only [illegible]. Now the rascal is burning hot and I'm almost incapable of keeping him under control. I hope you'll come and meet me by the first post-coach.

Constanze may indeed have been unfaithful, either during Wolfgang's many absences or when she went on holiday. From 1789 she frequently spent a week or more in the spa of Baden, near Vienna, to take the cure, nearly always accompanied by a family friend, Mozart's composition pupil Franz Xaver Süssmayr. One or two letters to Baden show that Wolfgang was worried about her behaviour — either with Süssmayr or someone else. The relevant names were either disguised by Mozart as 'N.N.' (short for Latin *notetur nomen,* meaning 'You-know-who') or subsequently erased by Constanze. In a letter he wrote in August 1789 to Baden, where she had gone this time to cure a foot infection, he sounds alarmed and worried. Announcing that he was about to take a coach to join her — even at the cost of neglecting essential work like revising *Figaro* and supervising rehearsals:

Dearest little wife. I will speak quite frankly to you. You have a husband who loves you, who will do everything he can for you. As far as your foot is concerned, all you need is patience; it will surely get well. I'm pleased that you are having a merry time — sure — only I wish that you wouldn't sometimes make yourself quite so cheap. In my opinion you are too free with N.N. . . . and it was the same with N.N. when he was still in Baden. Just remember that N.N. has not been quite as familiar with other women as with you, though he possibly knows them better than you. N.N., who is otherwise a well-behaved fellow, and is especially respectful to women — even he must have been misled by your behaviour into writing the most digusting and crude *sottises* in his letter. A woman must always command respect, or people will begin to talk about her. My love! Forgive me for being so frank, only my peace of mind demands it, as well as our mutual happiness. Remember that you yourself once confessed to me that you *too easily gave in.* You know the consequences. Remember also the promise you gave me. Oh God! Just try, my love! Be merry and happy and pleasant to me. Don't torture yourself and me with needless jealousy. Have confidence in my love — after all you have plenty of proof of it! You'll see how happy we'll be. Surely you believe me when I say that only prudent behaviour in a wife can enchain her husband — adieu — tomorrow I shall kiss you most tenderly. Mozart.

It has been suggested that the Mozarts' younger surviving son, Franz Xaver, named after Süssmayr, was in fact the latter's son, and the most likely date of conception falls within Mozart's absence on tour. To be his child, Franz Xaver would have had to be conceived immediately on Mozart's return from Germany on the 10th of November 1790, but even then would have been at least seventeen days premature. After Mozart's death, Constanze was left with two small sons to feed and educate but proved a better businesswoman than she had been a housekeeper. Among her letters to the publishers Breitkopf & Härtel, who were planning a biography, was one (August 28, 1799) mentioning her late husband's youthful indiscretions with his *Bäsle*. 'Of course they are tasteless, the letters to his cousin, but very jokey and deserve at least a mention. But naturally they could not be printed in their entirety . . . . I hope you won't allow anything to be printed without letting me read it first.' She sold many of his manuscripts, some piece-meal — a page here and a page there — so that some of his compositions have had to be painfully reassembled.

On the 26th of June 1809, Constanze married the Danish diplomat Georg Nikolaus Nissen who, like Wolfgang, had been her lodger and was collecting material for a Mozart biography. The ceremony took place in the Cathedral of Pressburg (now Bratislava) where they had fled from Napoleon's second siege of Vienna. They were soon able to return to Vienna, before moving to Copenhagen in 1810, where they lived until their return to Salzburg in 1821. Constanze proudly styled herself 'Frau State Counsellor von Nissen, formerly Widow Mozart'. Her second husband was an able business manager and financial adviser to her, helped her with the disposal and exploitation of Mozart's works and relics and made provision for the two boys. He also managed to achieve what Mozart had so signally failed to do — that is, to turn her into a tidy, house-proud woman, though she bore Nissen no children. By this time she was financially secure with a small public pension. When Nissen died in 1826, Constanze, curiously, had him buried in the same Salzburg grave as Leopold, the father-in-law she disliked so much. She and Nannerl never visited each other. Nannerl died, blind and almost bereft of speech, in 1829. Constanze, doubly widowed, continued to live comfortably and contentedly in Salzburg until her death on 6th March 1842.

GIACOMO ANTONIO DOMENICO MICHELE SECONDO MARIA PUCCINI

Born:	Lucca, 23rd of December 1858
Married:	3rd of January 1904 Elvira Bonturi-Gemignani (1860–1934)
Musical	Giacomo (Primo) Puccini (Lucca, 1712–1781)
Forebears:	Antonio Benedetto Maria Puccini (Lucca, 1747–1832)
	Domenico Vincenzo Maria Puccini (Lucca, 1772–1815)
	Michele Puccini (Lucca, 1813–1864)
Brother:	Michele Terzo (Lucca, 1864- d. Rio de Janeiro, 1891)
Son:	Antonio Puccini (Lucca, 23rd of December 1886 — died 1946)
Died:	Brussels, 24th of November 1924

No doubt Giacomo Puccini, like several other composers in this book, complained that his wife did not understand him. Elvira Puccini was a moody, shrill, ill-mannered shrew, given to tantrums and hysterical outbursts, and unappreciative of art, but she understood Giacomo only too well, just as Zdenka Janacek and Minna Wagner understood what motivated their husbands. Elvira knew that Giacomo was a compulsive womanizer: nothing in skirts was safe from his roving eyes and wandering hands, from English society hostesses to peasant girls — and Elvira was obsessively jealous — hardly the best recipe for a successful relationship. But had he not 'womanized' with Elvira in the first place?

Elvira Gemignani, née Bonturi, was the wife of a wealthy wholesale grocer, Narciso Gemignani. Some say that she was a found-again friend from Puccini's youth, others that she took a fancy to him and consoled him when he was depressed after the death of his mother. They began their affair after her husband suggested she take lessons from Puccini in singing and piano playing. Narciso's frequent absences from Lucca enabled teacher and pupil to develop their relationship, and she became pregnant. She was tall and striking-looking, with honey-blonde hair, shining dark eyes and big breasts; aged 24, she was two years younger than Giacomo, a handsome man with a straight nose, generous moustache and silky, chestnut-coloured hair. One of his eyelids had a slight droop, which gave him a quizzical aspect, emphasized by the way he wore his hat: always cocked at a jaunty angle. It was his 'thing' — photographs suggest that none of his contemporaries wore their hats at quite such an exaggerated slant. There was always a cigarette in his mouth or between his fingers — what Vincent Seligman (the son of his English mistress Sybil Seligman) called 'his *eternal* cigarette'. Puccini's speaking voice was described as alluring: *una voce bruna,* and had a seductive huskiness (which might have been the result of his chain-smoking or else the beginning of the throat cancer that killed him). His singing-voice was a light tenor, and when at rehearsal he wanted to indicate a woman's role he was able to break into an effortless falsetto.

Giacomo Puccini came from a distinguished dynasty of Lucca musicians, almost Bach-like in their single-minded pursuit of the family trade but fiercely loyal to the locality. His great-grandfather, also Giacomo, baptized on the 26th of January 1712, reached a high musical position in the then independent state of Lucca — so high that his emoluments equalled that of another important public servant, the Official Hangman (and in his orchestra there served a young cellist called Luigi Boccherini — 'nothing but a show-off', Puccini noted in his diary). He himself was the son of Michele Puccini, also a composer, as was 'our' Giacomo's brother Michele. The first Giacomo's son Antonio was born in 1747, and in turn had a son, Domenico, born in 1772. It was *his* son, Michele Secondo, born on the 27th of November 1813, who was the father of Giacomo Secondo, the composer of *La Bohème* and *Turandot*. Giacomo Puccini was the fifth child but the first son; and incidentally all of the foregoing male Puccinis were important enough to be accorded biographies in *Grove*: at least four Puccinis appear in the record catalogues. Another Puccini musician must be mentioned: a third Michele, our Puccini's elder brother who emigrated to Brazil in 1889 and worked as singing teacher and composer in Rio de Janeiro, but died only two years later, in 1891, in a yellow fever epidemic. Had Giacomo joined him there, as he at one time planned, the history of opera might have taken a different course.

When Elvira was no longer able to hide her pregnancy in the autumn of 1886 she left Narciso Gemignani to live with Puccini in Milan (where he was by then working) and took her young daughter Fosca with her — leaving a son, Renato, with her husband. Elvira and Giacomo moved to Monza, where their son Antonio (Tonio) was born on the 23rd of December 1886. The Puccini and Bonturi families were outraged by the ensuing scandal and forbade him to bring Elvira and their bastard child back to Lucca. In addition, his great-uncle called in a loan that had enabled the young Puccini to study, telling him that if he could afford to keep a mistress he could afford to settle his debts. Giacomo and Elvira were effectively banished from Lucca, even after they had legitimized their union; but marriage was not possible until 1904, when Elvira's lawful husband died. All this time Puccini must have had scores if not hundreds of love affairs, while living as man and wife with Elvira. What with his womanizing and her jealous rages their partnership made an explosive mixture. They lived on the edge of a volcano under constant threat of eruption, with emotional fire and brimstone all around them. His condition was probably satyriasis (the male equivalent of nymphomania, than which it is more common, yet less often mentioned). Elvira had some kind of hold over him which biographers have failed to explain. They wounded each other constantly, and deeply, but always stayed together, or were reunited: Giacomo nicknamed her 'the Policeman'. Later, in 1915, he wrote her a staccato, let's-get-this-straight-once-and-for-all letter (translation based on Mosco Carner's biography):

Your suspicions mislead you into the most undignified investigations. You invent women in order to give free play to your Policeman's instinct. Everything appears serious, large, weighty to you, while it is nothing, a mere negligible nothing. You have never looked at these matters as do other women who are more reasonable. Good God! The world is full of such things. All artists cultivate such gardens in order to delude themselves that they are not finished and old and torn by strife [Puccini was then 56]. You imagine immense affairs. In reality it is nothing but a sport to which more or less all men dedicate a fleeting thought, without, however, giving up that which is serious and sacred, that is, the family. . . . Do not oppose me with that vehemence and assiduity that you have adopted. Everyone has within himself a measure of rebellion. It is natural. See to it that my house is not odious to me and burdensome, that I find here a cupful of jollity and calm, instead of this continuous and discouraging aggravation. Such a state embitters a disposition however good, irritates and renders the soul desirous of other and different sensations. The wife of an artist has a mission different from that of wives of other men. This is something you have never wanted to understand. Indeed you sneer when the word 'art' is uttered. This has always offended me and offends me still. I, more than you, want peace. I seek to continue to live with you and end with you a life that would have been less parlous if you had had more judgement and sense. Goodbye! I kiss you. Remain calm. Wait for me. I shall always be your Topizio.

The use of one of their nicknames was a signal for reconciliation (others were *Cecetta*, 'Little Pea'; *Cicina*, 'Little Fatty'; *Porchizia*, 'Piglet'; and *Topizia*, 'Little Mouse') but Elvira did *not* remain calm. When a young singer came to rehearse with Puccini, Elvira attacked her with an umbrella and chased her from the house. She put mothballs into the pockets of his trousers to make him smell repellent and, whenever she thought he was going to be with women, perhaps at an operatic rehearsal or discussion of roles, she laced his wine or coffee with bromide, supposedly an anaphrodisiac (English wives have been known to overload their straying menfolk's food with garlic to create an amorous *cordon sanitaire* round them, but this would not work in Italy). Another weapon in her armoury was to fill the house with her relations, who stayed and stayed and could be relied upon during quarrels to take her side. Her excuse was that as she was not allowed to visit them in Lucca they had to come to her. In 1900, he went on the attack again:

You are no longer the same, your nerves dominate you, you no longer smile, no longer look at one openly. I feel myself a stranger in my own house . . . . Oh, the beautiful intimacy of our first years! Now we pass months (at least I do) in a house which belongs to others. I do not say this to complain about Ida, Beppe, etc. No, they are good people, very sweet people. But their continuous presence in our midst has driven out our intimacy. You are always bored in the country, while I love it so. You have need of your relatives to make the heavy burden of green nature seem lighter . . . .

Elvira and Giacomo continued to live together until his death, but interruptions were frequent — what with walkouts and professional absences, many abroad. He knew also that he always had a safe haven in Lucca, for she would have been driven out by the Lucchesi had she ventured to follow him; so he bought property there. He was by then rich and famous and was welcomed as a worthy successor to his distinguished ancestors. His earlier cohabitation with Elvira and the begetting of a bastard child was never forgiven, but his increasingly indiscreet affairs earned him the secret admiration of most of the men of Lucca. Only his publishers, Ricordi, were dismayed each time news broke of another liaison: not for moral reasons but because they felt that every hour Puccini spent in bed with a woman was an hour not spent with a score at his desk (or rather, at his piano, for unlike most 'real' composers he needed a keyboard for writing his music).They complained that the women were a distraction from his work and sapped his strength (on the lines of football managers who before important matches take their players away from their wives to a secluded hotel — where they seduce chambermaids instead). What the publishers really worried about was the threat to their income. After all, they had invested in him as a valuable commodity; and in earlier years, before he was able to call the shots, had shown such faith in him that they gave him a regular weekly allowance against future royalties. In 1901, when Puccini was starting to work on *Madama Butterfly*, Giulio Ricordi wrote to the librettist Luigi Illica:

> . . . it is impossible that a man who is preparing his own physical and moral downfall with his own hands can compose. I write this with the greatest pain and sorrow. However, in Puccini's present state I don't believe he can possess that vitality of thought which is needed to give birth to a creation.

The publisher was wrong: Puccini's constant quest for the perfect mistress merely inspired him. Ricordi also tried, with Elvira's collusion, to get Puccini's sisters to intercede, but not even Iginia, who had become a nun, was able to win him 'back to the fold of Jesus'. At the turn of the century, during the gestation of *Butterfly*, he fell in love with a young Piedmontese law student called Corinna (second name unknown — she was referred to simply as 'the girl from Piedmont') and their involvement lasted nearly three years. He is thought to have built her a small mountain-top castle as a love-nest. Who is to say that Corinna did not inspire him as he worked on that story of amorous betrayal — a story based on a real-life tragedy that happened less than ten years before? The 'real' culprit was a US Naval Cadet called William Benjamin Franklin, who abandoned his Japanese concubine, Cho-San, and whose grief drove her to suicide. Franklin provided Puccini's Pinkerton.

Like Pinkerton, Puccini left Corinna in the lurch — not with a baby so far as is known, and instead of committing *hara kiri* she threatened to sue him for breach of promise. Again Elvira set off a domestic explosion, and threatened separation — and again drew back (during the Piedmontese affair he and Elvira were still living in sin). Later he dismissed the three-year relationship as 'the Turin affair'.

On a foggy and frosty night in February 1903 Puccini's car, driven by his chauffeur, skidded off the road and into a ditch. Puccini was trapped under the overturned vehicle and badly injured. His recovery was slow and he spent months in a wheelchair: by August he was still walking with two sticks. Although used to being pampered, he needed more constant attention, so Elvira engaged a nurse, Doria Manfredi, daughter of local peasants in Torre del Lago, where the Puccinis then lived — a mere child of sixteen. Her family had misgivings about agreeing to her taking the post, knowing Elvira's reputation for ill-treating servants and his for seducing them. But Doria's mother was recently widowed and penniless, with several other children to support. Doria took the post and proved to be a treasure. She had a sunny disposition, said Vincent Seligman (a near-contemporary of the young Tonio Puccini and the son of the Sybil already mentioned, another mistress), was willing and helpful and adored Puccini. She stayed on after Puccini's recovery, and for five years all went well: Puccini was apparently able to keep his hands to himself, in spite of the fact that Doria had grown into a striking beauty. Then, one evening, Elvira — always suspicious — saw them talking together in the half-dark outside the house. She flew into a rage and threw the girl out; but did not leave it at that: she put pressure on the local priest to have the Manfredi family drummed out of the village. A witness later declared that when Elvira saw Doria in the street she called her ' . . . a slut, a tart, a whore, and yelled that she had been her husband's mistress, and that she would take her to the lake and drown her.' Elvira also put it about that she had caught them 'in the act', which was a lie. Tonio, also convinced of his father's guilt, took his mother's side. Puccini unceasingly protested his innocence and now, preoccupied with *The Girl of the Golden West*, wrote to Sybil Seligman on the 4th of October 1908:

> My life goes on in the midst of sadness and the greatest unhappiness! I don't want to write to you about it, because I don't want to put it in a letter — I should like to talk to you and perhaps then my spirit would find solace. When you write to me, don't say I have written to you in these terms; but there are days when I should like to leave my home — but the opportunity never occurs because I lack the moral strength to do it. And yet, I *want* to do it — and I'm certain that you would understand if you knew the circumstances. As a result *The Girl* has completely dried up — and God knows when I shall have the courage to take up my work again!

A few days later he fled to Paris, from where he again wrote to Sybil — revealing a little more of the cause for his unhappiness:

> I'm all by myself and have taken refuge here! I couldn't stand it any more; I've suffered so much. Elvira has given Doria notice, saying that she is a . . . without a *shadow* of proof. Life at Torre had become absolutely unbearable for me; I'm only telling the truth when I say that I have often lovingly fingered my revolver! And everyone (including you) says that I am the happiest man in the world!

I'm going to stay here for a short while and then, out of force of habit, I shall have to return to that Hell. I'm so unhappy, though a little less so here because I'm away from them all.

By the end of the year he was back in Torre del Lago, and on the 4th of January wrote to Sybil:

I'm still in a state of the greatest unhappiness — if you only knew the things my wife has been doing and the way she has been spying on me! It's an appalling torment, and I'm passing through the saddest time of my life! I should like to tell you everything, but I don't want to torture myself any further; it's enough if I tell you that I don't want to live any longer — certainly not with her. To go far away and create a new life; to breathe the air freely and rid myself of this prison atmosphere which is killing me . . . .

The dots that leave that letter — and others — suspended in mid-air indicate censorship by Vincent Seligman, who in 1938 published Puccini's letters to his mother but cut out any passages that might have revealed their intimacy. Officially the Puccinis and Seligmans were family friends: the six of them spent several holidays together, but the intimate correspondence was kept from their respective spouses and her letters to him were evidently destroyed to keep them from Elvira (as with the Elgar and Janacek letters). Puccini wrote to her in Italian, with occasional bits of fractured English: sometimes he signed himself 'Noti boi'.

Elvira stepped up her persecution of Doria, but this time went too far. On the 23rd of January 1909, the girl took mercury sublimate (then used as a rat poison) and died after protracted agony. Elvira fled to Milan. An autopsy established that Doria was a virgin. Puccini now really poured his heart out to Sybil and for the first time told her the full story:

Elvira continued to persecute that wretched child, preventing her even from taking a walk, and telling tales about her all over the village — to her mother, her relations, the priest and everyone. All my friends and relations and I myself told her to stop it and calm down; but she wouldn't listen to anyone. I made my peace with her and told her to forget about the past and be satisfied that the girl was no longer in the house. She promised to do so; but the same evening I found her out of doors hidden in the dark, *dressed in my clothes*, to spy on me. I said nothing and left the following morning for Rome.

Elvira was supposed to go to Milan; instead she remained for three more days at Torre, and during that time did everything and said everything she could to the mother, repeating again that her daughter was a . . . and that we used to meet each other in the evenings in the dark. She told one of Doria's uncles that her own grandchild used to carry letters between us; and, meeting Doria in the street, she publicly insulted her in the presence of others. Her brother wrote to me in a rage that he would kill me because I was his sister's lover — and that my wife had said so herself. In a word, poor Doria, faced with

Hell in her own home and dishonour outside, and with Elvira's insults still ringing in her ears, in a moment of desperation swallowed three tablets of sublimate, and died after five days of atrocious agony.

You can imagine what happened at Torre; Elvira left for Milan the day of the poisoning; everyone was against me, but even more against Elvira. By order of the authorities a medical examination was made in the presence of witnesses, and she was found to be *pure*, so public opinion turned round entirely against Elvira. There are some other painful details which I shall omit. The position now is that I can go back to Torre, and I *shall* go back. But Doria's family have brought an action against Elvira for public defamation. We're trying to see if we can stop the action, though I'm not directly taking part in the negotiations. In any case, Elvira will never be able to go back to Torre — or she would be lynched.

The press, Italian and international, reported every gruesome detail of the case, and Puccini was becoming increasingly distraught: 'I can't get her out of my mind,' he wrote, 'it's a continual torment.' This time he left home for seven months, and Tonio (now aged 22) ran away without telling his parents where he was going; he ended up in Munich and, when they traced him, threatened to emigrate to Africa. Not till the following July was there a reconciliation of some kind, brought about because Tonio had fallen ill. Giacomo had always been disappointed that Tonio did not follow in his footsteps, but he showed neither aptitude for, nor even an interest in, music. His father bought him a violin, arranged for him to have lessons, and was delighted when the boy carried it about with him, and even took it to the lakeside — to practise on, as he thought. One day he found that Tonio had tied a little mast to the fiddle's bridge, rigged a sail to it — and used it as a model sailing boat.

In spite of the evidence of the post-mortem, Elvira still did not believe Giacomo's protestations that he had not been having an affair with Doria, and declared she would 'throw herself out of the window — if it were a little higher' (presumably it was a ground-floor room). The woman was clearly out of her mind. Even after Doria's terrible death she still thought only of herself and had the gall to accuse Giacomo of having 'permitted' that 'the mother of your son should appear in the defendants' dock, between carabinieri and police, just like a common criminal'. At first the Manfredinis rejected any attempts at bribery, as the Puccinis tried to persuade them to withdraw their complaint against Elvira. Eventually money prevailed, and they accepted what must for them have been a huge sum in 'compensation' for the loss of their only daughter and the family's reputation. Yet again Giacomo went back to Elvira, to allow her to continue to torment him.

And now for Sybil — his long-serving confidante. He first met her in the spring of 1905, at the home of the composer Paolo Tosti and his wife, at 12 Mandeville Place, West London. Sybil Seligmann, a pupil of Tosti's, was a London society beauty, the daughter of the pianist Zillah Beddington, had a fine contralto voice and fluent Italian. She had married a rich banker, David Seligman, and could afford to indulge her love for opera. She and David travelled to many performances abroad, either *en* famille, or she with her young son Vincent, or alone. She and Puccini had a passionate affair, which after a while (it is not known how long, because of the destruction of papers) changed into the closest of friendships. Right up to his final illness Puccini always found time to write to her, even during the most hectic rehearsals for his operas.

In the summer of 1911 another of Puccini's affairs almost brought a final break with Elvira. On the beach at Viareggio, he struck up a conversation with a beautiful German baroness, Josephine von Stengel, aged 26 (less than half Puccini's age) who had two small daughters and was separated from Herr Baron. Dieter Schickling, Puccini's German biographer (1989), traced a false registration in the Hotel *Goldner Anker* at Bayreuth to Puccini and Josephine, under the names of 'Sigr. and Sgra. Grase' of Turin. They went to a performance of *Parsifal* and were spotted in the audience by Cosima Wagner—who was afterwards firmly told she 'must have been mistaken.' The affair lasted several years but was fraught with difficulties — both for reasons of geography, as she lived in Munich, and prying eyes — not least Elvira's. By 1915 'Josi' (or 'Busci', as he nicknamed her) took the first steps towards getting a divorce, so that she could live with, and eventually marry, Giacomo. On the 16th of March she wrote to him that she had consulted her lawyer ('incidentally, he would like a signed photograph of you') who advised her to deposit her children with their Munich grandparents to enable them to set up house together at Viareggio. She was looking forward to being united with her 'Giacomucci', or 'Mucci': 'I would like to have your dear mouth and your tender eyes now.' Unfortunately, and soon after he had met Josephine, Puccini met a young girl called Blanka Lendvai, the sister of a Hungarian musician, Erwin Lendvai. Recently discovered letters prove that the friendship was not as innocent as Puccini claimed when Elvira found and tore up her photographs. The discovery came too late for Mosco Carner's otherwise exhaustive biography but was revealed in 1980 by a later biographer, Howard Greenfeld. 'I kiss your beautiful mouth . . . ,' Puccini wrote to Blanka — while writing almost the same words to Josephine — after all, he re-used some of his musical themes to good effect.

Puccini was also in love with Maria Jeritza (who figures in the chapter on Richard Strauss) — but was not her only suitor. She astonished Puccini by singing 'dying' arias while lying full-length on the boards, not in accordance with normal practice while propped up on one elbow or staggering about the stage, enabling the lungs to expand. Jeritza became known as *la diva prostrata* — 'the horizontal prima donna' though malicious tongues declared it was for another reason.*

And so it went on, to almost the end. In 1923 he wrote to Sybil, 'I have such a fear and such horror of old age!' and in the same letter speaks of his intention to

---

* When a diva complained to Sir Thomas Beecham during a rehearsal, 'How do you expect me to sing while lying flat on my face?' he replied, 'Madam, *I* have given some of *my* finest performances in this posture.'

seek out Professor Eugen Steinach, a Viennese doctor then enjoying some notoriety with his rejuvenation treatment involving monkey-glands:

> I think in March I shall go to Vienna to see that doctor! I've met a South American gentleman here 67 years old, who tells me that the operation is nothing at all and that the benefits are extraordinary — he says he feels as though he were twenty-five again, and that it no longer tires him to walk and his mind is fresh and agile, etc. etc.

It was the 'etc. etc.' that worried him most, and he also considered consulting Professor Serge Voronov in Paris, who actually transplanted the reproductive glands of monkeys to increase the libido. But in addition to his loss of sex-drive Puccini had been suffering from constant sore throats. Cancer was diagnosed, and he died only seven months later.

For a while Puccini was on bad terms with Arturo Toscanini, probably as a result of Toscanini's quarrel with Ricordi. After the conductor had refused to include one of Ricordi's own works in a programme, the publisher-composer lost no opportunity to decry Toscanini's abilities. He had the courage to say — rather perceptively in my view — that the 'God' among conductors was little more than a machine-like, inhuman interpreter in search of mindless perfection. Puccini quarrelled with him on politics (not, surprisingly, over a woman, for Toscanini was almost as predatory as Puccini, if less blatant about it). At one point Puccini refused to let 'that *pig* of a Toscanini' conduct his operas, because he had once made a derogatory remark about one of them.

After Puccini's death it fell to Toscanini to conduct the first performance of *Turandot*. Although the opera had been completed by Puccini's friend Franco Alfano, Toscanini ended the performance with Liù's death and stopped at the point where Puccini broke off — turning round in to the audience and saying, with tears in his eyes, 'At this point the master laid down his pen.'

CHARLES CAMILLE SAINT-SAËNS

Born:	Paris, 9th of October 1835
Father:	Jacques Joseph Victor Saint-Saëns (b. Dieppe, 19th of March 1789)
Mother:	Clémence Françoise Collin (b. 27th of March 1809)
Married:	Marie Laure Emilie Truffot 3rd of February 1875
Died:	Algiers, 16th of December 1921

Saint-Saëns's ancestors came from the village of St Saëns, near Lyons, where lived St. Sidonius Apollinaris, one of the obscurer saints, whose 'happiest years were spent with his wife and family on his country estates, administering them, hunting, fishing and writing', says the *Penguin Dictionary of Saints*. Take away the wife and family and you have Camille Saint-Saëns, except that his recreations were nomadic and a mystery wrapped in an enigma shrouded in a puzzle. He possessed an almost Mozartian musical precocity, with perfect pitch from the age of three, when he composed his first piano piece. He then followed the well-defined path of the cosseted prodigy. Aged ten, already an experienced performer, he made his first concert début at the Salle Pleyel, playing Mozart and Beethoven concertos. He came to the notice of Gounod and other musicians; and, like Gounod, was encouraged and supported by the singer Pauline Viardot. Liszt heard him play the organ and pronounced him the greatest organist in the world. Most gifted musical children also excel at other subjects, and Saint-Saëns was no exception: classical literature, Latin, geology, mathematics, archaeology, astronomy — his precocious mind devoured them all. He lived in momentous times, so it is startling but not surprising to find among his works a Hymn to Electricity (*La feu céleste*, 1900), To Airmen (*Aux aviateurs*, written in 1911 soon after Blériot crossed the Channel), To the Miners (*Aux mineurs*, 1912) and even a Workers' Hymn.

Saint-Saëns's father was a well-to-do lawyer, who died when Camille was a baby. He was brought up by his mother and his great-aunt Charlotte Masson, and seems to have absorbed his interests from almost exclusively female company. They pampered and kept him from rough boyish company, so that he would not be distracted from his studies. The woman closest to him all his life was not his mother but her aunt, who taught him the piano and introduced him to music. When she died at 91 in 1872 he suffered a mental breakdown — one of several, usually followed by mysterious disappearances. Saint-Saëns was regarded by his contemporaries as physically something of a figure of fun, and was a butt of caricaturists: he was short in stature, with a huge, birdlike nose, a tripping walk and a lisping voice. If one were to look for 'psychological' reasons for the genesis of some of his works one could cite his opera, *Samson and Delilah*, with its betrayal and mutilation of a male by a female — or the unsuccessful *Henry VIII*, where the king chops his wives' heads off. Another of his stage works is called *On ne badine pas avec l'amour* — 'One Does Not Joke About Love'.

Saint-Saëns remained a bachelor till 1875, when at the age of 40 he married Marie-Laure Truffot, the teenage sister of his friend Jean Truffot. They had two sons, both of whom died tragically in infancy — the first by falling out of a window. They quarrelled constantly and he blamed her for their deaths. In 1881, while they were on holiday, he walked out and never saw her again. She lived until 1950, when she died aged nearly 95 — and what mysteries she might have resolved.... Saint-Saëns disappeared from his home also on the death of his mother and contemplated suicide. He gave away his furniture and possessions and led a nomadic life until his death in 1921. He was inseparable from his manservant Gabriel and always travelled with him and his dogs — usually to Algeria (where he died) or to Egypt: sometimes as far as Uruguay (whose national anthem he composed). He never divulged his destinations and often travelled under a false name. Rumours suggested he was a pederast, and chose his exotic locations for the pleasures they offered, with minimal risk of exposure or disgrace at home — North Africa was always the favourite playground of the deviant Frenchman.

Another of Saint-Saëns's mysterious disappearances was reported on the 1st of June 1890 by the amused editors of the *Musical Times*, who took it as a light-hearted escapade.

M. Charles Sannois, *alias* M. Camille Saint-Saëns, whose eccentric disappearance has been the talk of Paris for the last couple of months, seems to have had a good time while he was away. Amongst other amusements he very nearly made his *début* as an opera singer in Las Palmas, in the support of a *prima donna* who was paid at the magnificent rate of two francs a night. He had volunteered his services gratis, had been accepted, and rehearsed his part. But at the last moment the manager went bankrupt, the francs were not forthcoming, the *prima donna* struck, and *Rigoletto* with M. de Saint-Saëns in the cast, had to be withdrawn from the bills. It is, however, quite refreshing, in these mercenary days, to know that there are eminent composers who will sing for nothing, and, what is more remarkable still, *prime donne* who will 'sing a song sixpence', or, to be to be more precise, at a wage which is about the ten thousandth part of what Madame Patti has received for a single night's performance.

ERIK ALFRED LESLIE SATIE

Born:	Honfleur, 17th of May 1866
Father:	Alfred Satie
Mother:	Jane (Jeannie) Leslie Anton, from Scotland.
Status:	Single
Works:	Mostly for piano, including the famous *Gymnopédies*.
Died:	Paris, 1st July 1925

Asked what he thought about love, Satie replied, 'I find it very comical,' and on another occasion, with more feeling: 'Love is a sickness of the nerves. It's serious, yes, very serious . . . . Myself, I'm afraid I avoid it.' It seems that he did so, successfully, all his life — except for one brief and concentrated affair in 1893 with Suzanne Valadon, the mother of the painter Maurice Utrillo, a former acrobat, trapeze-artist and model for painters like Renoir and Toulouse-Lautrec. She was a woman of wide experience, and probably felt a duty to rescue Satie from his bachelorhood. Besides, she was his neighbour, at 6 rue Cortot in Montmartre, and on friendly terms. Satie himself meticulously recorded the affair:

> On the 14th of the month of January in the year of grace 1893, which was a Saturday, my love affair with Suzanne Valadon began, which ended on Tuesday the 20th of June of the same year.

But although the relationship was brief it must have been tempestuous. At its conclusion he failed to inform her that his affections had cooled — instead he told the police, asking the startled *gendarmerie* to post a guard outside his house to prevent her from visiting him. Rollo Myers, who wrote the first English study of the composer (published in 1948), observed, 'There are many ways of breaking off attachments of this kind; the method chosen by Satie may have been original; it was certainly quite fantastically inelegant.' With Satie one can never be certain whether he was teasing or in earnest; but during the short-lived relationship his creativity blossomed, and in March he wrote his nine *Danses gothiques* 'to restore the great calm and tranquillity of [my] soul.' He also drew pen-and-ink portraits of Suzanne, whom he called 'Biqui', and one of these illustrated his song *Bonjour, Biqui, Bonjour!* which he composed on the 2nd of April 1893. In a letter to her he wrote:

> Erik Satie to Suzanne Valadon
> Paris, the 11th of the month of March 93
> Dear little Biqui,
> Impossible
> to stop thinking about your whole
> being; you are in Me complete; everywhere,

I see nothing but your exquisite
eyes, your gentle hands
and your little child's feet.
You, you are happy; My poor thoughts
are not going to wrinkle your transparent forehead;
any more than worry at not seeing Me.
For me there is only the icy
solitude that creates the emptiness in my head
and fills my heart with sorrow.
Don't forget that your poor friend
hopes to see you at least at one of these three renedezvous;
1. This evening at 8.45 at my place
2. Tomorrow morning again at my place
3. Tomorrow evening at Dédé's (Maison Olivier)
Let me add, Biqui, chérie, that I shall on no account get angry
if you can't come to any of these rendezvous;
I have now become terribly reasonable; and
in spite of the great happiness it gives
me to see you
I am beginning to understand that you can't always do
what you want.
You see, little Biqui, there is a beginning to everything.
I kiss you on the heart
Erik Satie
6, rue Cortot

In the summer of 1926, after Satie's death, his brother Conrad found among
the squalor and ancient dried dog turds (for Satie befriended and took home
strays, as is recounted in Pets of the Great Composers) some letters to Suzanne
Valadon which presumably he had never sent — shades of Beethoven's Letters to
his Immortal Beloved, of which he, too, kept either the originals or made copies.
He got in touch with the old lady, asking her if she wanted them. She replied:

Cher Ami,
Your very friendly letter arrived just as I was about to leave Paris — an
emergency forces me to put off your visit — if however you can — wait until the
last week in August, for I should be back in Paris by then. The meeting will be
a very moving one and so many memories are heart-rending indeed, and yet
very sweet to me.
Croyez, cher ami, en ma grande amitié.
Suzanne Valadon.

She read the letters — and put them on the fire.

FRANZ PETER SCHUBERT

Born: Vienna, 31st of January 1797
Father: Franz Theodor Florian Schubert
Mother: Maria Elisabet Katherina Vietz. Twelve children: four survived infancy
Died: Vienna, 19th of November 1828.

He was the most lovable of all composers. No-one ever wrote an unkind word about him, nor apparently did he utter one. He composed heartfelt and passionate music — but left not a single love letter. Instead, he seems to have sent his women-friends songs; he certainly found them easy enough to write. Perhaps it was better so: his letters would have been full of unrequited love. Chopin, Liszt, Mahler, Wagner and the rest, all wrote love letters — some embarrassing and a few obscene — and most kept diaries, but they were filled largely with accounts of their own triumphs. Schubert's diary (of which only a few pages exist) opens with a declaration of love, a hymn of praise — for Mozart and his music. After a private recital which had included some Mozart he noted:

> What a light, bright and lovely day this will remain for the rest of my life. As from afar the magic sounds of Mozart's music still softly haunt me. With what unbelievable power, yet how gently, Schlesinger's playing impressed it deep, deep into my heart. And so the soul retains these beautiful impressions which neither time, nor anything else, can erase, and which lighten our very existence. O Mozart, immortal Mozart, how many, how infinitely many, such glimpses of a brighter, better life you have brought into our souls . . . .

Schubert then reveals what Schlesinger played, adding almost as an afterthought that he himself had featured in the performance — playing variations by Beethoven and singing two of his own songs — but self-deprecatingly writes: 'There was unbroken applause for his music, less for mine.'

His voice broke at the age of fifteen, ending his membership of the Vienna Boys' Choir. We know the precise date, as he scribbled it into the margin of a score of a Mass which the *Sängerknaben* were rehearsing: 'Schubert, Franz — squawked for the last time, 26th of July 1812.' Two years later he composed his Mass in F (D105), already a veteran conductor, having been promoted to *Subdirigent* of the famous Viennese choir from the age of fourteen, and therefore conducted his Mass himself. The soprano who sang the solo part was a sixteen-year-old girl, Therese Grob, daughter of a silk-manufacturer. Schubert confessed his love for her in a letter to his friend, a man called Holzapfel, a letter which the recipient later described as 'long and enthusiastic' but which is unfortunately lost. Holzapfel reported that Schubert had described her as 'Hardly a beauty, but tall, rather well-built, with a fresh-complexioned, childlike, roundish face, and a beautiful soprano voice that reached top D.' The concert must have been a thrilling occasion: to have his first important work publicly performed when he was only seventeen, and the solo taken by an attractive sixteen-year-old whom he loved and wanted to please. Not much is known about the affair, except that, as a mere assistant schoolmaster, he was in no position to marry. The evidence of his infatuation with Therese is there for all to hear, in the music he poured out while under her spell. She inspired him to embark on an astonishingly productive period. During the whole of his short life he wrote more than 1,000 works, of which no fewer than 400 (most of them love songs) were created between 1813 and 1816, as a direct result of his love for Therese. The floodgates opened with the precocious *Gretchen am Spinnrade* ('Gretchen at the Spinning-wheel'), full of restless longing.

It was said that when the affair with Therese ended — we know not how — it took Schubert three years to get over it. She later married a baker called Bergmann and settled down in the suburbs of Vienna. Until quite recently her descendants treasured an album in Schubert's own hand, headed 'Therese's Songs'. But no letters. Two years later, he wrote in his Diary: 'Happy is the man who finds a true friend. Happier still, he who finds a true friend in his wife' — almost echoing the words of another Viennese bachelor, his older and more celebrated near-neighbour Ludwig van Beethoven, whom he dared not approach and to whom he felt close only when acting as torch-bearer at his funeral. It has been said that the two never met socially (and certainly there is no evidence in the Conversation Books that Schubert ever spoke to him, but he did visit Beethoven on his deathbed).

Schubert lamented his inability to find a wife when he was only nineteen: 'Nowadays the thought of marriage is full of terrors for a single man. But the alternatives are either sadness, or wanton sensuality.' In 1818, Schubert was invited by Count Johann Eszterházy to teach music and piano to his daughters at their summer palace in Zseliz. From there he wrote a number of delightful, light-hearted letters: 'The cook is rather loose, the lady-in-waiting thirty years old, very pretty [and] often my companion. The janitor is my rival in love.' When he first began to teach them music, the two princesses, Marie and Caroline Eszterházy, were still children, but when he returned to the summer palace, a relationship seems to have developed between him and Caroline, who had grown into a beautiful, sophisticated young woman of twenty. What her feelings were we do not know, though Schubert — probably misreading her naturally affectionate nature — interpreted it as love. Perhaps she led him on, assuming that he realized that a liaison between a humble music teacher and a Countess would have been out of the question. While at Zseliz with the Eszterházy girls, Schubert wrote several works in one of his favourite art forms, for two pianists playing together: not at two pianos but seated side-by-side at one keyboard. In Schubert's day — and in his life — the piano duet was of considerable sexual significance. Imagine yourself in a middle-class household of Jane Austen's time (roughly contemporaneous with Schubert's Vienna of the Biedermeier period). The wire-caged crinolines, which would have made piano duets impossible because people could not sit close enough, had given way to high-waisted, soft, body-hugging dresses. Freed from the cages, piano duettists could, as it were, sit cheek-to-cheek. Girls' dresses still went down almost to the shoes, so that young men who had led a sheltered life must have thought that women were solid from the ankles upwards. The female bosom had only just been liberated — temporarily, as it turned out — from tight-laced whalebone stays; arms were usually left bare. It was nearly 100 years before dancing was to become an activity permitting body-to-body contact; and all kissing between members of the opposite sex, other than a familial peck on the cheek, was done in private. Against such a background of formalized lust, mixed piano duets were, for adolescents, almost as provocative as what the Americans later called 'heavy petting'. Men and women could play beautiful and emotional music together, in private, with their arms and thighs touching — perhaps even on occasion — it hardly bears thinking about — crossing hands which required reaching across, and brushing against, one's partners body. Schubert's friends could not believe that he allowed himself to feel so strongly about an unattainable young woman and were, for once, unfeeling to the point of cruelty; and one of the chief members of the Schubert circle, the poet Eduard von Bauernfeld, wrote a mocking little verse about the love affair with the young Countess:

Schubert's besotted. The object's a lady, no less.
His pupil. He loved her as soon as he met her.
But he gave himself to one not a Countess —
In order to try to forget her.

Schubert's love for Caroline Eszterházy appears to have lasted for several years. Eduard von Bauernfeld wrote: '*I'm* still in love with Clotilde, *Moritz* with his Nettel. *Schubert* is laughing at us both, but he himself isn't quite cured [of love] yet.' Her identity is confirmed in Bauernfeld's Diary, February 1828: 'Schubert seems to be seriously in love with the Comtesse E. I like it. He is giving her lessons.' The girl Schubert 'gave himself to' was someone more attainable, Josefa (or Josefine) Pöcklhofer — nicknamed Pepi — a young lady-in-waiting at the Eszterházys' palace, in whose arms he found consolation. In another letter Schubert describes Pepi as 'amenable'. He later met her again in Vienna; or maybe she followed him there in the autumn of 1824, when he was back among his circle of close friends. One of these, the painter Moritz von Schwind, wrote to the poet Franz von Schober: 'Schubert is here. Sends you many greetings. He's well, and in heavenly high spirits, newly rejuvenated by happiness. . . .' Johanna Lutz, another member of the Schubert circle, declared: 'What he urgently needs is a male friend . . . . ' — a noteworthy remark in the light of recent theories which attempt to 'out' Schubert, claiming that he was the 'Queen Bee' in a hive of homosexual poets, artists and musicians. They certainly got themselves into many scrapes, including some political ones for which they were raided by the police (Viennese police spies were constantly trying to sniff out suspected student subversion), and, as homosexuality was severely punishable, it would necessarily have been carried on in secret; but there is no evidence of any physical relationships. Certainly the tone of the letters that passed between the young men were full of declarations of love, with much 'I greet you and kiss you from all my heart,' but this was characteristic of the *Sturm und Drang* period and young men followed the romantic ideals of the novels of 'Jean Paul' (pseudonym of Johann Paul Richter). Besides, the Schubert circle was a mixed-sex, near-secret society, not without its internal jealousies. Eduard von Bauernfeld wrote in his Diary in March 1827: 'Schwind and Schober more and more in conflict. Schober's total laziness and his affair with a woman of our circle are the main reasons for it.' Nearly all Schubert's close friends subsequently married, and his brother Ferdinand had two wives — successively — fathering enough children to staff a small chamber orchestra. One tragic revelation — tragic only for Schubert, as it turned out — might have lent a little weight to the homosexual theory, namely that Schubert and his beloved Franz von Schober were both infected with venereal disease in the same year, 1822. Schober was known as a womanizer and is thought to have led Schubert astray by taking him to his favourite brothel. The onset of Schubert's illness, with its first alarming symptoms, led him into a deep depression, so that he shunned all company. However, it produced some of his most magical songs, including *Du bist die Ruh*. The *Unfinished* Symphony also dates from that period; and while we know that he left it incomplete only because he put it to one side (possibly forgot about it and wrote something else instead), it is not inconceivable that his spirits deserted him when syphilis was confirmed. It killed Schubert at the age 31, whereas Schober's appears to have lain dormant — or else was misdiagnosed in the first place: at any rate he lived to the age of 87.

Schubert's nickname was Little Mushroom. He was short — just over or just under (reports vary) five foot (150 cm) tall — but gave the appearance of being even shorter, his head rather big for his body. He was shortsighted, so that he seemed to peer at people through his glasses, which he found so indispensible that he slept with them on his nose. A doctor, G. F. Eckel, described him:

> Small and stocky, with strongly developed bones and firm muscles, without angularity and rounded. The neck short and strong; shoulders, chest and hips broad, nicely curved. The fairly big, round and strong head was enveloped in brown, luxuriantly curled hair. The face, of which the forehead and chin were the predominant features, was not beautiful but expressive, with firm features. His gentle, and if I am not mistaken, light brown eyes, which when he was excited could be fiery, were overshadowed by protruding, bushy eyebrows which, because he often screwed up his eyes, as the shortsighted do, seemed smaller than they really were.

Another close friend, the composer Anselm Hüttenbrenner, describing Schubert to Liszt in 1854, wrote: 'Schubert's exterior was noticeably likeable . . . rather corpulent . . . . ' — and Bauernfeld once addressed him in one of his letters, in 1825: 'How are you, my fat friend? Your belly will have got bigger by now.' Wilhelm von Chezy rudely called him 'Lump of Lard' (*Talgklumpen*). Although Schubert's shyness made him feel unattractive to women, they always surrounded him as soon as he started playing; and said they preferred his company to that of taller men. Perhaps — like Brahms and Beethoven — he was so afraid of close relationships with respectable women that he sought the solace of prostitutes. Contemporary reticence ensured that Schubert's (like Brahms's) love life remains a mystery. Hüttenbrenner kept an intimate diary concerning the circle's amatory adventures but destroyed it in 1841. Von Chezy, who, though a friend, was not close, left this significant statement in his reminiscences: 'Unfortunately Schubert's lust for life lured him into paths from which there is usually no return, at least no healthy return.' Franz von Schober, his fellow-roisterer in taverns and, according to some writers the man who introduced him to the pleasures of promiscuity without warning him of its dangers, recalled in 1868 that Schubert led an 'excessively lustful and sensual life [and] went wild, overstepped all bounds, and knocked about in low dives — though of course he composed his most beautiful songs there.' In a letter dated 15th of July 1819 Schubert confided in his brother: 'In the house where I live there are eight girls, nearly all of them pretty. You can see that one has one's hands full.' Unless he was boasting, these are hardly the words of a shy young man. The word 'syphilis' was never mentioned, and the posthumous diagnosis was made only on circumstantial evidence. But when in 1986 some newly discovered diaries by members of the Schubert circle were examined, one cryptic entry confirmed it. It was written by Bauernfeld, in August 1826 (when Schubert was in and out of remission): 'Schubert half-ill (he is in need of "young peacocks" like Benv. Cellini). Schwind is morose, Schober indolent as usual . . . . ' It is known that Benvenuto Cellini hoped for a cure through a diet of young peacocks. The expression became a kind of euphemism, a veiled way of mentioning that someone had the disease.

Towards the end of his life, Schubert dedicated the most beautiful — certainly the saddest — of his piano duets to Caroline. It alludes melodically to Mozart's song of loss at the beginning of the last act of *The Marriage of Figaro*. But while in the opera the loss is make-believe, that of a pin significant only to the plot, in Schubert's F-minor Fantasy (D940) it was his love that he lost. The Fantasy is one of the works usually described as 'valedictory' and shares with the A major Piano Sonata (D959), written only weeks before his death, a sudden harmonic cry of pain in the closing bars: a barely resolved discord as full of searing anguish as an entire Mahler symphony.

Even at the end of his life Schubert was still grieving for Caroline Eszterházy, though he pretended otherwise. After his death she remained unmarried until 1844, when, in her late 30s, she accepted the proposal of a French count, but the marriage was anulled soon afterwards. Perhaps she secretly grieved for her piano duet partner, just as he had done for her.

ROBERT ALEXANDER SCHUMANN

Born: Zwickau, 8th of June 1810
Father: August Schumann, b.1773
Mother: Johanna Christiana Schnabel, b.1771
Married: Clara Josephine Wieck
Children: See below
Died: Endenich, nr. Bonn, 29th of July 1856

CLARA JOSEPHINE SCHUMANN

Born: Leipzig, 13th of September 1819
Father: Friedrich Wieck (1785–1873)
Mother: Marianne Wieck
Married: Robert Alexander Schumann
Children: Marie, 1st of Sept 1841; Elise, 25th of April 1843;
             Julie, 11th of March 1845; Emil, 8th of February 1846 (d.1847); Ludwig,
             20th of January, 1848; Ferdinand, 16th of July 1849;
             Eugenie, 1st of December 1851; Felix, 11th of June 1854
Died: Frankfurt am Main, 20th of May 1896

This chapter is about the great spouse of a great composer; and the description can be applied either way. Although Clara Schumann was the most renowned woman pianist of the nineteenth century, she never gained the fame she deserved as a composer. For one thing, in spite of her almost superhuman reserves of energy, she had little time for composition; for another — she was a woman, and during her lifetime her compositions were hardly taken seriously.

Clara was marked out to be a pianist even before she saw the light of day. She was the daughter of Friedrich Wieck, a noted music teacher who specialized in creating child prodigies. As soon as he knew his wife was pregnant he decided he would make the child, whether male or female, into a piano virtuoso. Wieck was so sure of his methods (based on those of J. B. Logier and involving a patented machine which forced the hand into the correct position) that he guaranteed results to parents who sent their children to him. Child prodigies were in demand: they were a good source of income for their families — the younger the child the greater the income. The Germans call them *Wunderkinder* — 'wonderchildren' — whereas the English have always taken a more realistic view: 'prodigy' comes from the Latin *prodigiosus*, 'a monster, a monstrous or abnormal thing'.

Wieck hoped to turn his own offspring into a kind of demonstration model to show his clients what he might do with theirs. Although he loved his daughter, his pedagogy was rooted in cruelty bordering on sadism. The method had never failed him, and its continuing successes merely confirmed his view that hard work and strict discipline were sure to produce results — though in reality he based his work on much the same principle as the old circus practice of breaking children's joints to ensure their later suppleness. Beatings and other punishments were nothing out of the ordinary in everyday schooling; and one may assume that a teacher's own children would have been treated even more harshly than those of fee-paying parents.

Wieck was a tyrant in his household, and in 1824 his wife divorced him. Clara was thus separated from her mother at the age of five, which made her unusually introspective. In addition to the gruelling piano lessons he gave her several times a day, Wieck also supervised her practice and monitored her every movement. When she started giving concerts away from home, he put his other pupils into the hands of an assistant and travelled with her. He shared her hotel bedrooms, dressed her, wrote her diary entries (full of moral precepts) and, as she began to grow up into an startlingly pretty adolescent, shielded her from the attention of males. All the while he continued to inflict physical punishment: a prodigious monster himself who, like many a strict teacher, had no difficulty in justifying to himself the sadism he enjoyed was 'all for the pupil's good.'

On the 9th of September 1827 Clara gave her first concert at which she played a Mozart concerto. It took place four days before her eighth birthday, but Wieck, using the traditional licence surrounding prodigies, described her as seven years old. A year later there was a musical evening in the salon of a Frau Agnes Carus of Colditz Castle, then being turned into a lunatic asylum — Frau Carus's husband was a doctor specializing in mental illnesses. Clara Wieck and her father were among the guests, and she played a piano trio by Hummel, to universal approbation. Herr Wieck showed his own approval in a manner entirely characteristic of him: instead of praising his daughter he grudgingly told her she had made 'only a few mistakes'.

Also at that *soirée* in Colditz was Robert Schumann, the son of a bookseller in Zwickau, who was waiting to enrol at Heidelberg University and would have described himself first as a poet and only secondly as an amateur pianist. He was present because he was infatuated with Agnes Carus, eight years older than himself, whom he had met in his home town (where she had relatives). Schumann liked to accompany her when she sang Schubert songs and play piano duets with her — and playing piano duets with women, as Schubert (who was then still alive) well knew, was a highly charged experience. No wonder Schumann wrote in his Diary: 'Sitting alone at the piano with her for two hours made all dormant feelings well up mightily. She must have seen it in my eyes. I will go to bed and dream of her. Good night, Agnes. . . .' — but on the 19th of August 1828 his subconscious libido worked overtime, as he records that he had dreamt of Agnes *and* Clara (a different Clara, surnamed Kurrer, otherwise nothing is known of her). He noted in his Diary, 'Musical duets can easily turn into duets for two hearts . . . four-hands piano playing remains the greatest enjoyment', and on another occasion called it, 'Duet for 4 legs': a rare flash of humour for this over-sexed but over-earnest young man.

Agnes Carus was not his first — or only — married woman friend. There was Frau Miersch, whose husband was the owner of a delicatessen shop and patisserie and 'quite under her thumb'. She allowed him many a favour and (to recount just one adventure in the nineteen-year-old Schumann's own disjointed words) on Sunday the 19th of April 1829 found her 'sleepy' but willing to offer 'red-hot kisses' while 'all pissed'; followed by 'embraces round the loins' — and all under the nose of her husband. In Schumann's affections there had been — or still were — Nanni Petsch ('Clara's companion, cunningly ingenious, discreet' — Diary, September 1837), Lidy Hempel and another unnamed girl, about all of whom he fantasized steamily in his Diary ('Lidy often hungers for love from me'). In 1831, there are references to 'a beautiful Dutch girl' (who has 'a Greek profile and is vivaciously seductive' and 'makes eyes like nobody's business') and visits to a 'Julie'; also (in 1837) the earlier Clara, who has given rise to some minor confusions of identity with the 'real', life-long Clara. There was also an 'English girl' — apart from Robena Laidlaw (who was Scottish, but Scots were, and still are, thought of as 'Engländer' in Germany).

Schumann wore his emotions on his sleeve and, in keeping with the romanticism of the time, was easily moved to tears: when he heard of Schubert's death he 'cried all night'. His feelings as a sixteen-year-old youth, torn between Nanni and Lidy, are comprehensively described in the Diary entries at the beginning of 1827:

2nd of January 1827: I often thought of my Lidy Hempel — the hopes and fears — more I'm unable to say, and if I did it would have to be platonic matters. My most blissful dreams often conjure up this divine girl to me. . . . Even if reality is sad, one can still dream. . . . I also think of Nanni Petsch — if only I were in the clear with her. . . .

4th of January 1827: Invited to Bodmers for a glass of wine. We spoke of mundane things. The conversation moved to Lidy: she was described in glowing terms. . . . I'm unhappy . . . the most dreadful doubts about her arise. . . . I thirst for her glances.

20th of January 1827: Here I sit and think of that blessed Tuesday. It was the 16th of January, and we were celebrating Nanni's birthday. I spent many an hour in her company, dreaming — it was my first, ardent love: and I, happy one, was loved by her. But all day Lidy's apparition floated before my eyes: I can't forget her —

— which he follows with a mawkish 150-line poem. The same poem also mentions ecstatically a girl called Mili, and the way her big breasts bounced up and down as she danced. By no means all the entries were concerned with his longings. There is homespun philosophy, some poetry, observations about his contemporaries, their music and their playing, as well as descriptions of works of art he saw. In

Munich, at the age of seventeen, he went to see a new sculpture group in the Leuchtenberg Gallery and found 'the [Three] Graces of Canova lacking in nobility'.

The musical evening in the Carus salon brought about Clara's first meeting with Robert Schumann, only recently arrived in Leipzig. He discussed literature with her: Wieck insisted that his pupils read books as well as music. Schumann had been learning the piano since he was seven, and his parents were hoping to persuade Wieck to accept him as a student. Clara was captivated by this soft-featured, handsome and romantic young man and later looked back on the meeting with sentimentality. She knew it was a turning-point in her life — which, in one way or another, it doubtless was, though one wonders how her career would have developed had she not met him. He, on the other hand, pretended not to have noticed her. Ten years later, when they were retracing the progress of their falling in love, as lovers do, he had forgotten about the soirée, and wrote:

> My first recollection of you goes back only to the summer of 1828: you were trying to write, at least you were were going through the motions, while I was studying Hummel's A minor concerto; and you kept turning round to look at me.

Did he really not remember his first encounter with Clara? But then, as he himself had noted in in his Diary in June 1828, when he thought he was in love with Agnes Carus: 'Where love is concerned men have a weaker memory than women; women know every little gesture, every glance.'

When Wieck heard young Robert play he immediately offered to teach him, promising his mother that within three years he would 'make him into one of the greatest living pianists'. And so, in October 1830, at the age of twenty, Schumann moved into Wieck's house as a boarding pupil. Wieck had remarried in 1828 — much to Clara's dismay, and she disowned her stepmother, a subconscious way of punishing her father. In Robert she found an exciting new big brother in her home, someone she could look up to. Schumann regarded her in a less brotherly way, though she had not reached puberty. He spent time with her and read poems by Heine and ghost stories by E.T.A. Hoffmann to her.

Schumann's piano technique was always inferior to Clara's. She had from an early age submitted to her father's draconian methods and the mind- and-finger-numbing practice he demanded — no thoughts of 'Repetitive Strain Injury' then. Robert found Wieck's methods repellent, especially the relentless practice-by-repetition — though he acknowledged that it was necessary for the 'calm, cool, collected and sustained conquering of technique'. Clara was more advanced than Robert also as a composer. By 1830 her first compositions, *Four Polonaises*, had been published when Schumann had not even made up his mind to become a composer, and two years before he got a work into print. By an irony she dedicated them to Henriette Voigt, with whom Schumann was secretly in love and whom he called 'my Leonora', and 'My Soul in A-flat'. She remained his confidante and adviser in amorous matters until her early death and was the only outsider he told of his engagement to Ernestine von Fricken.

Schumann professed not to be impressed with Clara's compositions, and when a reviewer in the journal he edited, the *Allgemeine musikalische Zeitung*, damned them with faint praise, including the words, 'After all, we are here dealing with the work of a woman,' he did not interfere with the judgement. A century after her death, as more of her compositions are published, performed and recorded, the world has become aware of her true gifts as a composer, and future generations may come to regard them as superior to many of her husband's. Robert was a dreamer, a self-consciously introspective poetical fantasist, a chronically depressive hypochondriac who was always analyzing his own feelings, while oblivious to those of others. Clara simply got on with her work.

While Robert Schumann was still in his teens — well before he took up residence in Wieck's house — he was already familiar with 'the jolly goings-on in the bath-houses' of Heidelberg and Leipzig and recorded in his diaries various sexual exploits, including 'finger games under skirts'. That could have been when he contracted syphilis, which is what biographers now believe he suffered from, although it has not been conclusively proved (if he did have it he not only produced some remarkably healthy children but also left his wife unaffected in spite of their active sex-life). In 1832, he had trouble with his hands, probably caused by mercury poisoning, a substance used in the treatment of syphilis, and later had his tendons cut to increase his keyboard stretch. When Robert was lodging in Clara's house, her father claimed to notice signs of his mental instability and would have exaggerated them to Clara so as to warn her against becoming involved; what father likes to see his daughter paired with an unstable young man of whom wicked stories were circulating? (He was probably aware that Schumann's sister Emilie had recently died at the age of nineteen, mentally and physically handicapped). Heidelberg and Leipzig were not big cities, their musical and intellectual circles small, and scandals travelled fast. But to the outsider, to everyone other than her father, Robert and Clara seemed made for each other. In 1832, when at thirteen she was giving a concert in Robert's home-town of Zwickau, his mother said to her, 'You must marry my Robert one day'. Even while nurturing his love for the pre-pubescent Clara, Robert Schumann had a sexual affair under the Wiecks' very roof. At eleven Clara was too young — and besides, was under her father's constant surveillance — but there was a girl he called Christel, the affectionate diminutive of Christine, also nicknamed 'Charitas'. She was probably a live-in servant, as Robert referred to her only by her first name in his Diary and never mentioned a family name, let alone a family, which he would have done had she been a fellow-student. The Diary reveals that Christel/ Charitas came to his room almost every day — which suggests she was a chamber-maid. No-one of her name is recorded as a pupil of Wieck's; and when he moved out of Wieck's house she came to visit him in his new rooms. On the 18th of June 1831, Schumann confided to his Diary that he made love to Charitas for the third time — 'one-and-a-half-times'. On the 13th of June she came to him again, but he records that she was bleeding heavily with a period. Charitas keeps appearing in the Diary until her place was taken — at any rate in its pages — by Robena Laidlaw (of whom more later), though Charitas had long been a willing partner. Other entries record 'some beautiful hours in her [Clara's] arms', though that was probably a romantic exaggeration — or another Clara — as full sexual intercourse with Clara Wieck probably did not take place until a few weeks before their marriage. There are many more occasions when he described himself as *knill* — 'pissed' — and records one hangover after another — also his dangerous habit of smoking a last cigar in bed before falling asleep. His eye for pretty women is shown by many diary entries of chance encounters with girls, or glimpses of them at windows — encounters that often went no further than a description of their looks ('she looked round at me for a long time') perhaps followed by a 'pleasant dream'. If a name is mentioned, it is usually only a Christian name. One affair seems to have been carried on entirely through the lovers' respective windows — his and hers, opposite. What could he have been up to?

During most of his married life Robert wrote down every occasion on which he had sex by means of a 'secret' mark in the margin of his Diary and the Household Account Books, useful for checking dates, in case of symptoms of veneral disease or the onset of yet another pregnancy. He used a symbol which could be interpreted either as a capital F (the vernacular German word has the same initial) or a semiquaver — a mere passing-note, a short and barely-perceived *acciaccatura.* . . . 'Christel in one minute' suggests that where sex was concerned the 'calm, cool, collected and sustained conquering of technique' Wieck so strongly recommended for his piano playing still eluded him. The relationship with Christel continued for several years, concurrent and overlapping with his courtship of his wife-to-be as well as affairs with other women. Moments after he had knelt before little Clara to protest his eternal love and quoted romantic poetry at her he was back in his room and on his knees again, this time before Christel and in a more purposeful posture.

In 1834 Wieck noticed that Clara, now fifteen, was showing signs of calf love for their lodger. He immediately sent her to Dresden on the pretext of her having lessons in musical theory. Schumann lost no time consoling himself, not only with Christel but also another of Wieck's live-in pupils, the seventeen-year-old Ernestine von Fricken, who had joined the pedagogic ménage earlier in 1834. She was the daughter — or so Schumann thought — of the rich Baron Ignaz von Fricken, from Asch (he commemorated the affair with a set of piano pieces based on the German names of the notes that spelt the town — later used in *Carnaval: scènes mignonnes sur quatre notes*). What Schumann did not know was that Ernestine was not the Count's daughter but the illegitimate offspring of his sister-in-law, Countess von Zedtwitz, by a man described as a *Drahtzieher* (literally 'wire-puller,' meaning a wire manufacturer). Schumann thought she was an heiress, and, money being a powerful aphrodisiac, he proposed to her. When the Baron heard about their affair he hurried to Leipzig to remove Ernestine. The lovers, however, resisted his attempts at being parted and became secretly engaged. By the time Clara returned to her home in July for the christening of her new half-brother (her father's child by his second wife) she noticed that Robert and Ernestine were being treated as a couple and were together standing as joint godparents to the new baby. Clara showed her jealousy in no uncertain terms, though she recognized that Ernestine loved Robert. In December Schumann went to visit the Frickens' home, still unaware of his fiancée's illegitimacy, but by the following August, when he found out that she was neither daughter nor heiress, his affection cooled. By New Year's Day 1836, he had extricated himself from the engagement. She felt hurt and humiliated, especially as Schumann had taken her virginity, but he told her that he had all along loved only Clara, to whom he wrote, 'You are my oldest love.' Eventually the Baron did adopt Ernestine, and, in November 1838, she married a relative of her mother, a Count Wilhelm von Zedtwitz-Schönbach, so she got her real surname back; also her inheritance, as her adoptive father had registered her as his legal child. Her husband died after only eight months, leaving her comfortable, both financially and in society. Schumann may have temporarily renewed their affair, for he wrote wistfully of Ernestine in the Diary even after his reconciliation with Clara and shortly before his marriage to her. In 1836 and/or 1837 he had a fling with an eighteen-year-old Scottish beauty, Robena Laidlaw (1819–1901). Although only sixteen she was Court Pianiste to the Queen of Hanover. The Diary reports that they reached a 'quick understanding'. A meeting is recorded in the Rosenau, the Rose Gardens in Leipzig, and a boating trip during which he promised her a rose: 'I searched long but could only find a rose which is not worthy of you. But I will send you a remembrance of the Rosenau.' This turned out to be his *Fantasiestücke*, op. 12, dedicated to her. An article in the *Strand Magazine* in 1904 reported that after her recent death in London, letters from Schumann were found among her effects, together with a single withered rose: 'Schumann gave me this rose at the Rosenau, 1836.' She may have misremembered the year, as Schumann's diaries refer to her in 1837. Also in that year there is a mysteriously anguished reference in the Diary to Clara, and angry ones against 'the old man', meaning Wieck: 'Another thing — on the 4th of August, Ernestine — her letter — our meeting — farewell for ever — previously wicked relationship with the *faneuse* — and the discovery in the cellar.' What discovery in the cellar? Was she, figuratively, the female haymaker (French *faneuse*) or was there another affair, with a country girl? Certainly the *faneuse* occupies several Diary entries, but in a cryptic manner. We shall never know, but in 1838 he wrote, 'Yesterday I re-read a few letters from Ernestine and wept bitterly.' Tears came easily to Schumann.

When Robert and Clara declared publicly their love for each other, Friedrich Wieck redoubled his campaign against Schumann by spreading various rumours (some of which were no doubt true but defamatory all the same) to blacken his reputation and prove to the world that his loose life-style made him unsuitable as a husband. In 1836 he forbade all contact between them and by January 1836 took her away to Dresden; but in February had to absent himself for a short time.

Robert took the opportunity of secretly joining her, and the two lovers spent five days together (give or take the odd boating trip with Robena Laidlaw). Wieck found out and was furious and, when back in Leipzig, decided on a diversion by encouraging Clara to see more of her singing teacher, Carl Banck. Sure enough, she developed an affection for him. Schumann vented his rage against the interloper in his *Allgemeine musikalische Zeitung* by inventing a semi-fictional character called 'Knapp' — the German word for 'barely' or 'inadequate'. It gave Robert the excuse for consoling himself with Christel (Charitas) once more. The Diary contains numerous entries like 'Charitas came completely' and reports her to be 'full of fire and flames.' Then disaster struck. Robert discovered lesions on his penis, and he and Christel went to consult a cellist friend and former fellow-student who had become a physician, Dr Christian Glock. He may have prescribed *Tierbäder*— 'animal baths', which were recommended to Schumann also when he suffered with his fingers. The treatment involved the insertion of the affected part into the flesh of newly slaughtered animals.*

Christel eventually became pregnant and gave birth to a daughter, though paternity cannot safely be ascribed to Schumann. There is a terse entry in the Diary for the 17th of January 1837: 'A little girl (on the 5th, I think).' Even as far into his courtship of Clara as October 1838, and in spite of all the romantic effusions he was writing to and about her, Schumann still hankered also for Ernestine: '27th of October. Wrote a letter to Clara but without enthusiasm or love. Re-read a few letters from Ernestine, which made me cry bitterly. You can imagine, dear diary, how often I am depressed and sad.'

When Clara reached the age of eighteen on the 13th of September 1837, Robert wrote to Wieck and formally asked for her hand. Wieck refused, calling him 'inadequate'. He had not yet done anything of note: why had he not produced any masterpieces, like *Der Freischütz* or *Don Giovanni*? He took his daughter on another concert tour, this time to Vienna. But by 1839 he allowed her to organize her own tours and travel without his personal chaperonage. This gave Robert the opportunity of arranging meetings, and they were reunited in Leipzig. In the summer they appealed to a court to have the paternal ban overturned and gained the support of Wieck's ex-wife, Clara's mother. The hearing took place on the 18th of December. Fortunately for the lovers, Wieck lost his temper in court and annoyed the judge, who ruled against him. All charges Wieck laid against Schumann were dismissed — except one, that he was a drunkard. Still 'the old man' (as both Robert and Clara called him) did not give up. Between the judgement and his appeal to a higher court Wieck had a hate-pamphlet printed and distributed, containing hints — no direct accusations — that Schumann was suffering from syphilis; and started a campaign of vilification

---

* In Beethoven's Conversation Books the composer is told of a Habsburg *Kaiser* who was such a sickly child that his doctors ordered him to be sewn into the carcass of newly slaughtered pigs, which were afterwards smoked and given to the poor — hence the (still popular) Austrian *Kaiserfleisch* — now made from pork loin.

against his daughter, too. The matter dragged on, and by August the court had given them their licence. As a final act of defiance they chose the day before her 21st birthday (when she came of age anyway) and married on the 12th of September 1840. The night before the wedding, Robert gave Clara his song cycle *Myrthen*, op.25: Myrtle Blossoms — the flowers held sacred to Venus and traditionally used for wedding garlands. Almost exactly a year later, on the 1st of September 1841, their first child, Marie, was born. It was a blissful time for them — his Year of Song, full of outpourings in his favourite medium. A second daughter, Elise, followed on the 25th of April 1843. At this time Robert began to note down in the Diary various symptoms clearly suggesting more than his customary hypochondria. Names of doctors figure, but no diagnoses. However, in 1842 he was told he was suffering from 'over-exertion' and *Nervenschwäche*— the dreaded but imprecise 'neurasthenia' doctors diagnosed when at a loss. Schumann's final decline was under way. His diaries indicate an increasingly troubled and confused state of mind — though it did not impair his sex drive. Robert and Clara's marriage was happy, and more children followed — in 1843, 1845, 1846, 1848, 1849, 1851 and 1854 — plus several pregnancies that did not reach full term. In both the Diary and the Household Account Books he recorded the occasions on which they had sex, with the F-sign in the margin. He also entered every tiny expenditure, including the housekeeping money he carefully allocated to Clara. As she was the principal breadwinner, she must have handed her earnings over to him and allowed him to give back to her what he considered necessary—with an occasional small 'extra sum to Clara', meticulously recorded. So is the occasional bill marked 'Income Tax'. The Schumanns were not well off but they kept nannies and children's maids (whose meagre pay is entered, along with the school fees and milk money). A barber came daily to shave Robert and was paid infrequently and late.

Domestic help was essential for the children's well-being, as Clara, already celebrated as a pianist and in international demand, spent long periods away from them on tour. The year 1843 began with a long-overdue conciliatory letter from 'the old man'; and, heavily pregnant with her second daughter Elise, Clara risked the bad weather and worse roads to visit him in Dresden. After Schumann's *The Paradise and the Peri* was performed there, and proved a resounding success, Wieck finally admitted that he had done Robert an injustice and grudgingly accepted him.

From February to May 1844, and again in 1864, Clara toured Russia, and played at Court. On her return from the earlier trip their third daughter was conceived. Clara had a great following in Britain and visited London and provincial cities on several occasions, both during Robert's life and afterwards. She was invited to play before Queen Victoria but disliked the way she talked through the performance.

At the end of 1844, the Schumanns moved to Dresden, where Wagner had been Court Kapellmeister since 1843. True to his nature, Wagner made a pass at Clara, but she took an instant dislike to him and rejected his advances. The two couples never met again socially.

Schumann's Piano Concerto op. 54 received its first performance at a joint concert he gave with Clara in Leipzig in 1846, but a subsequent tour to Vienna earned a disappointing reception. Soon after their return home their little son Emil — at that time the only son — died of a 'glandular complaint'. A few months later, Robert was devastated by his friend Mendelssohn's death and went into intermittent bouts of depression. He was becoming aware, also, that while he ruled the roost at home, artistically he was playing second fiddle to the more successful Clara. Much as he loved her he was not pleased when he found (and duly recorded in the Diary) that on a riverboat trip word went round that 'Clara Wieck was on board' while his presence had gone unnoticed. (The *Musical Times* later described the first London performance of one of his works as by 'Mr Robert Schumann, the husband of the celebrated pianiste . . . .')

Schumann's laconic Diary entries are often tantalizingly uninformative, more like one-word reminders of events he may have intended to enlarge upon later. In his earlier years he had a hypochondriacal preoccupation with his feelings, his state of mind and every tiny pain or discomfort — headaches and mood swings from one extreme to the other — or, after yet another drinking session, hang-overs — for which the German word is *Katzenjammer* ('Yowling Cats') — and often 'the shits'. Later, when his health disintegrated, the neurotic hypochondriac turned into a stoical sufferer. The year 1852 was a bad one for him, and Clara was obliged to neglect the children as well as her concert work to take him on spa 'cures'; yet in spite of all his woes, the F-signs continued to appear regularly, and poor Clara dragged herself from one pregnancy to another. Spa treatment in the Dutch resort of Scheveningen led to a miscarriage (though Peter Ostwald, in his fascinating study, *Schumann: Music and Madness*, suggests that some of her miscarriages may have been 'therapeutic abortions.'). By 1853 Schumann shed some of his depression, apparently helped by a bout of 'table-shifting' — i.e. spiritualism — and Robert and Clara were able to take part in the Lower Rhine Music Festival, where they heard, met (and both immediately adored) the 22-year-old violinist Joseph Joachim. He introduced to Robert and Clara the young Johannes Brahms, and they formed a close friendship. Brahms was still unsure of himself, but they encouraged him, and Schumann, by then an influential music journalist, recommended his compositions to publishers. Brahms promptly fell in love with Clara, while carefully concealing his feelings. When he wished to dedicate some works to Clara, he first asked Robert's permission.

During the happier years of Robert and Clara's marriage, they kept a joint album (later inscribed by Clara 'For our Children, to be carefully preserved: Dresden, the 13th of June 1845'), into which they pasted about 150 letters, pictures and prints and wrote messages and poems to each other; also locks of hair, dried flowers and other souvenirs. The album is now in the Saxon State Library, Dresden, a poignant record of their all-too-brief happiness.

Clara's youngest child Felix was born on the 11th of June 1854, three months after Robert was declared insane and taken to an asylum. Later sugges-tions that Felix was Brahms's son can be refuted with almost total certainty, for the child would have been conceived on either the 26th of August, or else the 2nd, 6th or 14th September 1853 — all of them days on which F-signs appear in Schumann's journals. By the 3rd of October Clara knew she was pregnant, when Robert wrote down the two words, 'Clara's certainty' — and entered another F-sign to seal the certainty. But there were ominous entries indicating that his mental state was deteriorating — doctors' visits, and 'mysterious failure of my hearing mechanism'. A bout of 'table-shifting' in August coincides with the note, 'Somewhat better.' An F-sign on the 10th of February 1854 coincides with 'in the evening a very strong and embarrassing hearing impairment' and the final one, on St Valentine's Day, is followed by 'amazing suffering — Dr Hasenclever — no better.' Schumann's instability became more and more pronounced, and his Diary and Household Account Book entries cease altogether. At noon on the 27th February 1854 — Clara hurried to fetch the doctor, asking the twelve-year-old Marie to keep an eye on her father. Marie later wrote:

I was supposed to sit in mother's little sitting-room and see if father, whose room was adjoining, wanted anything. I'd been sitting at mother's writing-desk for a while when the door opened and my father stood there, wearing his dressing-gown, the long one with the green flowers. His face was completely white. As he saw me he clapped both hands to his face and said, 'Oh God!' — and went back into his room. For a short while I was rooted to the spot when I remembered why I was there. I went into father's room — it was empty — and the doors leading to my parents' bedroom and from there into the hall, they were wide open. I rushed to my mother, who was still with the doctor, and we searched all the rooms in the apartment. It was clear that my father had disappeared.

Wearing only his dressing-gown and bedroom slippers, Schumann had rushed from the house, run to the bridge over the Rhine and jumped into the freezing river. His leap was seen by fishermen, who pulled him into their boat, rowed him ashore and took him home. From that moment he was never left alone, with two male attendants guarding him day and night. He heard voices, as well as strange music (he wrote one piece down but it made little sense) and was moved to an asylum at Endenich, where he stayed to the end of his life. From that very day, the 27th of February 1854, the handwriting in the Household Account Books changed from Schumann's to Brahms's, as the younger man touchingly took on the daily chores for Clara: 'Housekeeping, Postage . . . . Letter to Dublin . . . half-bottle Moselle wine . . . coal . . . firewood . . . etc.'

The director of the Endenich Lunatic Asylum treated his patients' relatives with a curious high-handedness, refusing to let Clara visit her husband on the pretext that it would be too upsetting for him — while apparently not considering her feelings. She therefore did not see him for two-and-a-half years — so as not to upset the director's 'cure'; though in any case she had to support her children with the income from concert tours. Brahms was a constant source of help, financial as well as practical, and, almost apologetically, sent gifts. As Schumann's condition deteriorated, he and Clara found solace playing his D minor Piano Concerto together (in the original two-piano version as a Piano Sonata), which he had written at the time of Schumann's suicide attempt. In September 1856 Brahms wrote to his friend Julius Otto Grimm:

> I was with Schumann for his birthday. I found him strangely altered, suddenly, and it was for the last time. Frau Clara came from England. Immediately on her arrival she found there was worse news from Endenich. Eight days before his death (on Wednesday) we received a telegram. 'If you want to see your husband again alive hurry here at once. You will find his aspect gruesome, however.' We drove there. He'd had a fit, which the doctors believed would lead to his death immediately . . . . I went up to him but he was evidently in great turmoil and distress, so that I as well as the doctors advised Clara against seeing him and persuaded her to leave. Schumann just lay there, taking no food except the odd spoonful of wine and jelly. But Clara's suffering was such that by Saturday evening I *had* to suggest to her to see him. I thank God now and for ever that she did, for her peace of mind. She saw him on Sunday, Monday and Tuesday morning. That afternoon at four he died. I shall never experience anything so moving as that reunion between Robert and Clara. He lay there, with his eyes closed, and she knelt before him, more calm than one would have believed possible. He had still recognized her, earlier. Once he had tried to embrace her but managed to put only one arm round her . . . . He slipped away quite gently, so that one was hardly aware of it.

After Robert's death, his wedding-ring was nowhere to be found. Two years later a note was discovered which he had written before attempting to drown himself.

> Dear Clara, I am throwing my wedding ring into the Rhine. You do likewise, and both rings will surely be intertwined eventually.

In 1870, Clara and Robert's son Ludwig, aged only 22, was admitted to a lunatic asylum, just as his father had been 26 years earlier. His grandfather, like Robert himself, also suffered from unspecified 'nervous disorders'; and in 1887, Clara had to look after Ferdinand's children as he had become a morphine addict.

In the winter 1873–4, Clara's rheumatism prevented her from playing, and she had to cancel her regular concert tour of Britain. She bore no grudges against her father for his appalling treatment of her when she was a child and, after his death in his late eighties, wrote in her Diary: 'Although we disagreed in many things, this could never affect my love for him, a love which all through my long life has been heightened by gratitude.' That was the measure of this noble and gifted woman.

Clara's half-sister Marie (1832–1916) also became a pianist and minor com-

poser but her brother Friedrich Allwin Feodor (1821–1885) disappointed his
father by working happily as a humble orchestral violinist. After Clara died, on
the 20th of May 1896, Brahms — himself with less than a year to live — wrote his
Four Serious Songs, op. 121, to texts from St Paul's Letter to the Corinthians. He
sent them to her daughter Marie but enclosed a note warning her,

> Don't play them through, because at present you would find the words too
> moving. Just put them to one side, as they are intended as a memorial for your
> beloved mother.

They end with verse 13 of the First Epistle:

> And now abideth faith, hope and love;
> these three.
> But the greatest of these is love.*

*In the Scriptures the Greek word is *agapé*, non-erotic love, while the German version of the
Bible used by Brahms has, *Aber Liebe ist die größte unter ihnen.* The King James Bible interprets it
as 'charity': 'But the greatest of these is charity'. Incidentally, Sir Malcolm Sargent orchestrated
the accompaniment of Brahms's *Four Serious Songs* (originally composed for voice and piano) to
occupy his mind while his young daughter was dying.

BEDRICH/FRIEDRICH SMETANA

Born:	Litmysl (then Leitomischl), 2nd of March 1824
Father:	Frantisek Smetana (1777–1857)
Mother:	Barbora Lynkova (1791/2–1864)
Married:	1st, 27th of August 1849, to Katerina Kolarova (1827–1859)
Children:	Bedriska b. 7th of January 1851, d. 6th of September 1855
	Gabriela, 26th of February 1852, d. 1854
	Zofie 24th of May 1853 Katerina b.25th of October 1855, d. 1856
Married:	2nd, 10th of July 1860, to Bettina Ferdinandova (1840–1908)
Children:	Zdenka, b. 25th of September 1861, Bozena 19th of February 1863
Died:	Prague, 12th of May, 1884

The eighteenth-century musical traveller and historian Charles Burney in 1770 described the Bohemians as 'the most musical people of Germany, or, perhaps, all Europe': a reputation that was almost entirely due to their enlightened use of music in both churches and schools: every village priest seemed to double as a composer and music teacher, and music was a 'core' subject in every school. But there were other national talents, too, for example the famous Pilsener Beer, produced by the brewery at Plzen in the service of the Counts Waldstein and later the Czernins — familiar names as patrons of Viennese music of the classical and romantic periods. Frantisek Smetana, master brewer in charge of the operation from the turn of the eighteenth century, neatly combined the arts of brewing with music making, being an enthusiastic amateur violinist. Unusual among the artisan class, he was by 1825 prosperous enough to occupy his own grand house in the market square of Leitomischl which later became the Town Hall (though it must be said that he made a fortune supplying the occupying Napoleonic forces with beer: Beethoven's brother Johann also prospered as a 'collaborationist', as a supplier of medicines). Chief Brewer Smetana was an important man in the town.

The family's name is not unduly rare — one of Beethoven's physicians was a Dr Smetana (and his lawyer a Dr Bach) — and it means 'sour cream*'; but Frantisek's son Bedrich, the eleventh child, was destined to make it known world-wide. It was he who gave Bohemia its national musical voice.

To put Bedrich Smetana's birth date into the perspective of his times, he was born a year before Beethoven's Ninth Symphony, as was Anton Bruckner. At home he was called Friedrich, as the family spoke German, and he kept his diary in German: only later did he think of himself as a Bohemian and was obliged to learn to speak the language.

---

* Many Czech families bear 'silly' names, which they chose when their Habsburg masters forced the population register for taxation purposes.

In 1831, the family fortunes moved a step up when Frantisek Smetana bought an idyllic country property in Ruschkolhotitz (Ruzkova Lhotice in Czech), although hard times later forced him to sell it and revert to being a tenant-brewer. Bedrich wrote in his diary: 'When I reached the age of four my father taught me how to keep musical time. In my fifth year I went to school and learned Violin and Piano-Forte' (it is said that at five he led a domestic performance of a Haydn string quartet). He also began writing down tunes that came into his head. As an exceptionally bright child he was sent at fifteen to the *Akademisches Gymnasium* (i.e. Grammar School) in Prague, where, according to his diary, he lived in spartan conditions. 'I ate in an inn for 21 crowns daily — provided I had money. Often I went to bed hungry; once I had nothing for three days except a small cup of coffee for breakfast with a bread roll, and then no more for the rest of the day. It took me months before I got near a piano.' He was, however, able to enjoy the musical life of the city, and go to concerts and opera — all new experiences for a village boy.

The young Smetana was unprepossessing — pictures always show an amiable but sad-looking, hang-dog face with big spectacles — but he had an eye for the girls and candidly recorded in his diary any amorous approaches, rejections or conquests he made. As he was too poor to give his intended girl friends presents or love tokens he presented each with his special home produce: a polka or a waltz (Chopin also had a good line in waltzes as courtship presents). He was modest and unambitious and saw himself as little more than a dance composer supplying the immediate neighbourhood with music, usually polkas, for the bands that played in inns and in the town squares. If the waltz towards the end of the nineteenth century was the characteristic dance of Vienna, the polka was the musical emblem of Bohemia; and as the province was a reluctant member of the Austro-Hungarian state, its people treated it as a kind of dance of independence.*

Smetana's love offerings cost him little more than the few sheets of music-paper the polkas were written on and, at the same time, affirmed his national pride. The *Louisa Polka* was followed by the *Elisabeth Waltz*, the *Marina Polka* and the *Katerina Polka*. There were girls called Lida and Clara — though both the *Lida Polka* and the *Clara Quadrille* are lost, perhaps destroyed by Smetana during the sadness that surrounded the end of his Clara affair (their second names are not known): 'Clara conquered me but now I am released. I shall celebrate my victory by freeing myself from her destructive clutches which would otherwise have held me prisoner and tortured me. We have separated. Adieu, Clara!' At the age of nineteen, having matriculated, Smetana left school determined to become a musician, to the disappointment of his father who wanted him to be a brewer like himself and join his uncle in making Pilsener; or, better still, a civil servant. Young

---

* The dictionaries say it is 'a lively dance of Bohemian origin' but the word is almost certainly a contraction of 'polacca', a Polack, or Polish dance. Another possible, if far-fetched, explanation traces it to *pulka*, Czech for 'half'. The dance did, however, spread from Prague where the *Oxford English Dictionary* says, it was danced in 1835, then in Vienna in 1839, Paris in 1840 and London (on its way across the Atlantic) from 1842.

Smetana's affections were switched from Clara to his childhood friend Katerina (nicknamed Wild Kate when they were both at school). She was a gifted young pianist, the daughter of a civil servant, Karel Kolarov. For her Smetana wrote more important works than mere album-leaf polkas. Again he confides in his diary: 'Slowly that strange feeling has blossomed into love. May it flower for ever! You are curious, dear little book, to know who it is that lives in my heart. Let me tell you, it is Kate, yes, Katerina — a virtuoso who has at last captured my affections!'

Bedrich Smetana and Katerina Kolarova were married on the 27th of August 1849, when she was 22. Several daughters were born, at little more than yearly intervals, but three died tragically at an early age. The death at four-and-a-half from diphtheria of Bedriska (German form Frederika, diminutive Fritzi) was the saddest of many bereavements they suffered: even as a baby she had shown remarkable musical awareness, able to sing in perfect pitch, and her loss was almost unbearable for him and Katerina. Her death inspired his first major work, the elegaic Piano Trio in G minor. The first two movements contain a plaintive, chromatic descent down the interval of a fifth, a moaning sigh of pain; and grief runs through the entire work. Gabriela was born in 1852 and died aged two of tuberculosis; and a third, Katerina, born in 1855, lived only eight months. Zofie, born in 1853, was luckier and survived her childhood to marry a forester, Josef Schwarz.

Bedrich's wife was a simple, even-tempered and good-natured young woman but she suffered from chronic ill-health after the birth of her first child and was eventually found to have tuberculosis.

Smetana became involved in the revolutionary movement of 1848 and found life in Bohemia uncongenial. After a meeting with Liszt, that veritable musical Baedeker, Smetana was convinced he had to seek his fortune abroad. In October 1856 he departed for Sweden to take up a teaching and conducting appointment in Göteborg. He was invited to take over the conductorship of a choral society called Mådagssångövningssällkapet (and presumably managed to get his German-Czech vowels round it), opened a music school and gave private piano lessons. He was captivated by a young married woman, the 29-year-old Mrs Fröjda Benecke (nicknamed Feda), a niece of a singing-teacher and Cantor of the Göteborg Synagogue. They had in common the fact that she looked after a sickly husband, and he an ailing wife. He found her aloofness, combined with a certain cold Scandinavian charm, irresistible: the attraction proved mutual, and they fell in love. Their relationship soon became a full-blown affair. She inspired a number of compositions, one of which, a Polka of 1858, was renamed 'Vision at a Ball', presumably referring to their meeting, and he incorporated into it her nickname the note-row F.E.D.A. His Polka op. 12 No. 2 is dedicated to Fröjda, and the Polka op. 13 No. 2 to his wife Bettina. They are not the simple strophic dances their name suggests, but Smetana's answer to the large-scale Waltzes and Polonaises of Chopin. In the summer of 1857, Smetana's father died, and he returned home for the funeral. By the autumn he had resumed his work in Sweden and, braving the harsh northern winters, his wife joined him. Her arrival put a stop to his affair with Fröjda, but Mrs Smetana did not stay long. Her health declined further, and he decided to take her back to their own country, with its milder climate. On the 19th of April 1858, they had to break their journey at Dresden, as Katerina became too ill to travel any further, and she died on the same day. In his diary he wrote, 'It is all over. Katy, my dear, deeply beloved wife, died early this morning without our being aware of it until alerted by her stillness. Farewell, my angel'. At the same time Smetana was racked with guilt for having neglected her during his stay in Sweden and taken up with Fröjda. Later he wrote in his diary: 'I now feel lonely and abandoned. Only now do I realize how precious she was to me.'

Three months after his wife's death, Smetana fell in love again. Bettina (Betty) Ferdinandova was already part of the extended Smetana family, his brother Karel's sister-in-law and the nineteen-year-old daughter of an old family friend. Smetana probably chose her because he was lonely, overlooking her lack of interest in music. She respected him as an older friend and minor celebrity but did not love him. Her parents, however, were delighted by the prospect of welcoming a budding genius into the family and persuaded her to accept Smetana's hand. Smetana's own misgivings must have been kindled by an extraordinary act of tactlessness on her part. In continuation of his well-tried bachelor practice he wrote for his bride his *Bettina Polka* and presented it to her. But, unlike all the other young ladies, she rejected it out of hand — perhaps she wanted a symphony. Like the Piano Trio, with its grief-laden figure mentioned earlier, this polka, too, has its musical allusions: descending triplet passages depicting Betty's tinkling laughter — a pre-echo of 'Dorabella' in Elgar's *Enigma* Variations.

When Smetana returned to Sweden in 1860 it was with Betty and his step-sister Zofie, but his heart was no longer in the work offered by the country where, earlier, he had seriously considered taking up permanent residence. Smetana's Swedish-nationalist symphonic poem *Haakon Jarl* is one of several works which bear witness to his Scandinavian commitment; but he felt that his native Bohemia needed him; and Fröjda was no longer a magnet. Had he not given way to these feelings he would have become a Scandinavian composer — which could have delayed the advent of Czech musical nationalism by half a century.

In May 1861, Smetana and the now pregnant Bettina returned home, where on the 25th of September their daughter Zdenka was born. Success was slow in coming, with many disappointments, and even the *Bartered Bride* took time to be accepted.

He was struck down by various illnesses: throat troubles, rashes and ulcers, and worse, his hearing began to give him concern. In Sweden Fröjda organized a collection so that he could afford to consult the finest ear specialists in Austria and Germany. Not that they had much to offer: indeed some of their treatment was little better than the quackeries Beethoven endured half a century earlier. At 58, he twice suffered a temporary loss of memory and speech and was ordered to stop composing or even thinking about music, and to live in totally silent surroundings: poor advice, as silence made him all the more aware of his agonizing tinnitus, an internal top E permanently ringing in his ears.

The tinnitus 'note' — inaudible to anyone else — is poignantly illustrated in Smetana's E minor string quartet, entitled 'From My Life', completed at the end of 1876, and explained in his own words:

1st Movement. My inclination towards art in my youth, captivated by romantic feelings, my unspeakable, unimaginable yearning for something I could neither imagine nor describe but which also held a forboding of misfortune to come. The long note in the Finale arose from this opening; and it is the same fateful whistling sound in the highest register in my ear which in 1874 heralded my deafness.

2nd Movement. A kind of polka, which takes me back to the cheerful days of my youth, when I poured forth dance numbers.

3rd Movement. Largo sostenuto, reminds me of my blissful happiness, of love to a girl who later became my faithful wife. [i.e. 'Wild Kate']

4th Movement. Describes the awakening of national music, my proceeding along this path until interrupted by an ominous catastrophe; the onset of deafness; a glance into the sad future; a small ray of hope, but it is swamped with pain. So that's what this composition is about. I have set it for four instruments who, as it were, play together in close friendship, as if talking about it to each other. I find it very depressing. That's what it means and no more.

In 1879, while Smetana was completing his cycle of symphonic poems, *Ma Vlast* (My Homeland), he wrote, 'I have a fear of madness. I've become so depressed that I sit here for hours, doing nothing at all except think of my ill luck.' Smetana's behaviour became increasingly irrational. In summer he insisted on walking out dressed in furs, and in the street made frightening faces at passers-by, as if to warn them away. Sudden episodes of frustration manifested themselves in violence, and he began to smash furniture and window panes. On one occasion he threatened members of his family with a revolver. Often he babbled meaningless phrases, of which only odd words were discernible, like 'the country', or 'in the wood' or 'by a pond', or the names of Liszt and Wagner. Sometimes he conducted an imaginary orchestra, or uttered sudden loud cries imitating the bass drum. He imagined all kinds of threats and became deeply suspicious of everybody, accusing his bewildered wife, who had devotedly looked after him, of stealing his savings-book. For this imagined act of treachery he tried to start divorce proceedings. In 1884, he made an attempt at composing an opera, *Viola*, but the notes refused to comform to his meaning. He was finally taken to an asylum, where he died on the 12th of May 1884 and was buried at Vyserad — one of the places immortalized in *Ma Vlast*.

His daughter Bozena died in 1941 at the age of 78 in an old people's home, suffering from exactly the same degenerative illness as her father, which suggests that there is little basis for the notion that Smetana's dementia was caused by syphilis.

ALESSANDRO STRADELLA

Born:	Rome, 1st? Ocober 1644 (baptised 4th of October)
Father:	Cavaliere Marc' Antonio Stradella
Murdered:	Genoa, 25th of February 1682

Alessandro Stradella, composer and rakehell, was a worthy successor to Carlo Gesualdo, the sixteenth-century Prince of Venosa who gained his notoriety half a century earlier. But whereas the Prince, who murdered his wife and her lover, escaped public justice as well as its Italian privatized form, the vendetta, Stradella failed to elude the killers and became a murder victim himself. Both wrote beautiful music, both tended, later in their turbulent lives, to write strange and wonderful harmonies ahead of their time. While Gesualdo never suffered even temporary eclipse, Stradella's neglect is only now being rectified, with almost a glut of recordings. He was born in Rome on the 1st of October 1644, the youngest of four children of a low-ranking nobleman, Cavaliere Marc' Antonio Stradella, who had been created Marchese of Vignola only the year before Alessandro's birth. As a boy he sang in the Church of San Marcello and soon began to produce compositions notable for their maturity and originality. He was orphaned in 1655 at the age of ten or eleven, but was able to earn his living as a chorister. In 1663, still only in his teens, he caught the attention of Queen Christina of Sweden, for whom in that year he composed a Motet. He entered her service as boy *servitore da camera*, also acting as her lutenist, violinist and singer; the eighteenth-century English music historian John Hawkins says he was also 'an exquisite performer on the harp'. Stradella was employed by the Queen in Italy, where she had taken up residence, finding the Italian weather more congenial than that in Sweden, not to mention the artistic and religious climate. She abdicated her throne, converted to Catholicism and set up a breakaway court in a Roman palace: not for political or subversive reasons but to safeguard her status as an ex-queen. Later Stradella served the Colonna family, for whom her wrote a large number of theatre works.

Perhaps it was his unsettled and unprotected youth which gave him the propensity for getting into scrapes; and being deprived of motherly love from an early age drove him into the arms of a succession of women. The few things known about Stradella are mostly, in some way or another, disreputable. Helped by occasional periods of patronage, he seems chiefly to have led the life of a playboy, working when he felt like it. Part of his income may have been the result of embezzlement rather than patronage. When he was 25, in 1669, he conspired with a shady cleric, the Abbot Antonio Sforza, and a fiddler, Carlo Ambrogio, to steal a great sum of money from the Roman Church. His spectacular success, both as a composer and with women, made him numerous enemies. His music was largely neglected until the late ninteenth century, when his works began to become available in specialist publications. In the previous century, Corelli, Alessandro Scarlatti and Handel were aware of the riches to be found in Stradella's works and trawled them for ideas. Handel, who stole other men's tunes as Wagner did other men's wives, often helped himself to bits of Stradella and adapted them for his own purpose: perhaps on the principle that stealing from a thief is a less heinous form of theft.*

In the spring of 1677, Stradella incurred the displeasure of Cardinal Cibo after accepting a 'very large' bribe from an 'old and ugly woman' to arrange a marriage between her and the Cardinal's 'nephew' (which in those days and in that religion usually meant 'son'). That is the official reason given for Stradella's being obliged to flee the city, though a more likely explanation would be yet another seduction of a pupil. Stradella resolved to move to Turin but on his way there he seduced, and eloped with, a young Venetian noblewoman, Ortensia Grimani, whom he had been hired to teach. It was a double misjudgement: not only was she herself a member of an illustrious family but she had also (in the words of an eigthteenth-century source) '. . . submitted to live in criminal intimacy with a Venetian nobleman': the mistress, in fact, of Alvise Contarini, a powerful gangster, a mafioso before his time who instituted a blood feud against Stradella. Thus, having seduced a woman who was a wronged sister as well as a suborned mistress, he laid himself open to revenge from two flanks; and revenge duly came. 'The frequent access of Stradella to this lady, and the many opportunitites he had of being alone with her, produced in them both such an affection for each other, that they agreed to go off together to Rome. In consequence of this resolution, they embarked one very fine night, and by the favour of the wind effected their escape. Upon the discovery of the lady's flight, the Venetian had recourse to the usual method in that country of obtaining satisfaction for real or supposed injuries; he despatched two assassins, with instructions to murder both Stradella and the lady, giving them [the assassins] a sum of money in hand and a promise of a larger one if they succeeded in the attempt.'

The hired killers were told to go to the Church of San Giovanni Laterano, where Stradella and his mistress were about to perform an oratorio composed by him. They were to pose as members of the audience and then, on the way out after the performance, to waylay and murder them. Fortunately it was Orpheus taming the wild beasts all over again. For 'the performance having begun, these men had nothing to do but to watch the motions of Stradella and attend to the music, which they had scarce begun to hear, before the suggestions of humanity began to operate upon their minds. They were seized with remorse and reflected with horror on the thought of depriving of his life a man capable of giving such pleasure to his auditors. In short they desisted from their purpose. They waited for his coming out of the

---

* But no; Handel also stole from his friends. In any case musical borrowings in those days were neither illegal nor reprehensible: some composers felt flattered to be quoted. There were also musical coincidences: for example, an aria in Stradella's *La forza d'amor paterno* anticipates Beethoven's opening theme of the Eroica symphony.

church and then courteously addressed him and the lady, who was by his side, first returning him thanks for the pleasure they had received at hearing his music, and informed them both of the errand they had been sent upon; and concluded with the earnest advice that Stradella and the lady should both depart from Rome the next day, themselves promising to deceive their employer and forgo the remainder of their reward by making him believe Stradella and his lady had quitted Rome on the morning of their arrival'.

In successive decades, even centuries, interest in Stradella's colourful life and his reputation as a seducer seems to have eclipsed his music. In his own time, and in spite of the tales that were told about him, his reputation as a musician was unequalled. Wherever he went, the nobility sought out his talents as a teacher, especially young women. Unfortunately, like Alexander Zemlinsky with Alma Mahler, Stradella did not confine his tuition to crotchets and quavers. His final adventure was with a member of the Lomellini family. When her brothers found out that he had been teaching her more than music they hired a gang of men who pursued and waylaid him. He was stabbed to death by unknown assassins on the night of February 25 1682. He is buried in the Chiesa delle Vigne in Genoa. One of his last works was a Cantata, *L'Accademia d'amore*. Hawkins says that when news of Stradella's assassination reached Henry Purcell, and he learned that jealousy had been the motive, 'he lamented his fate exceedingly; and in regard to his great merit as a musician, said he could have forgiven him any injury'. 'Which those,' added Hawkins 'who remember how lovingly Mr Purcell lived with his wife, or rather, what a loving wife she proved to him, may understand without farther explication.'

Many stories exist about Stradella's musical philanderings — some no doubt fictitious. However, it seems established that he survived two assassination attempts, recovered from injuries inflicted in both, and then succumbed to a third. Friedrich von Flotow wrote a blood-and-thunder opera about his life, *Alessandro Stradella*, which was produced in Hamburg in 1844 and still occasionally surfaces in the German repertory. However, the music is all Flotow's own: he probably never heard a single note of Stradella. Now, however, symphonies, arias, oratorios and madrigals by Stradella are available both in printed form and on record.

RICHARD GEORG STRAUSS

Born: Munich, 11th of June 1864
Father: Franz Joseph Strauss (1822–1905)
Mother: Josephine Pschorr (1837–1910)
Married: Pauline de Ahna (1862–1950)
Died: Garmisch-Partenkirchen, 8th of September 1949

They are a familiar phenomenon, those apparently ill-matched couples, a bossy and domineering wife and an easy-going husband: couples of whom friends say, 'If I were in his place I'd have left her years ago.' Such wives are not usually stupid but unperceptive — incapable of understanding that their behaviour might embarrass friends and bystanders. They never allow their husbands to tell a joke or relate an event without correcting details and seem to revel in their partner's dicomfiture, both in private and in public. They lose no opportunity of displaying to outsiders — whether close friends or railway porters — that they are the boss. Many highly successful men, distinguished in their own field and by no means weaklings, allow themselves to be cowed into domestic submission by wives with not a fraction of their accomplishments.

Richard Strauss was already a man of substance and growing reputation before he even met Pauline de Ahna. He had always been easy-going: more the resigned, shoulder-shrugging Austrian than the heel-clicking German. His birthplace, Munich, in the province of Bavaria, is so near to Austria as to share almost the same accent and much of the traditional musicality of Salzburg, as well as Austrian *Gemütlichkeit*; a quality Strauss possessed to an uncommon degree and which pervades *Der Rosenkavalier*.

Richard and Pauline Strauss's friends would shake their heads as they witnessed yet another one-sided scene and wondered what he saw in her other than a loud-mouthed, bullying harridan. Yet Strauss was devoted to Pauline and endured her embarrassing outbursts with patience. Alma Mahler reported in her *Reminiscences* how at a concert in Strasbourg in May 1905 Strauss threw a rare tantrum against a singer, Kraus-Osborne, calling her, among other things, a cow. The singer's husband, who was present, nearly challenged him to a duel. Alma reported that the normally so calm Strauss was 'foaming at the mouth and, after the Mahlers had pacified him, said, "Phew — I must write to my wife about this, because she thinks I never lose my temper."' Ida Dehmel, the widow of the poet Richard Dehmel, wrote in her diary on the 22nd of March 1905:

> I spent only one hour in the company of Frau Strauss de Ahna, in Pankow, Parkstraße 25, where she was on a visit with her husband. Kessler and von Hofmannsthal were there. In that short time, and in front of total strangers, she managed to utter so many ignorant, tactless and crude indiscretions that it was the absolute lowest anyone could have experienced from a woman. 'Yes;

men,' she said [Mrs Dehmel reproduced Pauline Strauss's peasant accent], 'the main thing is to keep a tight rein on them.' At the same time she made a gesture of reining in a horse, while making whipping motions with the other. When she heard the other men praise Strauss for his *Zarathustra* and *Eulenspiegel* she screamed in a fury, 'You're only encouraging him to write more stuff like that, and being played everywhere, too! Who likes it? I don't. Can't see anything in it!'

Mahler spoke of the Strauss's marriage with distaste. Their relationship is such, he said, 'that one has to look for evidence of masochism'.

Pauline de Ahna was a professional singer, the daughter of a recently ennobled German general. She was always conscious of her new-found rank and of the 'de' before her maiden name (considered a slightly snobbier prefix than 'von'). Richard, on the other hand, never even bothered to soften his rather vulgar Bavarian accent, reflected in that of the Viennese Baron Ochs in *Der Rosenkavalier*. If Pauline inherited her father's military peremptoriness it did not rise above the rank of the strident sergeant-major who bawls out pseudo-authoritative statements in a silly voice. She had an opinion on everything and never missed an opportunity of expressing it. Strauss usually deferred to her with apparent respect. Pauline's parents were not only music lovers and amateur performers but also collectors of famous musicians. As Strauss was by that time famous, they were delighted by their daughter's choice, in spite of the fact that he was the son of a mere horn player and an equally bourgeois mother — a dynasty which, like Smetana's, was founded on the brewing of a famous lager.

The young Richard was handsome, and widely hailed as as successor to Brahms — musically speaking, therefore, the grandson of Beethoven. He was only 23 when he met Pauline — while carrying on an affair with Dora Wihan, the wife of a cellist in the Munich Opera. His father, who was principal horn player in the Court Orchestra, knew about it and was half shocked and half pleased, a common fatherly reaction as a son reveals himself to be a fully-functioning man.

To distract him from Dora, Richard was introduced to Pauline by Strauss's maternal uncle, Georg Pschorr, at his estate near Munich — a carefully arranged matchmaking exercise to divert Richard from the clutches of a married woman. Pauline took singing lessons from him (no doubt she soon told her teacher how a voice should be produced). Having set her cap at him she captured his heart without difficulty. Strauss's tone-poem *Don Juan*, the most overtly erotic musical work since Wagner's *Tristan and Isolde*, was probably inspired by their love, which also provided him with inspiration for the completion of his first opera, *Guntram*. Later, in *Ein Heldenleben*, she is portrayed as the hero's 'helpmeet', lovingly, in the form of a ravishing violin solo (when a squawking soprano saxophone would have been more true to life); and later in *The Sinfonia Domestica* — in which we also hear their new-born son's crying.

After Strauss obtained an assistant conductorship at the Weimar Opera under Hans von Bülow, he managed to get his wife into the company as a minor soprano in 1890. In the following year she sang the part of Elisabeth in Wagner's *Tannhäuser*, with the approval of the now widowed Cosima Wagner. Cosima, always scheming, may have had an ulterior motive in engaging Pauline. She had had her eye on young Richard for some time and, by cultivating Pauline's friendship, managed to get them both to stay at the Wagners' lair at Wahnfried Frau Wagner had no designs on Strauss himself (as a prospective husband to step into Richard Wagner's shoes, he was far too young) but was motivated by self-interest. Her plan was to alienate Strauss's affection away from Pauline and towards her own, still unmarried, daughter. She wanted him as a musical son-in-law, and to add him to her stable of conductors.

Cosima had not reckoned with an adversary as formidable as Pauline de Ahna, and her plot misfired. Its failure meant that they were never invited back to Wahnfried. This lost Pauline the chance of singing there, and Strauss never joined the select group of Bayreuth conductors. Had Frau Wagner succeeded, German opera at the turn of the century might have turned out differently, because Stauss would have had to spend more time in the orchestra pit than at his desk.

The Strauss's engagement was announced in characteristically stormy fashion, during the preparations for Strauss's *Guntram*, in which Pauline was singing. At the dress rehearsal she made one of her scenes, threw her score at his head, flounced off the stage and retired to her dressing room. Strauss followed her, closed the door behind him and, in vain, tried to pacify her. The rest of the cast listened to her tantrums and became anxious for his safety. They held a meeting and voted to ostracize her by refusing to work with her again. Fräulein de Ahna, they decided, must be expelled from the company. The pair eventually emerged from the room looking red-faced and tear-stained, respectively — it is not recorded whether the heavy score actually hurt him — and Strauss announced to the astonished company, 'Ladies and gentlemen. We are engaged.'

The marriage turned out even stormier than the rehearsal, but he stoically bore her moods and tantrums, even her telling him how to compose, telling him how to conduct and how to train singers. He was willing to give in to her, people said, because by her bullying, she made him work, whereas he preferred to play cards. She also relieved him of tedious chores, like paying household bills, and kept admirers at bay. She made him take off his shoes before he entered 'her' house in case he dirtied 'her' carpets and always spoke as she thought — without an ounce of tact. Their friends pitied him, yet admired his refusal to be embarrassed. Norman Del Mar in his biography of Strauss reported that after the first performance of *Die Frau ohne Schatten*, Pauline loudly declared it was the most stupid rubbish she had ever heard and refused to be seen walking home with him. If someone called her 'Frau Doktor Richard Strauss', she screamed, 'Frau Doctor Strauss de Ahna, if you please!' Toscanini was fond of saying, 'To Strauss the composer I take my hat off; to Strauss the man I put on three hats.' And an eyewitness reported that 'the statement was always accompanied by a gesture with both hands'. Strauss's librettist, Hugo von Hofmannsthal and his wife, as well as

Gustav and Alma Mahler, detested her and never lost an opportunity of saying so. A particularly fierce domestic quarrel was imortalized in an opera. One day, at breakfast, Strauss opened a letter addressed, to Herr Kapellmeister Strauss, Joachimsthalerstraße No. 17. Pauline, who was looking over his shoulder, saw that it was a love note on scented paper. Its tone was intimate and affectionate, and it alluded to some free tickets:

> *Darling Love! Dooo get me the ticket. Your faithful — Mitze. My address is: Mitze Mücke, 5 Lüneburgerstraße.*

'*Mitze Mücke*' was a Berlin prostitute, as he discovered later. Pauline fell into one of her rages. He protested that he had never even heard of the woman, let alone offered her tickets or been to bed with her. Pauline accused him of lying. She moved out, started divorce proceedings and refused to speak to him. Strauss assumed that the note was meant for a Kapellmeister Edmund Strauss, who worked with him at the Berlin Opera House; but he, too, denied any knowledge of the woman. Eventually the truth emerged. The intended recipient was neither Strauss but a Kapellmeister Stransky, who was conducting at the Kroll Opera House. One night he and two colleagues — an Italian tenor and his manager — drank at the bar of the Hotel Bristol, when they were approached by a hotel prostitute who, realizing from their conversation that they were musicians, asked them for free tickets (Berlin tarts must have had good taste). Either they mistook the Italian's fractured German pronunciation of 'Stransky' for 'Straussky' or perhaps he did write down his name for her (and in continental handwriting *n* and *u* are often indistinguishable). When she searched the telephone directory she found no 'Straussky' but Kapellmeister Richard Strauss in the Joachims- thalerstraße. Eventually, Pauline accepted the explanation. The incident inspired Strauss's opera *Intermezzo*, unique in the operatic canon in that it portrays the composer's own marital troubles (just as the *Sinfonia Domestica* had depicted their domestic bliss). The breakfast letter incident opens the work. Strauss wrote his own libretto and worked on the opera from 1918 to 1923 (von Hofmannsthal having declined a collaboration as he found so public an airing of a private affair distasteful). *Intermezzo* is subtitled 'A Bourgeois Comedy', and Strauss enjoyed writing as well as producing it in Dresden, on the 4th of November 1924. The sets were copied from the Strauss's home in Garmisch, and before rehearsals began, he invited the soprano Lotte Lehmann (who took the role of the wife, 'Christine') to their house so that she could secretly study Pauline's stridency, which she faithfully reproduced on stage. To underline the *verité* of the plot, the two principal singers surprised everyone, including the real-life couple, by wearing masks depicting Richard and Pauline, who in the score are called Herr and Frau Storch. Strauss even introduced, by way of a tit-for-tat swipe at his wife, a character based on a male visitor whom she had once — innocently — entertained in her husband's absence. *Intermezzo* begins with a stand-up, ding-dong slanging match between husband and wife in the presence of an embarrassed maid servant, as the hero, a conductor, is packing his bags for a concert tour. Not only the characterization of the voices, but also the orchestral writing, reflects the chaos of domestic strife. Strauss's portrait of his wife as a petulant, spoilt loudmouth — and of himself as 'Robert', the patient and sensible husband — met with delighted approval. (Their maid Anna and their son Franz were given their own, real names). It was Strauss's revenge for all the humiliation he had had to endure, but he obtained it through music, without having to confront her. In their offstage life no serious infidelity seems to have clouded the marriage: not the slightest rumour was whispered — a rare thing among the artistic circles of the time. The first Viennese performance was conducted by Strauss himself, with designs and production by Alfred Roller and Lothar Wallerstein; Alfred Jerger sang the role of Kapellmeister Storch. At one point Jerger lost his temper with his stage wife and banged on the table with his fist. The real Frau Strauss was in the theatre and afterwards took Jerger to one side and said, 'That bit where you bang on the table with your fist. Better leave it out next time. My Richard never dares do anything like that at home.'

There is, however, a touching postscript to Strauss's apparently uneventful love-life. On the 23rd of November 1948, less than a year before his death, he completed the song *Malven* ('Hollyhocks') to words by Betty Knobel. He sent the manuscript by post to his old friend, the soprano Maria Jeritza, together with a request for a copy to be made and returned to him. She either forgot his request or ignored it. The existence of the song was known, tantalizingly, because the composer referred to it in his letters, but no-one knew its whereabouts: Jeritza regarded it as a secret between herself and the composer. Even after his death she refused all requests from scholars to examine it — the even more 'last' song than the *Four Last Songs*.

Only after Jeritza's death did anyone see it. It bore the inscription, 'This last rose for my beloved Maria'.

Among the roses, phlox, wreathed zinnias,
Hollyhocks rise above,
Scentless and lacking all glow of purple,
Like a pale, tearstained face under the golden light of Heaven.
And then, gently, the tender blossoms fall in the summer wind.

Strauss died in Garmisch-Partenkirchen on the 8th of September 1949. Pauline followed him eight months later, on the 13th of May 1950, heartbroken and without a trace of the old aggression. Friends said that when she no longer had him to scream at she lost interest in life.

ARTHUR SEYMOUR SULLIVAN

Born: London, 13th of May 1842
Died: London, 22nd of November 1900

Until recently that Victorian pillar of musical respectability, Sir Arthur Sullivan, composer of some 70 hymns including *Onward, Christian Soldiers,* numerous Anthems, the Biblical oratorio *The Light of the World* and the all-time religious hit *The Lost Chord,* would have have found no place in a book about composers' love lives. Today's prurient press would have described him as a 'confirmed bachelor;' but Victorians accepted that the private life of a man who had chosen not to marry was of no public concern. The barbs W.S. Gilbert and Arthur Sullivan aimed in *Patience* at Oscar Wilde sailed close to the wind, but when *Ruddigore* was given the subtitle *Robin and Richard were Two Pretty Men* — not a murmur of levity was heard. To the pure all things were pure: yet this chapter deals with Sir Arthur Sullivan and Aramis, Rachel, Louise, Fannie, Rem, Toot(s)ie, Mrs C., Miss C., Miss Violet, P.C., D.H., L.W., E. W., F.D., A.B.C, R., C., O . . . and the Girls at No.4.

In June 1966 the London auction house Sotheby & Co offered, as part of Lot 200, a collection of diaries and full scores in Sullivan's handwriting —'twenty volumes in black morocco with brass locks, which have been forced'. But it was not until the mid-1980s, when Arthur Jacobs published Sullivan's definitive biography, making use of the diaries, that a picture emerged of the composer's energetic life between the sheets. Suddenly we knew what Sir Arthur Sullivan 'did'. Moreover, he did it often and with numerous women, all of whom he recorded — painstakingly if not always lovingly, which is why his black diaries had locks. Almost everything in this chapter is based on Professor Jacobs's work, and it is difficult to see what any future biographer could add to his assessment of Sullivan — the man, his music, and his place in high Victorian art.

Like Robert Schumann, Sullivan used a code for the nights (or days) on which he had sex, including the number of times; and like Samuel Pepys, who also recorded such exploits, Sullivan used foreign terms: many a *Himmelische Nacht!* (always thus misspelled for *Himmlische,* and sometimes abbreviated '*Him. Nt!*') to recall some 'heavenly night' spent with either his long-term mistress Fanny, or another of a bewildering array of others. Parenthesized numerals following a woman's initials denote the number of times he achieved 'heavenly bliss' — though, as he never seemed to exceed the number '(2)' per night one wonders why he bothered to count. His preoccupation with numbers reveal an immature lover, perhaps unaware that his partners might have preferred duration to repetition — something Wagner knew well enough and illustrated in his music. But Sullivan also faithfully recorded with a nought '(0)' his occasional failure to score: 'L.W. 0!' or 'L.W. 0! disappointed ambition'. And no wonder, if the next entry is an indication of Sullivan's mastery of what the Germans call, in a different context, *Vorspiel*: 'L.W. *straight up!* Coffee at the restaurant. Shopped a little. V.S. Stayed at home and played poker all evening. Beautiful moon. *Himmlische Nacht!* (1).' One diary entry recorded a 'Long conversation' with E.W. but otherwise nothing more than 'a little bit "touched"'.

Abortionists also figure in Sullivan's diaries, as do brothels, one of them cryptically described as being situated at 'No.4'. Sullivan records the length of time he spent there, followed by the usual parenthesized figure. On the 10th of April 1882, he recorded that he was 'very tired'; after writing down the following events in a single day during a Paris stay:

> Arr. at 6 a.m. Descended at Grand Hotel — rooms 197–199. Adele came at 9. Breakfasted at Voisin's at 11. At 12 went to keep appointment at no.4 rue M.T. Stayed till 5.30 (2). Dined with Dicey and D.H. at Restaurant Poissonière. Took Dicey home, then D.H.(1). Then home myself, very tired.

Add to all this a steady procession of maid servants, some of whom were required to minister to his needs when other women were not available; but he did not always bother to record these encounters. They included Jane, Harriet, Janette, Ruth, Sarah, Louisa, Adèle, Delphine — and a Belgian girl, Clotilde, with whom he had a long and specially close relationship and who received the enormous sum of £1,000 in his will. His disagreements with Clotilde sound almost like marital squabbles: 'squalls' he calls them, after which he wrote, with relief, 'Domestic reconciliation complete! Oh, the bother of servants! It is enough to make one marry — but the cure would be more awful than the disease. I can get rid of servants but not a wife — especially if she is *my* wife.' When Clothilde went on holiday she cabled that she was bored, and would he join her. After Adèle left his employment he arranged a clandestine holiday with her in a Paris hotel. Telegrams like 'Meet me in Paris at . . . .' were not uncommon, for before the telephone became widely available, the rich recklessly entrusted their love notes to telegraph boys; telegrams were usually delivered within the hour. On one occasion L.W. ('Little Woman', his long-term mistress Fanny made a scene when she found an intimate cable from another woman on the breakfast table.

When he was about 21, he was guest at a grand house near Belfast, where a young girl fell in love in with him. In her letters she called him 'brother' but signed herself, pseudonymously, 'Aramis':

> Do you know, it strikes me that when you become a great man and an eminent musician, *my* letters may be published if your biography is written (which it is sure to be), and the idea is not a pleasant one. This is itself reason enough for destroying them, is it not, dear brother?

Arthur Jacobs thinks 'Aramis' was Annie Tennent, and that her feelings were not reciprocated. Perhaps his mind was already on Rachel Scott Russell, whom he wooed in 1867, at first through her mother by 'respectfully' dedicating a song to her — remembering that there were not only beautiful daughters in the family but also money. He was a frequent house guest, but her mother discovered their relationship and expressed her icy disapproval:

> It has come upon with a shock to learn that you could not be content on merely the terms of intimate friendship in this family. . . . It grieves me to tell you that under *no* circumstances could I ever consent to a different relationship. And therefore I ask you, if you *cannot* bring yourself to be satisfied with that which hitherto subsisted, to abstain from coming here till you can do so, and to cease all correspondence . . . I grieve that I reposed in you a confidence to which you were not equal. I did it in absolute good faith. . . .

Her younger daughter Alice was being wooed by the son of a wealthy MP, and mother had higher hopes for her daughters than a struggling minstrel. But she was too late, as Sullivan continued to meet Rachel at secret locations, one of them the office of the amenable George Grove (of *Dictionary* fame). Sullivan's nickname for her was Chenny; and in her cooing letters to him she signed herself 'F.D.' (for Fond Dove) and 'Your little Passion Flower'. At some point Sullivan also managed to stir the passion of her eldest sister, Louise, who had at first acted as go-between for her sister and her clandestine lover. She wrote letters to him beginning 'My dearest Arthur. . . .' and signed herself 'Your truly loving' and 'Your own devoted little Woman'. In one letter she admits that sex had taken place between them: 'You have taken as your right the only thing I have to give.' Rachel, too, made the depth of their relationship clear:

> Ah me! when I think of those days when cooing and purring was enough for us, till we tried the utmost — and that is why I fancy *marriage* spoils love. When you can drink *brandy*, water tastes sickly afterwards. . . .

Curiously forward sentiments for a young Victorian woman. But once he had experienced 'the utmost' with her, his feelings cooled. Rachel continued to write touching and increasingly despairing letters. This on his birthday:

> This is the first 13th of May since 1863 that I have not wished you 'many happy returns' with my hand held out to welcome you. It is so bright and sunny and the birds are singing — and God grant this may be a happy day for you — and with all my heart I pray that there may be many in store for you yet. I send you some of our flowers — they will bring back everything to you so vividly, as picking and choosing them has done for me. I knew you would not care merely for a bought thing — and so I decided to do what has no intrinsic merit of its own beyond being as much as the work of my own hands as it is possible for anything to be. Doctor Pole has arranged — as you know — your symphony — *my* symphony — for me and I thought it would please you if I made a copy of it for you. . . . I am sure it is full of mistakes, but you know you always scolded me for not copying accurately and I am not improved. I am too sad to write much as it seems to me so curious that you could resist my letters — but if it

saves you pain, God knows I would not ask you to do it. I am so utterly sad that I long to go away where the daily pain may be a little less. . . . I am doing a translation of that letter of Hiller's on Wagner and I will send it to you when it is done. But it is *so* difficult that I almost despair at times. Will you not write to me now? If I can help you in any way in copying or anything with your *Prodigal Son* do give it me to do. . . . Oh, Arthur, I pray God with my whole soul to bless you and to make you happy. The tears drop over the poor little face you used to love as I write. You know all I would say and cannot. God have mercy on us both.

In 1872, Rachel was married to a William Holmes and did not see Sullivan for a long time. When they met, his diary entry is cold and non-committal: 'Chenny came at 4.30 — stayed till 6.15. Had a long talk. She is very little changed.' In 1881, Sullivan records another brief reunion, in formal circumstances:

John Millais gave a splendid ball at his new house in Palace Gate, and there I ran up against Chenny! (R. S. R.) — whom I had not seen since her marriage and departure for India. We sat on the stairs talking for three hours! She is as handsome as ever.

But no numerals. Other initials came and went, and one D.H. was so unwise as to call on Sullivan at midnight. But D.H., Arthur Jacobs thinks, may have stood for 'Dear Heart', alias L.W., or 'Little Woman' — Fanny, the most important of the little women and the love of his life. After his death she referred to 'a friendship' of 23 years so they must have met around 1870. She was Mary Frances Ronalds, a New York society beauty born in Boston in 1839, the daughter of a rich American called Carter. According to one of her many admirers:

Her face was perfectly divine in its loveliness, her features small and exquisitely regular. Her hair was a dark shade of brown . . . and very abundant . . . a lovely woman with the most generous smile one could imagine, and the most beautiful teeth.

Sullivan called her Fanny or Fannie (in those days it was evidently still possible for an American girl to bear that name) and fell deeply in love with her. She was a fine sportswoman and a singer and spent much time in court circles in Paris, where she first met Sullivan (doubtless on one of his frequent trips to enjoy the beauties at No.4). She was not divorced but separated from her husband, who refused her a legal separation. Even after his death she and Sullivan did not marry — afraid, perhaps, that *their* brandy might turn into sickly water.

Sullivan 'set up' (as people said in those days) Mrs Ronalds in South West London, at first at 84 Sloane Street, later at 7 Cadogan Place, built in fashionable red brick. Frequent visits are recorded in Sullivan's diary. While their sex life had to be clandestine, they were often seen together in London society; and almost accepted as man and wife; though chaperoned in public by a woman of maturer years (Fanny's mother while she was alive). When Fanny accompanied him at public functions his diary calls her 'Mrs R', but when she appears as a sexual partner she is referred to by initials, or 'Little Woman'.

Fanny was highly regarded for her singing of Sullivan's great hit, *The Lost Chord*, and even the Prince of Wales, says Arthur Jacobs, was prepared 'to travel the length of his future kingdom to hear her sing it'.

At the end of 1884, while Sullivan was working on *The Mikado*, he feared that he and Fanny had some infection, or else she was pregnant.

11 December: Uncertainty changed to conviction.
12 December: Went to M. [consultant or high-class abortionist] alone.
13 December: Things very bad. Took D.H. to M. Usual course advised.
19 December: Signals of safety began
20 December: Signals of safety. Things going well
21 December: Out of the wood.

In the days of unreliable birth control the sight of the telegraph boy bringing one of Fanny's 'All Clear' telegrams would have been particularly welcome. With erratic antisepsis, even the most expensive abortionists endangered women's lives. Sullivan's recurring, chronic kidney trouble was also causing him (and perhaps Fanny, too, if it was venereal) pain and discomfort. Sullivan must have wrought havoc among the women he slept with; his behaviour, especially in foreign hotels and brothels, was nothing if not reckless. During his 23-year affair with Fanny, others appeared and vanished again with alarming frequency. Heaven only knows what presents he brought back from his travels abroad: an encounter in Shepherds Hotel, Cairo with a 'Miss C' was especially unwise.

In 1947, a 'Miss Violet' confessed to Leslie Bailey (author of *Gilbert and Sullivan and their World*, 1973) about her friendship with Sullivan when she was a girl and showed him a letter he sent her. She said he offered her a secret register office marriage (with which he surely had no intention of going through: he was probably merely placating her after having seduced her). 'Miss Violet' has been identified by Arthur Jacobs as Violet Beddington, whose sister, Sybil Seligman, became Puccini's mistress . . . (and Elgar's 'Windflower' was the daughter of Sir John Millais, mentioned above: so *la ronde* went round and round).

Sullivan reveals himself in his diaries as a snob and social climber who treated women as society accessories or sexual playthings. He had strong views about contemporary composers and performers, but these find little expression in his diaries; even after attending important first performances he recorded merely that he was there and heard them. Stranger still for a man who wrote the music for all those deliciously witty Savoy operas, he displays little wit in his personal jottings. If his bed springs ever creaked to the sound of laughter the diaries give no indication of it.

As the century entered its last decade, Sullivan's passion for Fanny, which he had for so long sustained and assiduously recorded, went into a decline. So indeed did he, with recurrent bouts of his old kidney complaint. In 1896, he forgot her birthday, making a feeble excuse ('I thought it was the 29th and it is the 23rd. . . .'). She took it as the signal that it was all over, and sent him a poem called 'In Remembrance' which ended:

> If I have ever made you glad,
> Have ever made one single hour
> Pass brightlier than else it had,
> Have planted in your life one flower —
> If I have ever had such power,
> I cannot now be wholly sad.

She signed it, 'L.W.' — but knew she was no longer his Little Woman. She might have added, 'I have sought, but seek it vainly/That one lost chord divine'. By the time of his death not long afterwards, his long involvement with Fanny had been acknowledged even by royalty (no strangers to illicit affairs), and Fanny was accepted almost as his widow. Perhaps because his rampant love life remained unsuspected, Fanny was accepted almost as his widow. Princess Louise, Queen Victoria's daughter, telegraphed to her during his last illness for news of Sullivan's condition; and the Queen sanctioned a burial in St Paul's Cathedral. The causes of death were given as 'bronchitis' and 'cardiac failure'.

Fanny did not receive any money in Sullivan's will but was invited to choose any objects she wanted; also, of course, 'their' song, which they had so often performed together: 'the original manuscript of *The Lost Chord*, and other musical and vocal scores she may care to have.' Fanny died on July 28 1916 in London, at 7 Cadogan Place, SW, where they had shared so many a *Himmlische Nacht*. It was rumoured that the manuscript of *The Lost Chord*, believed to have been lost, had been placed on her breast and buried with her, but this apparently is a romantic myth. It would have been fitting if *The Lost Chord* had been not so much lost as gone before.

MARIA AGATA SZYMANOWSKA

Born: Maria Agata Wolowska, Warsaw, 14th of December 1789
Married: ?? Szymanowski (name unknown)
Died: St Petersburg, 25th of July 1831

Maria Agata Szymanowska studied piano and composition in Warsaw, under Lysowsky and Gremm, and became the first professional Polish woman pianist. She made her debut in Vienna in 1815 and spent the next thirteen years touring every major city in Europe. From 1822, she became Court Pianiste for successive Tsarinas — a breakthrough for women, as all such posts had previously been held by men — and settled in St Petersburg from 1828 until her death in 1831. Her playing was praised for its technical mastery, its *cantabile* line, precision of execution and exceptional dynamic range — on 'grand' pianos still in their infancy. In addition to her pianistic and compositorial skills she must have possessed exceptional charm, because composers fell over each other to compose works for her. Beethoven's 39-bar Bagatelle (*Klavierstück*) in B flat, WoO 60, is thought to have been written for her, whom he described as 'the foreign lady'. The manuscript was at one time in her possession.

Although Agata was not one of the great composers — and is more notable for having been loved than loving — she is important as the pioneer of Polish romanticism and, most remarkably, provided the patterns for Chopin's Nocturnes, Mazurkas, Polonaises and Etudes, many of which are modelled on hers. Her compositions include not only works for piano solo, but piano and violin; as well as — unusually for a woman composer of the time — a fanfare for brass instruments.

She came from a Jewish family, which makes her employment at the notoriously anti-semitic Russian court all the more remarkable. Much of her life was spent travelling, so she had less time for composition than she might have wished. Her wide-ranging European concert tours gained her much renown, and her beauty and personality captured many hearts. Luigi Cherubini dedicated to her his C major Fantasia for piano, and she earned the admiration of Rossini, Pleyel and Glinka; also Schumann, who described her compositions as 'the most noteworthy ever produced by musical womanhood' (what would his wife Clara have thought of that remark?).

Szymanowska's greatest conquest was outside the musical profession, when she captured the heart of Johann Wolfgang von Goethe — late in his life, and by then more than forty years her senior. He fell in love with her, and under her spell wrote a series of poems, *Aussöhnung* (Reconciliation), one of which begins, 'Passion brings suffering'. When he met her, and especially when she played to him, he described himself as being once more 'unfolded' (*entfaltet*, which literally means blossomed-out, emerging from a cocoon) after a long period of emotional recession. Goethe was then in his seventies and at the same time passionately in love with a nineteen-year-old, Ulrike von Levetzov. The poet seriously considered marriage to Maria Agata, though he consulted his doctor first — not for the sake of her marital happiness but to ask him if wedlock might place be too much strain on his delicate health. The doctors seem to have advised against it, and after a 'very last kiss', he and Maria Agata reluctantly parted. No doubt he expected her to outlive him, but she died in the cholera epidemic of 1831, which also took the philosopher Hegel at the height of his fame. No family relationship has been claimed between Maria Agata Szymanowska and the later Polish composer Karol Szymanowski (1882–1937), but as Szymanowska's husband is a nebulous figure ignored by the reference books (who must have left the scene before Goethe's offer of marriage) one cannot be certain.

PYOTR ILYICH TCHAIKOVSKY

Born:	7th of May 1840
Father:	Ilya Petrovich Tchaikovsky (1795–1880)
Mother:	Alexandra Andreyevna Assier (1813–1854)
Brothers:	Nikolay Ilyich (1838–1910); Ippolit Ilyich (1843–1927)
	Modest Ilyich (1850–1916)/Anatoly Ilyich (1850–1915) Twins
Sister:	Alexandra Ilyinisha (1842–1891)
Married:	Antonina Ivanovna (1849–1917)
Died:	6th of November 1893

Tchaikovsky was handsome, gifted, charming and rather shy, a combination often irresistible to women. He was flattered by their interest; but although he tried at least twice to form relationships he found their proximity repellent and physical contact unthinkable.

'Coming out' would have been unimaginable in Tchaikovsky's time, and meant disgrace and exile in Siberia. It would also have been impossible for a known homosexual to obtain a post at the Conservatoire.

His early years were spent almost entirely in the company of women. He idolized his mother and was inconsolable when separated from her. He was deeply attached also to his French-speaking Swiss governess, Fanny Dürbach, who called her delicate and strikingly beautiful charge 'my porcelain child'. He really did look like a piece of Dresden china. He was distraught when in 1848 she returned to Switzerland — the farewell letter the eight-year-old sent her was rendered illegible by his tears. In the following year, his mother wrote to Fanny, 'He is totally changed, he lounges around listlessly and I don't know what to do with him. I feel like weeping.' Towards the end of that year a new governess, Petrova Petrovna, was engaged, who was more sympathetic. In 1850, he wrote to Fanny, 'I spend all my time at the piano. It brings me consolation when I'm sad.' His mother sent him to St Petersburg, to a junior school preparatory for law studies. On his first day, she accompanied him to school, but when she prepared to leave, he clung to her skirts and, screaming in terror, had to be forcibly parted from her. He ran after her coach and tried to stop its wheels by putting his hands into the spokes. Soon afterwards his mother died in the cholera epidemic of 1854. He was only thirteen.

> I shall never get used to the idea that my mother is no more, and that I shall never have the opportunity of telling her that I still love her as deeply as ever. . . .

And later he wrote:

> On this day exactly 25 years ago my mother died. It was the first great sorrow

I experienced. Her death left the greatest impression both on me and my fate. She died in the bloom of youth, quite suddenly, of the cholera . . . . Every minute of that frightful day remains as vivid as if it had happened yesterday . . . .

His grief made him again turn to music for solace, as he had done when Fanny deserted him. There was further grief when he lost a young friend during a scarlet fever epidemic — events which probably established the pattern of his melancholy tunefulness based on the 'dying fall' of a descending scale — in *Onegin* spanning an entire octave. At school, he was soon overcome with grief again when his best friend died. It seemed that one blow was to follow another, but he found consolation in a friendship with another schoolmate, Alexei Apuchtin, probably also a budding homosexual: he confessed they were drawn to each other by 'strange feelings'.

Tchaikovsky made two attempts to adopt a heterosexual lifestyle. When he was 28 he encountered the celebrated Belgian mezzo-soprano Désirée Artôt, who was then in Moscow on a concert tour, and persuaded himself he was attracted to her; a woman with a strong, masculine face who was anything but a beauty. In a letter to his father in January 1869 he wrote, 'There has developed a certain mutual tenderness and we discussed the possibility of marriage. All things being equal, the wedding should take place next summer.' Désiree was older, in her mid-thirties and boyish (later Strauss's first Berlin Oktavian, the 'trousers role' in *Der Rosenkavalier*). To his brother he wrote, 'I am very much in love with her.' Modest must have been startled by this development, as he not only knew of his brother's predilections but shared them — without being so guilt-ridden. But such things were illegal and they had to make their references cryptic: Tchaikovsky in a letter to his brother speaks of 'the Sword of Damocles that hangs constantly over my head,' and of 'this thing' and the things he did, which he secretly coded 'X' and 'Z'. Désiree left Moscow — whether still engaged to Tchaikovsky or not we do not know, as no letters seem to have passed between them — but only a few months after her departure he was surprised and slightly hurt, though probably relieved, to hear (not from her) that she had married the Spanish baritone, Mariano Padilla y Ramos, in Sèvres, a subsequent city on her tour itinerary. Later it emerged that Tchaikovsky's friend, the pianist Nikolai Rubinstein, had tipped her off that Pyotr might not come up to her expectations as a husband. The Romance in F minor, op. 6, was written for Désiree, part of the song-cycle that contains his best-known song, 'None but the lonely Heart'; and he further tried to purge his failure with Desirée by composing the passionate Fantasy Overture *Romeo and Juliet*.

Tchaikovsky's growing fame and good looks gained him many female admirers but *they* invariably had to make the first move. In 1877, he confided in his friend Nikolai Kashkin:

During the early or middle of May I received a longish letter, a declaration of

love for me. It was signed by A. Milyukova, who told me she'd already loved me
when she was a student at the conservatoire, some years before.

Her letter was what would now be called fan mail. She said that she admired
him and often thought about him. He replied, politely thanking her for her kind
attention but not encouraging her further. She wrote again, more strongly, saying
that she was trying to control her feelings but that she could not bear the thought
of his leaving the city without her, that she had felt compelled to turn down a
declaration of love from another former fellow-student — in short, that she
wanted no other man but him, the object of her adoration. Her next letter, as
printed in David Brown's biography of the composer, reveals a woman unhinged.

I've been in the most agonizing state for a whole week, Pyotr Ilyich, not
knowing whether to write to you or not. I see that my letters are already
becoming wearisome to you. But will you really break off this correspondence,
not having seen me, even once? No, I am convinced you will not be so cruel. Do
you, maybe, take me for a frivolous person or a gullible girl, and therefore
place no trust in my letters? How can I prove to you that my words are genuine
and that ultimately I would not lie in such a matter?

Tchaikovsky's letters to her were destroyed, but he must have tried gently to tell
her that he was not the marrying type. She was undeterred.

After your last letter, I loved you twice as much again, and your shortcomings
mean absolutely nothing to me. Perhaps if you were a perfect being I would
have remained perfectly cool towards you. I am dying of longing and I burn
with a desire to see you, to sit with you and talk with you, though I also fear that
at first I shan't be in a state to utter a word. There is no failing that might cause
me to fall out with you . . . .

Little did she know. An older woman might perhaps, even in those days, have
understood Tchaikovsky's signals. But to a starry-eyed 28-year-old like Antonina
Ivanovna he was an irresistible challenge. It made her all the more determined.
She could hardly have imagined what anguish was in store for them both.

Having today sent a man to deliver my letter I was very surprised to learn that
you had left Moscow, and longing descended upon me even more. I sit at home
all day, pace the room from corner to corner like a crazy thing, thinking only
of that moment when I shall see you. I shall be ready to throw myself on your
neck, to smother you with kisses — but what right have I to do this? Maybe you
take this for effrontery on my part . . .?

She told him she did not make a habit of pursuing strange men; that she was no
'groupie' or a loose woman. And furthermore, that she was a virgin.

I can assure you that I am a respectable and honourable woman in the full sense of the word and that I have nothing that I would wish to conceal from you. My first kiss will be given to you and to no-one else in the world. Farewell my dear one. Don't try to disillusion me further about yourself, because you are only wasting your time. I cannot live without you, and so maybe soon I shall kill myself. So let me see you, and kiss you, so that I might remember that kiss in the other world. Farewell. Yours eternally, A. M.

About two months after Antonina's first gushing letter — followed by a veritable flood in the same vein of desperate infatuation — Tchaikovsky capitulated and married her. He had recently told Modest that he might be forced to take such a step.

> From today onwards I shall do everything possible to marry someone. I know that my inclinations are the biggest and insurmountable obstacle to my happiness, and I must fight with all the strength I can summon against my nature. I shall achieve the impossible and get married this very year; and if I cannot find the courage I will in any case renounce my old habits . . . . The thought that those who love me have sometimes cause to be ashamed of me wounds me mortally. It's happened a hundred times and will happen many hundreds of times more. All I want is to enter into a marriage, or even some connection with a woman, so as to shut the whole pack up. Although I despise them, they are capable of causing sorrow to those who are close to me. But I am too fixed in my habits and preferences to be able to discard them like an old glove. I have no strength of character, and since my last battle I have already given in to my inclinations three times.

He sought refuge from his turmoil by composing *Francesca da Rimini*: and hearing it in the context of that letter gives it new meaning. He had recently struck up a friendship with another woman, Nadyezhda Filaretovna von Meck. Like Antonina she had made the first move. She was a widow who had been a prolific breeder, of whose numerous children no fewer than eleven survived (the Soviets would have declared her a Stakhanovite Mother and given her Order of Lenin). The arrival of the last child unwittingly killed her husband at the age of 45, his death brought about by his discovery that their eleventh, Ludmila, was not his but that of his secretary. He was so upset that he had a heart attack, though it may have been a hushed-up suicide. Through an intermediary Mme Meck sent Tchaikovsky a message telling him how much she admired him and invited him to re-score some of his own music for violin and piano for performance in her salon, where she held frequent musical parties. For this rearrangement, a modest task by any reckoning, she offered an unusually large fee. Tchaikovsky needed the money and complied immediately. It was a ruse on her part to gain his attention; yet there is no indication that she had her eye on him as a replacement for her husband, or even hoped to make him her toy boy.

Friday, 30th of December 1876. Permit me to convey to you my sincerest

gratitude for such a swift execution of my request. To tell you how much delight your compositions afford me . . . might appear to you ridiculous [but] my enjoyment is so precious to me that I do not wish it to be ridiculed. Therefore I will only say, and I ask you to believe this literally, that with your music I live more lightly and more pleasantly. Accept my sincerest respect and sincerest devotion,
Nadyezhda von Meck.

Tchaikovsky was rather wary and replied formally.

I am sincerely grateful for the kind and flattering things you have been so good as to write to me. For my part I will say that, for a musician beset with failures and disappointments of all kinds, it is comforting to think that there is a small number of people who love our art so warmly and deeply. Sincerely devoted and overflowing with esteem, P. Tchaikovsky.

Mme von Meck could not praise him enough.

Your music is so wonderful it transports me into a state of utter, blissful happiness. I seem to float above all things earthly, my head reels, my heart beats madly and my ears drown in the magic of such music . . . . Oh God, how great is the man able to induce such moments of happiness . . . .

It was the start of one of the most remarkable friendships in the history of music. For Tchaikovsky — perhaps for both of them — the ideal relationship. In February 1877, she enlarged on what she had written to him earlier.

I would explain to you a little about the somewhat unusual affection which I harbour for you, but I am fearful of taking up your valuable time. So let me content myself by telling you that these feelings — may they be never so abstract — mean a great deal to me, because they are the best and the purest man is capable of. For this reason, Peter Ilyich, you can call me a fantasist, or even a madwoman, but you must not make fun of me. It would all be ridiculous if it were not so sincerely and deeply felt.

She kept reiterating that far from wishing to arrange a meeting she would do everything to prevent it. 'The fascination you hold for me is as great as my fear is of getting to know you in person'; and that disillusion followed all intimacy. He kept her informed about his fiancée.

I must tell you something about my future wife. She is called Antonina Ivanovna Milyukova. She is 28 years old and fairly good-looking. Her reputation is impeccable . . . seems very nice and capable of making an irrevocable attachment.

It sounded simple and straightforward: a young man had found a bride.

Nadyezhda sent him her congratulations. Only later did she confess that she had found the news 'bitterly unbearable'.

Nadyezhda von Meck, during a long and increasingly intimate correspondence, made it clear that she herself, widowed after a tedious marriage, eleven children and even more confinements, was not seeking a physical relationship with her young correspondent. They never met, and — at her insistence — went out of their way not to meet, even when geographically quite close to each other. They could thus carry on a correspondence that was intense, often almost passionate, without risk of involvement. Fond as Madame von Meck was of music, she appears to have been even fonder of young musicians. There was something of the trophy-huntress about her (except that these usually collect musicians they can exhibit in their salons, and Tchaikovsky never set foot in hers). She was a kind and generous woman, a multi-millionairess who put her money at the service of music: posterity owes much to her. For fourteen years she supported Tchaikovsky; and he accepted her generosity with no more than a token protest.

> Let me say it once and for all, Nadyezhda Filaretovna, I declare without false shame that from you I will take everything that you wish to offer to me. I know you are rich, but wealth is a relative concept. A big ship makes big waves. You have much means, but for that reason alone you also have great expenses. What pleasure you gave me today with your letter, my new wonderful Nadyezhda Filaretovna! How endlessly happy I am that you liked the symphony — that you could relive the thoughts that filled my brain as I was working on it, and that my music has found a way to your heart. . . .

The new symphony was No. 4 in F minor but Madame von Meck would not allow him to dedicate it to her. He simply wrote across the score, which is full of autobiographical allusions, 'To my beloved Friend'; and when they wrote about it they always called it 'our symphony'. When announcing his impending marriage he told her he was taking this step after careful consideration, and for two reasons. One was that Antonina refused to let him go and had threatened suicide, and that it was therefore his duty to stop her. (Antonina had even dropped hints of a breach of promise action, claiming that he had compromised her virtue: 'You saw fit to visit a single girl and thus entwined our destinies. If you do not make me your wife I shall kill myself.'). The other, more compelling, factor was that he was giving in to the wishes of his family, who had long been waiting for him to take a bride — unaware of both his and Modest's homosexuality.

> My decision [he wrote to Nadyezhda] was supported by the fact that the sole dream of my 82-year-old father and all my relatives was that I should marry. And so, one beautiful evening, I went to my future wife, told her openly that I did not love her [Tchaikovsky underlined these words] but that, whatever else happened, I would be a staunch and grateful friend . . . .

Like many men in such a predicament he convinced himself that it could be an amicable working arrangement, that his wife would accept him as a brother, companion and lodger; and that she would dutifully keep house. He told her that there would be no physical relationship, a condition to which she consented. Of course it did not work. A traumatic train journey on which they embarked at the start of their honeymoon, although much exaggerated in subsequent film and television 'biographies', set the scene for their disastrous marriage. After only a few hours Tchaikovsky decided he could not bear his wife's company. When they met friends in the street, Tchaikovsky would simply ignore her and neglect to introduce her as his wife. He told Nadyeshda that he had to escape, and she quickly sent him the money for a trumped-up trip to the Caucasus, 'for a cure'. He was close to a collapse. To Nadyezhda he wrote, 'Death seemed the only way out, yet I could not contemplate suicide.' He decided he would die by making himself ill, to 'catch his death of cold'.

> Every evening I took walks, wandering aimlessly for hours on end through the deserted streets of Moscow [a century later this would have been called 'cruising'] and one such night I was approaching the River Moskva when sudenly, in a flash, I conceived the idea that I would purposely catch a cold which would lead to pneumonia and kill me. Under cover of darkness, unseen by anybody, I waded up to my waist into the water. There I remained as long as I could bear the cold. Then I clmibed out, convinced I had caught my death of cold. When I got home I told my wife I'd been fishing and had fallen in. But my constitution was so strong that the icy water had no effect on me.

He made a trip to Switzerland, where he spent a month, then moved to Paris, and finally to Italy, where the *Souvenirs de Florence* and the *Capriccio Italien* were conceived.

> Physically my wife has become totally repugnant to me [underlined]. Yesterday morning, while she was taking a bath, I went to Mass at St Isaac's Cathedral. I felt the need to pray . . . . You ask whether I have known non-Platonic love, too. Yes and no. Put this question slightly differently and ask, did I ever know the happiness of love fulfilled, I would answer, no, no, no! I believe, incidentally, that an answer to that question is to be found in my music. But if you ask me whether I have known the whole force, the infinite power of love — then I would reply, yes, yes, yes!

The trouble was that the kind of love he felt did not, at the time, dare to speak its name. In 1879, when the marriage was long over, Nadyezhda wrote to him:

> . . . do you know, when you married it was terribly hard for me, as if you had broken my heart. You will never understand how jealous I am of you, in spite of the fact that we have never met, never had any personal contact. Do you not understand that I am jealous of you in the most unforgivable way, just like any woman who is jealous of the man she loves? What a wicked woman I am. I

delighted in the fact that you were unhappy with her! I reproached myself for it and I don't think I let it show in any way, yet the feelings were there and could not be banished. I hated the woman simply because she did not make you happy — but I would have hated her a hundred times more if she had. I thought she robbed me of what should have been rightfully mine, and mine only, which I thought was my right, as I loved and valued you more than anyone in the world. If this worries you, forgive me for confessing it. I have said it at last. . . . Forgive me — and forget all I have said: I am not in a normal frame of mind. Goodbye, my dear friend — forget this letter but do not forget your heartily loving N von Meck.

He wrote to her:

Your letter touched me deeply. The happiest moments of my life have been those in which I realized that my music touched the heart of people I loved, whose approbation I valued more than fame or mass appeal. I need hardly say that you are the person whom I love with all the intensity my soul is capable of, as I had never in my life met a human spirit which responded so sensitively to every one of my thoughts, to my every heartbeat. The love and sympathy of my distant friend has become the foundation of existence. And when I compose I always imagine to myself that you are the one who is listening. You have no reason to fear that the affectionate sentiments you utter in your letter might turn me away. As they come to me from you my only thought is that I am not worthy of them.

Nevertheless, when after a year's correspondence Nadyezhda suggested that they might abandon the respectful address *Sie* and use the more familiar, singular *Du* (they corresponded in German), he replied:

As regards the transition to 'Du', I simply can't summon up the will to adopt it. It would embarrass me, addressing you by the intimate 'Du', for it would create the kind of intercourse which I want to avoid in our relationship. In any case, whether we address each other as 'Sie' or 'Du', my feelings of the deepest, eternal love for you remain unaffected. So YOU decide how it should be!

They remained on formal 'Sie' terms. In August, 1879 coincidence brought them within a few yards of each other in a theatre in Florence. Each knew the other was there, but they did not speak. Tchaikovsky was terrified she might come closer and fled. She was not offended, for she knew that both wanted it that way.

Their correspondence continued, and although he wrote about Antonina he could not bear to write her name, referring to her as *eine gewisse Person* — in German an expression of contempt: 'a certain person'. They both travelled a great deal, and their letters traversed Europe, Italy, Russia, Austria and Switzerland, were eagerly awaited and impatiently opened. They knew each other intimately, yet remained pen-friends — and she showered him with presents and money.

Suddenly things changed, and no-one knows why. When he was on a concert tour in Tiflis he was devastated by a curt letter from Nadyezhda saying that her circumstances were now different and that his regular allowance would cease. It was suggested that she had suffered a mental breakdown, and that her children had forced her to write the note, under threat or duress; and for a time he even supected that it might have been a forgery, concocted by some enemy. He replied, hurt but with dignity.

> My dear, precious friend. The communication you sent to me deeply saddens me, not for my sake but yours. These are no mere words. Certainly, I would be lying if I said that such a big cut in my income has no effect on my economic circumstances. It does, but to a far lesser degree than you might suppose. In the last few years my earnings have increased significantly and will doubtless continue to grow. Please don't worry on my account. In God's name believe me that this economic loss has not given me even the most fleeting anxious moment . . . . Your closing words, 'Do not forget me and think of me some-times' hurt me a little, but I can't think you meant them to be taken literally. Are you really suggesting that I think about you only so long as you are in a position to send me money? Could I forget for a single moment what you did for me, and the debt that I owe you? I can say without exaggeration that you saved my life. I would certainly have perished if you had not come to my rescue. . . . From all my heart I kiss your hands and beg you never to forget that no-one cares more about your well-being . . . . Your Pyotr Tchaikovsky.

Four years after the nominal end of their friendship, she took to her bosom (again metaphorically) the eighteen-year-old Debussy, whom she called 'my little Frenchman'.

As for Antonina, she vacillated between giving and refusing Tchaikovsky a divorce, tormenting him for three years, though she agreed to keep away from Moscow and out of his sight. In 1881, he discovered that she had given birth to an illegitimate child, which provided him with grounds to divorce her. The break was irrevocable and absolute, yet he was afraid of completely antagonizing her in case she made his homosexuality public — and lived in daily dread of this for the rest of his life. He resolved to spend as much time as possible abroad in self-imposed exile and on one trip, in 1892, sought out his old governess, Fanny Dürbach, whom he had not seen for more than 40 years. He felt no acrimony for Antonina and never tried to blame her. 'Looking back on the brief time together I see that I did not play an attractive role in it. My wife certainly deserves to be pitied.' She certainly did. Probably unstable from the beginning (else how could she have pursued Tchaikovsky in the first place, or agreed to marry him?) Antonina was put into a lunatic asylum in 1897 and died there in 1917. Tchaikovsky slowly recovered as the trauma of his marriage faded, and worked on his sixth symphony. But the old enemies X and Z continued to torment him. He started a new relationship, with the nephew of a courtier, and this time his secret was about to be exposed — not just to his friends and acquaintances but to Alexander III himself. The courtier, Prince Stenbock-Fermor, wrote to the Tsar complaining that Tchaikovsky had been 'paying too much attention' to his nephew. Letters to the Tsar went through the hands of secretaries and one of these, Nikolai Jacobi, happened to be a former student with Tchaikovsky at law school. Instead of forwarding the letter, Jacobi decided to prevent it reaching its destination. He convened a Court of Honour consisting of six lawyers, all former members of the School of Jurisprudence — a tribunal without legal force. It met on the 19th of October in Jacobi's apartment, Tchaikovsky was summoned and confronted with the evidence. They gave him a choice: ignore the complaint and face the consequences, or avert a scandal by committing suicide. Another former pupil, the attorney August Gerke, obligingly agreed to procure poison for him, thought to have been arsenic. The story would be that Tchaikovsky, depressed as usual, had recklessly drunk a glass of unboiled water — and this version was accepted for nearly a century. After all, had he not previously courted death by wading into the River Moskva? Eyewitnesses said that Tchaikovsky almost ran from the meeting, white-faced and without saying a word.

Under Article 995 of 1885/6, homosexuals were punished by loss of civil rights and exile to Siberia; but if this law had been strictly enforced, several members of the Imperial family and numerous courtiers would have had to be banished — so there was a strong likelihood that in view of his position as the country's leading composer, the authorities would in any case have hushed up the offence. His last symphony, the *Pathétique*, on which he was working at the time, was without doubt intended as a requiem for himself (indeed the symphony contains a quotation from the Russian Orthodox Requiem). Its first performance was on the 28th of October 1893, and on the 6th of November he was dead. The cause of death was given as cholera, which had also killed Tchaikovsky's mother. The disease raged almost out of control in every part of the world and was as feared as AIDS is today: victims were immeditaely encased in lead-lined coffins and quickly buried to reduce risk of infection. Tchaikovsky's coffin not only remained open but numerous friends filed past him to pay their respects. Some bent down and kissed his face — hardly the way to behave in the presence of a cholera victim. Rimsky-Korsakov, who was amongst the mourners and had been led to believe that the cause of death was cholera, actually remarked on the friends' behaviour.

The true story has been gradually pieced together only in recent decades, and was fully revealed by David Brown. Modest Tchaikovsky was one of very few who knew the truth, and it was he who proposed the title, *Pathétique* for the symphony — a title more appropriate than concert-goers knew. The work contains what Brown, described as '. . . the agonies of the finale, with its obsessive clinging to two descending melodic ideas supported by some of Tchaikovsky's most plangent harmonies. The result is the most explicit emotional declaration in all Tchaikovsky's works, a mixture of anguish, brooding and sorrow, which finally retreats into the subterranean gloom in which the whole symphony had started, fading into oblivion.'

WILHELM RICHARD WAGNER

Born: Leipzig, 22nd of May 1813
Father: (nominal) Friedrich Wilhelm Wagner (d. 1813)
             (putative) Ludwig Geyer (1779–1821)
Mother: Johanna Rosine Geyer, née Pätz (1774–1848)
Married: 1st Wilhelmine (Minna) née Planer (1809–1866)
             2nd Cosima von Bülow, née Liszt (1837–1930)
Children: Isolde, b. 10th of April 1865; Eva, b. 17th of February 1867; Siegfried, b.
             6th of June 1869
Died: 13th of February 1883

Wagner was — there is no getting away from it — a thoroughly unpleasant man. Few saints figure in this book, but Wagner was exceptional: selfish, self-important and pompous to a ludicrous degree; and emotionally, politically, intellectually and financially utterly dishonest. He twisted facts to suit his opinions, exploited and manipulated those he loved as much as he tried to control those he despised and tried to get his own way by the grossest flattery. He wheedled money out of anyone foolish enough to part with it, without the slightest intention of paying it back unless taken to court. When creditors pursued him, he passed unsecured cheques or simply left town. He almost made a habit of attaching himself, leech-like, to rich men, sponging off them and living on their generosity — and then humiliating them by seducing their wives. So calculating was he that he took advantage of the young, mentally unstable and homosexual King Ludwig of Bavaria by hinting that he was a homosexual himself, just in order to get money and patronage out of him. He was so completely convinced of his own genius that he took it for granted that the world owed him, the Greatest Artist Who Ever Walked This Earth, a living. Unfortunately, one must concede that, loathsome as he was, the world is the richer for him.

Wagner's personal magnetism cast a spell on all who came into contact with him. He fired men intellectually to devote their lives to him, even those who did not understand his music or whom he was cuckolding. He must have exerted a remarkable sexual attraction, though as soon as women surrendered to him he exploited their emotions with calculated ruthlessness. As a proto-Nazi he reviled Jewry and wrote a polemical book against Jews in Music (*Das Judenthum in der Musik*), because he resented any Jews who achieved success in 'his' art. At the same time, he captivated individual Jews, like Hermann Levi, who became his favourite and favoured conductor. *Das Judenthum in der Musik* and other Wagner polemics not only influenced Hitler's racialist thinking but inspired his very actions: Wagner advocated 'racial cleansing' (*Rassenreinigung*) as early as 1881, half a century before Hitler did. Even Hitler's *Endgültige Lösung* ('Final Solution'

— of the Jewish 'problem') was adapted from Wagner's term, *Die grosse Lösung*, though Wagner's 'Great Solution' was merely the expulsion of Jews from German lands. With an uncanny pre-echo of the holocaust he suggested that a theatre should be filled with Jews, locked and burnt down during a performance of Lessing's 'pro-Jewish' play *Nathan der Weise* (and when such an event actually happened — see Bruckner's chapter — both Wagner and his second wife Cosima expressed their satisfaction as will be seen later). The Nazi slogan *Deutschland erwache!* ('Germany awake!') was coined not by Hitler but Wagner: Hitler was merely quoting. Even Hitler's adoption of an excretory brown as the National Socialist colour, to be worn by the Brown-shirt thugs, was inspired by the title of Wagner's Diary, *The Brown Book*. It was probably all Oedipus's fault.

Wagner was born in the Jewish quarter of Leipzig in 1813, the illegitimate son of a Jewish painter and actor called Ludwig Geyer, whom his mother married in 1814, a year after Richard's birth. To Wagner he was a love-hate figure who not only haunted him throughout his adult life but also coloured his relationship with women. The Germans, both before and during the Nazi period, did their best to deny Wagner's non-Aryan paternity (as they did that of the Johann Strauss family) but it has now been established almost beyond doubt.

Like Wagner's natural father, his first wife Minna (short for Wilhelmine) Planer was active on the stage, in a minor sort of way. She was four years older than Wagner and a barely competent actress, who had gone into the profession more because of her looks than her talents (today she would probably have been a fashion model). They met in Lauchstädt, when Wagner was musical director with a travelling troupe. He saw her, found out where she lodged and took a room in the same house. Minna's most notable performances probably took place on the casting couch. By the time she was fifteen she had given birth to an illegitimate daughter — whom she passed off as her sister. As her fellow-lodger and, soon, her lover, Wagner thought of himself as a slayer of evil dwarves, like something out of one of his future operas, this particular evil dwarf being Minna's current lover; and worse (or better), he was Jewish. Rather than let her fall into his clutches Wagner decided to marry her himself. He laid siege to her with an assault of love letters which, if the sentiments had been genuine, would be those of a man besotted (though in reality they were more in the nature of exercises for future effusions to other women, just as other composers perfected their double counterpoint by constant practice). They married in 1836, but in the following year she eloped — twice — with an actor called Dietrich, only to return to Wagner three months later. It was not a good start to the marriage but worse was to come: there is little doubt that Wagner ruined her health and her beauty, and reduced her to a pathetic, yet extraordinarily dignified, figure. Just before the wedding he wrote:

My dear sweet bride, thus I greet you and no morning shall pass, henceforth, when I fail thus to greet you. My pain and longing for you, which have turned me into a mere shadow of my former self, have made it quite clear to me — as if there had ever been any doubt about it — irrevocably and immovably; I can no longer live without you . . . but now I am experiencing a certain peace, safe in the knowledge of my resolve to bind you for ever to me . . . etc., etc.

The translation does little justice to Wagner's stilted prose (which re-emerges repeatedly in the absurd libretti he wrote for his operas). As a minor theatre conductor he was barely able to support himself, let alone Minna, their parrots and dogs. Neither Wagner nor she were made for marriage, and soon his extravagant daily greeting petered out. Her sickliness moved him not to sympathy but impatience and annoyance, and soon he began bitterly to resent her pale presence. 'I could not find words to convey to my utterly exhausted wife how I regretted it all,' he confided to his diary. Minna bore his taunts and insults with quiet resignation and tried to counter his indifference with affection. This was rejected; and eventually he discarded her altogether. It was exactly how he had treated his first love, a girl called Jenny, whom he quickly courted and as quickly abandoned: 'She was not worthy of my love,' he declared. When he finally left the household he continued to send Minna a monthly allowance; which was no hardship to him, as the money was not his but 'borrowed' from friends, who were ordered to send it direct to her. A letter dated the 5th of October 1865 shows some consideration, though he refused to read her letters — in case they 'disturbed' him.

> Dear Minna! Excuse the delay [in payment]. It shall not happen again. My request to pay it was not heeded. I have not read your letter. I found the one you wrote to me last spring so depressing that I decided not to upset myself unnecessarily. If you have anything to say to me about them [the payments] please ask Pusinelli [a doctor-friend and one of several sources of the cash Wagner sponged]. I shall always try to do anything in my power to see to your comfort.

In spite of the fact that he supported Minna, stories were beginning to circulate that because of his neglect she lacked the necessities of life. Only about two weeks before her death in January 1866, Minna wrote to the press to counter rumours printed in the *Münchner Weltbote*.

> In response to an erroneous article in the *Münchner Weltbote* I can truthfully state that up to the present time I have been in receipt of an allowance from my absent husband, Richard Wagner, which has freed me from worries about my subsistence.
>
> Mrs Minna Wagner, née Planer.
>
> Dresden 9th of January 1866

Wagner's marriage to Minna dragged on, *de jure* if not *de facto*, while he was already in the throes of a passionate affair with a young Scottish woman. There was also a second Minna in Wagner's life, the celebrated, notoriously promiscuous, singer Wilhelmine Schröder-Devrient, whom he managed to tap for 1,000 thalers after she sang the role of Adriano in his *Rienzi* in 1841. He wrote: 'The slightest contact with this extraordinary woman gave me an electric shock, and for a time I heard and sensed her presence when the creative urge came over me.' Not only the creative urge, and not only Wagner's: she also set off urges in Weber and Beethoven, to name only two. Before long, however, the relationship foundered on jealousy, professional and personal. Wagner gave the role of Elisabeth in *Tannhäuser* to his niece (or 'niece') Johanna Wagner (related through his brother but only by adoption) in preference to Schröder-Devrient, who felt slighted as only a diva can and instructed her lawyer to sue Wagner for her money. Had the relationship continued we might now have a Wagner opera called *The Saracen Maid*, which he intended to write especially for her. But Schröder-Devrient herself was overtaken by financial disaster, when her current husband (she had many), a Prussian officer named von Döring, decamped with her considerable earnings. In Wagner's eyes, Schröder's new-found poverty considerably lessened her sex appeal.

The year 1842 brought into his grasp Henriette Wüst, who was married to an actor, Hans Kriete. She sang Irene in *Rienzi*, and soon the Wagners and the Krietes were on dinner-party terms ('Richard Wagner begs you to put a capon in the oven in good time as he has no desire to be roasted himself.'). Wagner had been a witness at their wedding, and the fourfold friendship survived for some time — until Wagner 'forgot' the tidy sum he had borrowed from Kriete, and she turned nasty towards him.

During the 1840s there was also a woman called Alwine Fromann ('no longer in her first youth', wrote Wagner) who did not have much beauty or money, but influence at court (as 'reader' to Princess Augusta of Prussia) — and influence at court promised the possibility of money. 'She was always loyally devoted to me . . .' and he offered her the opportunity of joining him and Minna in a *ménage à trois*, but she declined. And so it went on, and on.

The was also a 'lassie from Scotland,' Jessie, formerly Miss Taylor, daughter of a wealthy London solicitor and a Scottish widow. When Wagner met her she was the wife of Eugène Laussot, a wine merchant—whom, naturally, he screwed for money, somehow persuading him with other friends to provide him with a 'pension'. To Liszt, his father-in-law-to-be, whom he also pumped, Wagner wrote on the 6th of February 1850:

> I hope this is the last time that I shall have to mention the word money between us. I'm about to go and see Mme Laussot.

To his wife, on the 2nd of March 1850, he wrote from Paris:

> It is unimaginable that anyone could be more kind-hearted, more noble-minded and sensitive than our [sic — *our*] friend Jessie Laussot. I think you would be really surprised, my dear wife, if you could observe the deep impact your husband's music is making on healthy, unspoilt, generous minds.

Little more than a week later:

> Will you be angry with me if I tell you that I have decided, quite suddenly, to accept the most urgent and cordial invitation from my friends at Bordeaux? They have even sent me the travelling-expenses. . . .

And then:

> Here I am now in Bordeaux and longing for a letter from you in which you must tell me, I very much hope, that you are not cross about my coming here. . . . I'm very happy here, although I long with my whole heart for you and our home! Believe me, I know of no greater bliss than to live in peace and quiet, together with you, in our cosy nest. I cannot describe the divine kindness and love of these people here! Perhaps they, or at least the wife, will visit us some time to see for herself that we are happy and want for nothing . . . .

The rapport between Wagner and Jessie had been immediate and total. In *My Life* (the frank and self-glorifying autobiography which his second wife, Cosima later dutifully took down to his dictation) he wrote:

> Her [Jessie's] instant receptivity was astonishing; she would immediately and, as it seemed, correctly, understand things which I barely hinted at. She could sight-read with the greatest facility . . . she played Beethoven's great B flat sonata for me and really surprised me . . . .

There was a small problem, though — to which he had a simple, peremptory solution:

> My admiration, sparked off by that discovery of such a natural, outstanding talent, turned to a sudden embarrassment when I heard her sing. Her harsh, shrill falsetto was fierce and gave no evidence of genuine feeling. I was so taken aback that I could not help begging her to refrain from singing in the future.

Their love blossomed, so apparently she did not take his *Singverbot* amiss. The presence of her husband was a minor inconvenience, fortunately relieved by his frequent absences on business. Minna must have known perfectly well what was going on. Mme Laussot wrote to her, on the 4th of April:

> Herr Wagner has made us extremely happy with his visit. I believe that his stay here has not been disadvantageous to him, either. The weather has always been at its best, and I do hope he will retain happy memories . . . .

Minna scrawled over the letter the German equivalent of 'You lying cow!' Jessie was not totally honest when she said that Herr Wagner had made 'them' very happy. M. Laussot was anything but happy when he discovered his wife and Wagner together and threatened to 'put a bullet through Wagner's head'. Wagner's reaction was characteristic: he expressed 'astonishment that a man could bring himself to hold on to a wife who no longer wanted him'. He decided he would leave Minna and elope to Greece with Jessie. Their passage from Marseilles was booked, but at the last moment the couple cancelled the trip. He wrote to Liszt:

> My proposed trip to Greece has come to nothing. There were too many obstacles and I could not surmount all of them. If I could have had it my way I should have left this world altogether.

To the woman who had introduced him to Jessie, Frau Julie Ritter, he wrote about Minna, explaining his change of heart:

> She now understands the strength of her love . . . . Thus she appears to me as an entirely brand new wife, different from the old one.

To Minna he tried to offer excuses and explanations which, in their lame disingenuousness and sheer *chutzpah* (a word he may have learnt at his father's knee) are hard to beat:

> I was so dreadfully perturbed and thoroughly shaken that, whatever happened, my only thought was to get as far away as possible. I decided to go to Greece forthwith. . . . I felt the urgent need to write to you, but what I was unable to write to you was the truth . . . . It would have been insanely cruel to disclose to you what was going on, as I myself was without the slightest notion of what it was. All I knew was that I wanted to get away, to the wide world . . . . My intention was to treat you as any humane physician would. . . . I was convinced that the news of my going to Greece would give you at least some peace of mind, since it would make you understand that I was not just leaving *you* but rather, so to speak, *the whole world*. Forgive me if I assumed wrongly! My intentions were good . . . . Truly, my heart was troubled, and the worst of it, I was forced to lie to you. If you do not believe me utterly and absolutely, as I should be believed, you will only make yourself very miserable. I shall not impose any conditions for my return to you [!] since I am aware of your state of health, so I have decided to return *unconditionally*. [!!]

He recalled what he wrote to Minna in 1847:

> What is a youthful passion compared with such an old love? Passion is beautiful only when it culminates in love of our kind; in and for itself it is suffering! But a love like ours is pure joy — and a brief separation makes this plainer than anything. But heaven preserve us from a long one. Isn't that so, old thing?

Minna annotated the letter, as was her custom:

> This is full of lies and and offensive observations. Our reunion is due to my love, which is so deep that I am able to forget and forgive what has happened.

He was reunited with Minna, unconditionally as he said, but in Zürich; not Germany, where he was wanted by the police (whether for political dissent or unpaid debts matters not for our purpose). He pretended to be contrite and (as he wrote to a male friend) returned to Minna 'without horse-whip and turban' — the Arab symbols of male marital authority. It was not to last, of course. In 1852, Wagner met Mathilde and Otto Wesendonk (also written Wesendonck), a rich and socially well-connected couple, and assiduously cultivated their friendship — having first mentally cast an eye over his putative bank balance and his wife's, beauty. Minna wrote to a friend:

> You know what he was when I married him. A forlorn, poor, unknown conductor out of a job! As regards his intellectual development, I have the satisfaction of knowing that everything that he has produced was written while I was with him; and the fact that I understood him is attested by the way he always read to me the draft of his poems, his compositions, scene by scene, or played them over to me and discussed them with me . . . [but] I always had the painful feeling that he was also breaking away from me.

At first it was the usual two-married-couples friendship between the Wagners and the Wesendonks, but events soon followed the well-trodden path: Herr Wesendonk became his benefactor and Frau Wesendonk his mistress, though officially the friendship continued. Responding to a dinner invitation, Wagner wrote a note entirely characteristic of his blind selfishness:

> (Easter 1853) Loveliest Good Morning to you! My poor wife has been taken very ill. I therefore accept the invitation for myself alone . . . . Yours R. W.

Compare this with the letter he wrote to the Wesendonks on a similar occasion, when his dog Peps was ill. (see Pets of the Great Composer). For Wagner the relationship with Mathilde may have been just another affair, but it changed the course of European music. Wagner set to music some of her poems, now known as the *Wesendonk Songs,* which crystallized the luscious chromaticism that later became the hallmark of *Tristan and Isolde.* Those yearning harmonies illustrate perfectly Wagner's ideal of sexual coupling — the perpetually postponed orgasm. His harmonies constantly shift towards a seemingly inevitable conclusion (in musical terms, to resolve in the 'home' key) only to be turned aside at the last moment by a single-note shift, to embark on yet more writhing, chromatic ecstasy (long before Wagner such a device was known as an 'interrupted cadence', but involving only two chords, not three hours).

While working on *Tristan* Wagner wrote some significant letters to his Mathilde — revealing not only his own opinion of himself (with which she must have been familiar by then) but also, to posterity, that he was sailing close to self-parody:

> Child! This Tristan is going to be something Tremendous! That last act — I'm frightened the opera will be banned. . . .

Never before had sexual intercourse been so vividly and unmistakably represented in music. It was Wagner's most original invention. Yet he was beginning to
compare himself to God — and ludicrously even claimed to know the approximate date of the Creation.

> Child! Child! Dearest Child! The Master has done it again. I have just played
> through the first half of the Act and had to say to myself what our dear God said
> to himself when he found that It Was Good. Like God about 6000 years ago I
> have no-one to praise me. . . .

> A thousand Blessings [!]   R.W.

When he had completed the whole of *Tristan* he wrote to Mathilde:

> The great love duet between Tristan and Isolde has turned out beautiful
> beyond measure. I am overjoyed about it. . . . I lay it at your feet, and praise the
> angels who have elevated me to these heights.

The Wesendonk affair soon became public knowledge. Servants who had to
take secret messages between lovers, began to talk ('This woman is sending
messages saying "Has Herr Wagner slept well?" and "Come over. The hothouse is
very warm!"') Eventually Minna intercepted some of them, and this led to an
estrangement between her and Mathilde. Wagner saw it differently:

> I had to inform Minna that because of her disobedience and foolish behaviour
> towards our neighbour, Frau Wesendonk, our staying here had become most
> doubtful.

The discovery finally convinced Minna that she no longer had a place in
Wagner's life. But as Mathilde Wesendonk's usefulness to him also declined, the
affair ended. This time it was Mathilde who returned his letters, unopened.
Everyone was devastated, except Wagner, who probably laughed all the way to the
new opera house he was planning at Bayreuth, with other people's money. He
wrote to Liszt:

> I am at the end of my conflict . . . every choice is so cruel that I must have at my
> side the one friend that heaven has sent me.

Before long, heaven — and Liszt — complied and sent him another 'great
friend', Liszt's daughter Cosima. When they first met, in company, he reported
that 'on parting she gave me a shy but almost questioning look'. He took it as an
unspoken 'When shall we meet again?' She became the most enduring and
influential of his partners. He declared that she, at last, was the *real* wife and
companion he had been longing for all along (though she was by no means his
last love). She in turn devoted her remaining years, until his death and for nearly
half a century beyond it, solely to him and his work. She acknowledged his rank

as second to — but not far below — that of God. And yet all this might never have happened had Cosima (who was at least as devious as Wagner himself) not kept from him one vital piece of information: her mother, the Countess d'Agoult, was Jewish and had been Liszt's mistress between 1833 and 1844. But then so was Wagner, at least half-Jewish, and he managed to keep it from himself.

Cosima was 26 and although often called 'beautiful', it was the kind of beauty usually ascribed to horses: with a long nose (mercifully straight or the Master would have smelt a rat) and a narrow, bony face, but a regal bearing and presence.

At the time of their meeting she was married to the conductor and pianist Hans von Bülow, another of Wagner's close friends (and provider of 'loans') — who had conducted the first performance of *Die Meistersinger* and was later to conduct that of *Tristan*. The fact that he was a friend and ardent supporter did not trouble Wagner for one moment. If it was the world's duty to foster Wagner's art it was also a conductor's duty to relinquish his wife to him. When Cosima gave birth to a daughter (on the day von Bülow conducted the first rehearsals of *Tristan and Isolde*) she was christened Isolde and was presented ostensibly as von Bülow's child. Another daughter, Eva, followed two years later, this time acknowledged as Wagner's. It was not until 1913 that Cosima, proudly calling herself 'The Widow Wagner' (while behind her back she was known as *Die Despotin*, 'The Female Despot') was forced to concede in a squalid court case about money that her daughter Isolde could not have been von Bülow's child but was Wagner's. Yet she did not hesitate for one moment perjuring herself and had denied it.

By this time we are no longer surprised that, like Otto von Wesendonk, Bülow responded to his wife's affair not with outrage but remarkable generosity, patience and dignity. It was almost as if he felt flattered to have the Great Man share his marriage bed (or, more likely, he was secretly glad to be rid of the monstrous Cosima). Soon it was no longer a question of sharing her with von Bülow. Cosima left him and set up house with Wagner. In 1869, after much pleading on her part and Richard's, she and von Bülow were divorced. Yet his respect and admiration for Wagner remained undiminished. In the same year, before the divorce could take place, an illegitimate son, Siegfried Wagner, was born (himself to become a composer and conductor whose interpretations of his father's music are preserved on record). Richard Wagner did not marry Cosima until the following year — a perfect union: two thoroughly unpleasant people had found each other.

Few letters passed between Wagner and Cosima though she assiduously kept a diary — with the golden pen 'with which Richard had achieved the ultimate in human creativity', she said. At the early stage of their relationship, when he would have gushed love letters to her, the two were inseparable. Later they were separated only for brief periods, by which time his need would have passed. Nothing was heard from Jessie for nineteen years, when a letter arrived at their home. Cosima took charge of it and dismissed it with, 'Richard is very unwell, which makes me sad; on top of that silly letter from Mme Laussot, who wishes to explain to him what happened twenty years before! That irritates him, as it is all so utterly pointless.'

Soon there was to be another serious mistress; Judith Mendès-Gautier, the nineteen-year-old wife of the French writer Catulle Mendès and daughter of the poet and novelist Théophile Gautier. She entered his life only a few years after his marriage to Cosima (with him the traditional seven-year-itch was but a short incubation period), and he fell in love with her 'Greek profile and ravishing figure.' She wore her wild, long hair loose, spoke several languages (even translated from the Chinese) and could hold her own in any discussion about literature, philosophy or music. Wagner, by then approaching the final decade of his life, was as infatuated as a schoolboy; and moreover made a thorough ass of himself by behaving like one, showing off in the stupidest manner, climbing the highest tree in the garden and generally acting the teenager. Cosima wrote of Judith:

> She is such a tomboy that it almost embarrasses me, but at the same time good-natured and terribly enthusiastic. She practically forces Richard to play and sing to her bits from the *Walküre* and *Tristan*. The woman says and does everything I myself merely *feel*, deep in my heart — which makes me apprehensive.

As well she might have been, although the relationship appears not to have turned into a full-blown affair until a few years later, by which time Judith had been divorced from Mendès. Cosima pretended not to notice and still clung to her early resolve that whatever was good for Richard was good for Art and posterity. He wrote to Judith:

> My Love! I am sad. Today we [i.e. he and Cosima] have company again but I'm not going down to join them. Instead I busy myself re-reading a few autobiographical reminiscences of my life, which I once dictated to Cosima. You sacrifice yourself for your father, who is used to grand company. Alas! When I embraced you this morning was it for the last time? No, I shall see you again. I want to, because I love you. Farewell! Be good to me!   R.W.

That letter, dated 4th September 1876, uses the formal *Sie*. By May 1877, they had reached the intimate *Du*:

> Precious soul, dearest friend! And you did not visit me! But in truth you would not have enjoyed seeing me as I am, almost at the end of my strength from all my exertions, and as a result of all the disappointments I have had since I last saw you. Ah, it would have instilled new life into me if only I could have seen you again! That is true and remains true. Oh precious soul! Sweet friend! And still I love you! You will for ever remain what you are, the only ray of love in these days, days which for others are so full of joy but for me so unsatisfying. But you are for me a sweet fire, intoxicating yet at the same time calming. Oh

how I would love to kiss you again, Dearest, Sweetest One . . . . I wish I could heed what you said and forget you. . . . Dearest Soul! No more shouting and protesting! I think of your embraces as an inspiring intoxication, a matter for the greatest pride of all my life. It is the final gift of the Gods, who did not wish to let me perish with the false fame accorded to me by the performances of the *Ring*. But why speak of these miserable matters? I do not complain, but in my better moments I retain for myself such a sweet, balmy longing, a longing to embrace you and never relinquish your heavenly love. You are mine? Aren't you?

Later come demands for purchases from the Paris *boutiques* unprocurable in provincial Bayreuth. Kurt Pahlen, in his *Mein Engel, mein Alles, mein Ich* (a splendid collection of musicians' love letters) says there are dozens of pages filled with mundane requests of material and perfumes, interspersed with self-laudatory reports of the progress of *Parsifal*. The perfumes and fabrics, etc, were not for Cosima but for himself.

I must write to you again, because I forgot something. The slippers must have no heels! And something else. For my chaise longue I would love to have a wonderful, sensational coverlet, which I shall call 'Judith'. Listen to me! Try to find me some silk of the kind they call 'Lampas' or something like that. The background must be yellow satin — as pale as possible — strewn with garlands of blossoms — roses. The pattern not too big, because after all, it's not for curtains. It's to be used for smaller pieces of furniture. If there is no yellow, then a very light blue. Even possibly a white background would do, which might be easier to find. I shall need six metres! And all the foregoing for my 'good morning' working at *Parsifal*.

If Adolf Hitler chewed carpets, Richard Wagner was turned on by sensuous silks and satins — hangings, wall-coverings, bedclothes and dressing-gowns — in his favourite faecal brown whenever possible.

My Judith! When last you wrote to me you said, 'I've seen a piece of white silk, 2m 80cm, at 70 francs. And another of the same sort, 2m 50cm, at 60 francs.' Now that I read your letter again I realize I could after all make very good use of those two things in my study. Excuse my oversight and please have the goodness to see to it. The fabrics I sent by way of patterns are different ones and have no bearing on the material mentioned above. I still haven't received my beautiful coverlet! I expect a letter from you today. You are well? I wait! I wait! And do you still love me? I do, you. O beautiful one, beautiful one!

After two years the affair ran out of steam — or she out of silk. But incredibly there entered his life not only a second Minna but, concurrently with Cosima, a second Mathilde, surnamed Maier. Rudolf Sabor reported that she was 'blue-eyed and flaxen-haired' and hailed from Mainz. She was 29, and came to his notice in

1862. From their first meeting he bombarded her with letters, going into the *Du* mode almost immediately. Soon it was *Mein Schatz* — 'my treasure' — the German equivalent of 'My Darling'. He was still writing love letters to Mathilde, still stringing her along. Indeed he wanted her to come and live with him and Cosima, promising her a whole floor to herself in their house. Her mother had misgivings, so he tried to placate her by hinting that he wanted Mathilde as a kind of spare wife, 'in case anything should happen to my own'.

> One should envisage the possibility — God forbid! — of my wife's death. In that case I would request your daughter's hand. I can offer you only one excuse for this, somewhat unusual, request, and that excuse is as extraordinary as everything in my whole life. It is surely extraordinary that I won a King [Ludwig II] for a most lovable, dearest of sons; and so I wish for myself, chastely but profoundly, for a dear woman by my side.

When Wagner was living near Vienna there was a succession of amenable Austrian housemaids. They were invariably young and pretty, but some annoyed him beyond endurance. He wrote (Sabor's translation):

> I have had nothing but trouble with the girl whom I decided to take in. On the evening of her first day with me I asked myself how to get the poor thing out of the house again without hurting her feelings too much . . . . My God, no; such arrangements do not really work . . . . But I have got to know her elder sister . . . I might give her a try. She seems better educated, and I would be able to introduce her in all respectability to guests of an evening, let her make tea, etcetera.

Her sister proved a success — especially in the matter of the etcetera:

> The older sister moved in yesterday and turns out to be a pleasant, clever and warm creature. She keeps me company at breakfast and in the evening, and pleases me not so much by talking but by just being there. We shall see!

She was called Mariechen ('Little Mary'), and ministered to his every need. On the 6th of December 1863 he wrote to her from a concert tour, asking for a fragrant welcome and specifying what she was to wear for his return:

> Dear Mariechen! Next Wednedsay I shall be home again, arriving at the Vienna North Station (*Nordbahnhof*) at eight o'clock . . . . Now my sweetheart, make sure the house is in good order, for I am longing to relax in comfort. Everything must be neat and tidy and well heated. Most important, see to my study, make it comfortable, open the doors so that it gets nice and warm, and spray it with perfume. Buy the best you can get and make it smell beautifully. God how I long to relax with you at long last. The pink panties [*rosa Höschen*] are ready, I hope??

That was written a week after he and Cosima had vowed to 'belong to none but one another', and while he was also dallying with Mathilde II. His letter of farewell to the second Mathilde followed two and a half years later; and her character is said to be portrayed by young Eva in *Meistersinger*. He was now clearing the decks for the already-recounted affair with Judith, although Wagner never really needed his decks to be clear. There was always room for one more, and the chronology confuses with its multifariousness. Wagner's and Cosima's third child Siegfried was born on the 6th of June 1869, the year he met Judith. Siegfried was named after the hero in Wagner's opera and inspired the *Siegfried Idyll*, composed secretly for Cosima and played on the staircase outside her room on the 25th December, a combined Christmas and birthday present for her 33rd anniversary and a belated welcome for the boy.

Slowly, as he moved into his final decade, Wagner's hormones stopped raging, and Cosima must have breathed a sigh of relief. Chest pains had been troubling him for several years, but were not recognized as heart disease. He died in Venice, of a heart attack, in Cosima's arms, on the 13th February 1883, evidently still firmly convinced that in matters of creativity he was second only to God: the night before he died he had embraced his wife and (slightly revising his earlier notion of the date of the creation) murmured to her, 'Once in 5,000 years it happens!' Cosima declared that all she wished was to die. She outlived him by 47 years, during which time she ruled Bayreuth with a rod of iron, passing its administration to their son Siegfried only in 1907. By the time of her death in 1930, she had lent her seal of approval to Adolf Hitler, proud that he had heeded her husband's teachings. Race was a continuing (though no longer dominant) obsession for her, and she was delighted when in 1908 their daughter Eva married Houston Stewart Chamberlain, the foremost English propounder of Wagner's racialist theories. Fortunately, that particular streak of madness in the Wagner family eventually burnt itself out — along with the genius — and most of their descendants behaved with integrity when National Socialism threw the country's artistic policy into a twelve-year turmoil; some even fled Germany.

Mathilde von Wesendonk lived till 1902. When she heard of Wagner's death she wrote an Ode, to be declaimed at his funeral on the 18th of February 1883. It begins 'A cry of pain goes through the world . . .'.

Regrettably the Viennese housemaid with the pink knickers never wrote her memoirs.

CARL MARIA FRIEDRICH ERNST VON WEBER

Born: Eutin, 18th? November 1786 (baptised 20th November)
Father: Franz Anton von Weber (1734–1812)
Mother: Genoveva Brenner (1764–1798)
Married: Caroline Brandt 4th of November 1817
Died: London, 5th of June 1826

We do not know how Carl Maria von Weber first combined music with love, except that his happy-hunting grounds were the opera houses in which he worked. He was born in the last years of Mozart's life (whose wife and loves, the Weber sisters, were his cousins). Even as a youth he saw life in the raw when he scraped a living in Viennese taverns, singing popular songs to his guitar (though not quite as raw a life as Brahms's apprenticeship as a Hamburg brothel-pianist). So it was hardly surprising that Weber's first opera, composed in his youth, was called *The Power of Love and Wine*.

When he was not yet eighteen he became *Kapellmeister* of an opera company in Breslau, followed by a post in Stuttgart, where he fell in love with a girl called Margarete ('Gretchen') Lang, a soprano, the daughter of one of the violinists.

The composer's son Max Maria von Weber in 1864 published ('at the request of my mother') a biography of his father — three volumes of densely-written, florid, mid-nineteenth-century German, printed in small gothic type. There is much fascinating material, including some of the composer's own writings, but in the biographical parts Max naturally plays down his father's pre-marital entanglements (and would hardly have mentioned any post-marital ones) though he does hint at the relaxed sexual mores within his father's opera companies:

> As bad luck would have it, Weber developed a strong passion for the singer Margarete Lang. If he had tried to keep it in check or else contain it in lawful marriage, it would have made him look absurd and ridiculous in the circles in which he moved. Margarete Lang, or, as she always signed herself, 'Gretchen' Lang, was a daughter of the Munich violinist Theobald Lang and the famous singer Hitzelberger. She was then barely twenty, with a small, full figure. In addition to her musical talent she was blessed with an enchanting, teasing sense of humour which so matched Weber's that he felt irresistibly attracted to her and made her the centre of his whole world. It is not possible to determine what measure of intimacy the relationship between the two artists reached, but during the time he knew her he neglected the company of his fellow artists, even his visits to the tavern, and made so many excuses to be absent from his musical duties that it did not go unnoticed, even in the royal circles.

Weber's nickname for Gretchen was Pucicaca, and, says his son, they and their friends were constantly having parties and engaging in pranks. They both appeared in a cross-dressing operetta burlesque called *Mark Antony* in which Weber played Cleopatra and Pucicaca/Gretchen (whom Max Weber described as *üppig*, i.e. big-bosomed) the part of Antony. The farce, written for private performance, later led to the composition of his little comic opera *Abu Hassan*. Pucicaca is also immortalized in a comic song cast in the form of a jocular letter written in music notation and addressed to the composer 'His Excellency Herr Kapellmeister Danzi in Stuttgart': 'Give my regards to everybody, especially *la mia cara Pucicaca*.' In Stuttgart Weber wrote numerous songs, most of them for Gretchen; and after various adventures and appointments in other places, he eventually returned to Stuttgart. Other posts took him to Heidelberg, Darmstadt, Berlin and Weimar (where he met Goethe); also Munich, a place where he embarked on many, but largely undescribed, love affairs.

In January 1813 Weber moved to Prague, by any reckoning a prize job in relative operatic importance. It was here that he first started to get pains in his chest, exacerbated no doubt by his stressful work as *Generalmusikdirektor*. In every opera house this post has, almost by tradition, made enemies for its incumbent, and Weber was no exception. His endeavours to reorganize all aspects (including backstage workers, scene painters and wardrobe mistresses) brought him resentment and hostility. But there was the compensation that he was able to forget Gretchen and find solace in the arms of an older woman, a minor singer and ballet dancer. Her name was Therese Brunetti, 31 years old, married to a dancer (who, said the composer's son Max, 'acquired the unusual facility of being able to walk three paces up a vertical wall'). In thirteen (Max Weber said fifteen) years of marriage she had borne her husband five children. Therese had a voice suitable chiefly for soubrette parts — 'the roles often of coquettish paramours' as well as those given to the higher sopranos of lower quality, who — even if they do have a good voice — can make it sound purposely silly: Despina in Mozart's *Cosi fan tutte* is a good example. According to Max, Therese had a pale skin, reddish-blonde hair and a voluptuous figure (one of Weber's requirments in women). Therese was 'capricious and unscrupulous' and set her cap at Carl, hanging about the theatre to wait for him after rehearsals. Eventually he set up a *ménage à trois* with her and her complaisant husband ('who was half flattered by having the new Opera Director of genius frequent his house.'). Therese was a demanding and unpredictable mistress who took fullest advantage of her sexual powers over the impressionable young Weber and tormented him. Jealous quarrels were followed by reconciliations, only to turn into more violent quarrels. She took advantage of him by demanding money. His diary entries are terse and to the point:

8th of November. Terrible scene with Therese. It really is a hard fate that the first woman whom I truly and deeply love, thinks I am unfaithful . . . .
9th of November. With Therese. Unutterably painful declaration. I wept my first tears. Headache and fever.

14th of November. With Therese. Prolonged tension. At last reconciliation, which had an incredible effect on us both and blew away all ill-feeling. Such is the power of the spirit over the body!

23rd of November. She doesn't love me. Else how is it possible that she can speak with such warmth of her first love affair and mentions every detail of her enjoyment of it with such gusto and recounts her strange feelings during it and that she has not felt it with me. How can a woman be so unfeeling if she says she loves me? She can be with me for hours and then suddenly, coincidentally, she mentions this Hans and comes over all rapturous, full of wistfulness.

26th of November. With Therese. As I expected, she was loving and good and all is forgiven.

29th of November. With Therese. An embarrassing day. Not a word of concern from her.

This went on for a year. Weber's diary makes it perfectly plain that however much he loved her he also despised her for her behaviour, yet was unable to escape the obviously strong sexual hold she had over him. But help was at hand. On New Year's Day 1814 a new soprano joined the company, Caroline Brandt, nicknamed Lina or 'Muckin', (which I translate as 'Midge'). Suddenly Therese was forgotten, and Caroline became the object of his affection — eventually his wife and all-too-soon his widow. Like Therese she was a soubrette, small, with pale blonde hair and a buxom figure — and by all accounts a delightful person. They fell in love — though her mother disapproved of the young conductor and as-yet-little-known composer. Weber asked Lina to marry him, but she hesitated. He gave her an ultimatum that if she didn't, he would leave Prague — though he himself still had misgivings about settling down to an exclusive and permanent relationship: one of these being her public life on the stage (a job which carried inescapable undertones of the loose woman) and the other — her mother. He wrote to her: 'My wife must belong to me, not to the world; I must be able to support her without a struggle. No devil of a mother-in-law shall come between us . . . .'

When another actress joined the company he had a brief affair — or at any rate a flirtation — with her that estranged Caroline from him. Weber worked for a time in Munich, while she stayed behind. This time it was he who was jealous:

Oh my Lina! I don't understand you. I give myself to you in my letters as I always have done. Though of course, I can't bring your cold writing paper to life. . . . And what a talent you have for finding the bitterest, the most wound-ing expressions. . . . I am not pretending, I never betray anyone . . . only in my purest love did I speak to you. But I hate all mechanical assurances that sound like some sort of musical box of the lips. . . . I can't go on like this. God send you rest: I can find none. But when you look into the world, then think that, somewhere out there, there lives a being that will always love you above all else, even if you are not aware of it . . . .

After a brief absence a reunion in Prague led to their engagement. It was followed almost immediately by a series of partings, and one of these (while Caroline fulfilled engagements in Dresden) inspired him to write a song cycle dedicated to her and entitled *Die Temperamente beim Verluste der Geliebten* ('Expressions at the Loss of the Beloved'). At Christmas he was offered the directorship of the Dresden Opera, which meant another separation, as she continued working in Prague. It was precious time lost, as they were to have little more than seven years together. While he was writing *Der Freischütz* he confessed to Lina that he had found another love:

18th of May 1817 My much-loved Midge and Snowfoot. Today I must make a big confession to you of something you would never have expected of your Carl. And yet as a man of honour I have to tell you everything. Yes, dear Lina, I cannot any longer keep it from you that for the last few days I have found it impossible to write to you. A girl, whose allure I am incapable of describing to you, has quite captivated me and is, to cut a long story short, my mistress. This is doubly wicked of me because she is also the bride of another. But not only does it not help, it merely enslaves me more. Yes, I must reveal everything to you. She is always in my thoughts, every moment her image floats before me. I am besotted, I embrace her with red-hot passion, and I am sure she loves me too, because she sleeps with me and does not leave my side for a moment. Yes, she even left her father's house so as to belong only to me. Is there a bigger proof of love? I confess. Quite naked she came to me and I want to dress her in the finest clothes, to nourish her with my lifeblood. She has an irresistible urge to go on the stage, and I will help her to do so, although I know all the dangers that lurk. I often cry out, 'Oh, my beloved Agatha, will you remain faithful to me?'
So now you know my guilt. Judge me but don't condemn me. Who can help being overwhelmed by such feelings . . .?
Well, I wouldn't be surprised if you hadn't felt worried for half a second. Well then, give me a box on the ear, it's nothing, it doesn't hurt. But then you probably laughed. And yet it's true, dear little Midge, that damned huntsman's bride won't leave me alone. . . . The opera is really excellent after the new work I've done on it. . . . Let God pour His blessing on it, because it's giving me horrendous problems, and my poor little head is buzzing . . . .

If by then Lina had not fallen into a swoon she would have been relieved to realize that Carl was writing about his heroine Agathe, in *Der Freischütz*, (original title *Die Jägerbraut* — the Huntsman's Bride).

30th of August. Oh, huntsman's bride, away with you — and come back with lots of money, so that my other bride, the real one, can get herself nice things, and a comfy little nest.
21st of June 1817 You are right, Midge. We have been given plenty of laurel

leaves, but they won't spice a pig's head. Ah, if one could transform all the praises into butter and lard, sausages and eggs, that would be worth something, and then I could fill the kitchen with real food.

The celebrated Wilhelmine ('Minna') Schröder-Devrient (1804–1860), sang the part of Agathe on the 7th of March 1822 under Weber's direction. Later in that year she created the role of Leonore in Beethoven's *Fidelio* — when she was not yet seventeen: Stegmayer, the Viennese impresario, called her 'the enchanting Wilhelmine Schröder with the heavenly blonde hair'. 'Minna' sang in Dresden on-and-off until 1847, and according to Max Maria von Weber was his father's pupil; but Max drew a veil over what was almost certainly an amorous entanglement: Schröder was nearly as famous for her overheated sex life as for her singing and well known to have strung along a prolific procession of lovers, including Wagner and the senescent Goethe (who was fond of teenage girls) wrote a poem to her, though it is doubtful that he did more than that. Schröder was the daughter of a singer (the first German Don Giovanni) and an actress and performed on the stage as a dancer at the age of eleven. (Wagner's affair with her may have been purely financial: when she sang Adriano in his *Rienzi* he screwed her for a 'loan' of 1,000 thalers). Shortly after her death there appeared *Memoiren einer Sängerin* ('Memoirs of a Songstress') which purported to be the story of her sex life, ascribing to her in graphic detail every imaginable erotic variation, from sado-masochism to troilism and lesbianism, and claiming that she started having sex at the age of ten. It was probably a pornographic fabrication.

Weber and Lina did not get married until the 4th of November 1817, in Prague, and they had two sons.

In 1825, he received the most important invitation of his career, from Charles Kemble of the Theatre Royal, Covent Garden, to visit England. He and Lina desperately needed money, and when, on the 7th of February 1826, Weber said farewell to her he 'dropped one more tear, placed one more kiss, on the forehead of his slumbering children' — confident that a good income would be forthcoming. After Lina had waved goodbye to him as he sat in the coach, wrapped in furs against the cold, his feet in velvet-lined boots, she ran back into the house and fell weeping to her knees. Much later she told her son Max Maria, 'I could hear his coffin closing.'

His host in London was the composer and conductor Sir George Smart (1776–1867), who played in Salomon's orchestra during Haydn's visits to London, was a founder member of the Royal Philharmonic Society and conducted the first English performance of Beethoven's Choral Symphony. Smart welcomed him to his house at 91 Great Portland Street and looked after him with the help of Adolph Fürstenau, Weber's friend and principal flautist at Dresden. Both were concerned at his weak and sickly state. Weber was coughing blood, but to Lina he made light of the hardships.

March 27th, 1826. On the evening of the 24th and 25th my cough was a bit rough and tortured me spasmodically the whole day. Smart kept telling me to see a doctor, which I refused, because I know my cough. But on the 26th, just by chance, I met the famous chemist and physician Severin [Weber misheard the name: it was Thomas Savory, founder of the London retail chemist which still bears his name] who happened to be visiting and heard me croaking. I told him the whole long story, and his verdict was as follows. The whole thing, he said, was not dangerous at all. He would give me some pills to alleviate the spasmodic tickle and prescribed a rabbit pelt to put on my chest. Apart from that I was to do nothing, except be cheerful, to live well and eat properly. When I come home you'll have an extra rabbit in the house, because since this morning I've got fur on my chest.

The cheerful tone was forced, and in between reports of the wonderful success Weber had achieved at Covent Garden with his new opera *Oberon*, he occasionally hints at his true state of mind:

I'm horribly depressed. If I were not ashamed to do it I'd pack up and come straight home — although I know that I'm the same old grouser at home. And really, there's nothing to complain about here.

Weber never saw Caroline and his children again. His health deteriorated alarmingly, as the English climate aggravated his consumption. Smart recorded in his *Journals*:

Carl von Weber was found dead in his bed about ten minutes to seven on the morning of June 5th, 1826. Lucy Hall [a servant] slept in the room next to his, and he was asked to leave his door unlocked in case he required help in the night. In the morning Lucy came down to inform me that the door was locked and that she had knocked several times but had received no answer, upon which I sent for Heinke, and he came with Fürstenau. We burst open the bedroom door, when we found Weber dead, lying tranquilly on his side, his cheek in his hand. . . .

Fürstenau broke the news to the Webers' friend Charlotte von Hanmann, who was deputed to tell Caroline what she had half expected with every postal delivery. Weber was buried at St Mary's Roman Catholic Church in Moorfields, East London, on 21st June 1826, laid to rest to the strains of the last work composed by his cousin by marriage, the *Requiem* of Mozart, though eighteen years later his remains were returned to Dresden.

On the 1st of July Sir George Smart received a touching letter from Lina which he preserved in his *Journals*:

Esteemed Sir and Friend, You would attribute it to the overpowering grief at the loss of the best of husbands if I neglected every duty during the first days after the mournful event; if I thought of nothing but of my deplorable situation — of no-one but my departed husband. Mr Boettiger has been so good as to convey to you the expressions of my sincere and everlasting gratitude for the incomparable kindness and friendship which you have had for my dear husband . . . . May God Almighty reward you for all you have done for him and for us . . . . Farewell, honoured friend; may your dear life be happier than ours — we are forsaken. For ever gratefully Yours, Lina von Weber.

Pets of the Great Composers

The French composer CHARLES-VALENTIN ALKAN (1813–1888) wrote a *Funeral March on the Death of a Parrot*, published in 1859, scored for four voices, with accompaniment for three oboes and a bassoon. It is rare in the output of this composer, who usually wrote fiendishly difficult piano pieces. Clearly intended as a joke (why are very dead parrots thought to be funny?) it has sad undertones. Alkan's parrot shared its name, Jaco, with Wagner's, and doubtless hundreds of other parrots (it is the continental equivalent of Polly), and the entire text — worthy of Erik Satie — consists of the words *As tu déjeuné, Jaco? Et de quoi? Ah.* Parrots ran in the Alkan family. When his son, the pianist Elie Delaborde, fled from the Franco-Prussian War to London (where he would have found Charles Gounod, among others) he had concealed about his person and luggage 121 cockatoos and parrots.

In 1810, BEETHOVEN wrote to his friend Ignaz Gleichenstein enclosing a Sonata (thought to be the Piano Sonata Op. 78 in F sharp) for Therese Malfatti (one of the Immortal Beloved candidates) and added a little tale about the Malfattis' dog Gigons: 'You're wrong if you think Gigons only goes to you; no, I too had the good fortune to have him stick to me. He dined by my side in the evening, and then accompanied me home. In short he provided some very good entertainment . . . .' In the following year, Beethoven reported his 'room-mate' missing, and added, 'I miss him in my loneliness, at least in the evening and at lunchtime, when the human animal is obliged to take refreshment, which I prefer to do in company.' Beethoven's friendship with Viennese noblemen, who all rode around on horse-back, gave him the idea that he, too, should own a horse. He bought one though he could not afford to maintain it. Nor did he trust the animal, for he was never a keen rider. Needless to say, the horse was neglected, and he eventually got rid of it. Later a 'beautiful horse' was presented to him by his friend Count Browne in exchange for a dedication, but it met with the same fate: after riding it a couple of times he forgot about it. Animals are occasionally mentioned in the Conversation Books, usually one that happened to be in the eating-house or some other place where the recorded conversations took place. In the autumn of 1823 there is a reference to a performing dog: 'The dog played bravely' — not music, unfortunately: it had a walk-on part in a drama then playing in Vienna. In about 1787 Beethoven wrote a heartfelt *Elegy on the Death of a Poodle*. The text author's identity is not given, so he might have written the words himself. There is no indication of the identity of the poodle.

ALBAN BERG preferred cage-birds, probably canaries, to four-footed pets, and both he and his wife Helene loved all kinds. In a footnote to a letter to her on the 25th of September 1930 he writes, 'Pipsi ignores me completely. In the morning, when he is let out, he flies to the wash-stand and sits on the floor . . . .' and that 'The bluebird Pipsi is being a good boy, as always.' On another occasion: 'Saw that robin redbreast again today . . . .' After Berg's death Helene kept an aviary at her house in the Hietzing suburbs of Vienna, and she was always to be seen feeding wild birds. In 1918, he wrote to his wife: 'Today I had a curious dream: I was in a meadow, and a crow with its tail-feathers on fire flew helplessly past. She let me approach so I could help her, which I did by smothering the flames with my cap. She looked up at me with a dog-like look of gratitude. What could this mean?' On the 18th of May 1911 Berg reported: ' Just think, I met the decorator's pinscher, completely shorn' — and appends a drawing.

CHOPIN's Dog Waltz, op.64 No.1 in D flat, is so named because his mistress George Sand's dog was always chasing its own tail — worms, no doubt — while Chopin sat at the piano and improvised a sound-picture of the animal's antics. The pianist Vladimir de Pachmann, however, maintained that the story referred to the F major Waltz. Chopin's Cat Waltz is Op. 34 No.3 is said to have come about in the same way as Scarlatti's Cat Fugue (below), when his cat leapt on the keyboard.

DEBUSSY had several dogs, one of them called Xantho. On the 11th of December 1913 he (Debussy) wrote about Xantho from St Petersburg to his eight-year-old daughter, Claude-Emma, ('Chouchou'). Translation is by François Lesure and Roger Nichols.

> Ma chère petite Chouchou
> Your poor papa is very late replying to your nice little letter. But you mustn't be cross with him. He's very sad not to have seen your pretty little face for so long or heard you singing or shouting with laughter, in short all the noise which sometimes make you an unbearable girl, but more often a charming one. How is that genius M. Czerny [i.e. her piano practice] getting on? Do you know the 'air de ballet' for fleas? And old Xantho? Is he still digging up the garden? You have my permission to give him a thorough scolding! At the Koussevitskys' house in Moscow there are two lovely bulldogs with eyes like the frog in the salon (we're great friends, I think you'd like them) and a bird which sings almost as well as Miss [Maggie] Teyte. It's all very nice, but don't imagine I can forget you even for a second. Far from it, the only thing I think about is when I'm going to see you again. Until then, love and lots of kisses from your old papa. C.D.
> Be very nice to your poor mama; do all you can to see she doesn't get too worried!

As is stated in his chapter, ELGAR was a devoted dog-lover, although he could keep them only after the death of his wife Alice, who hated them; so he 'boarded' a dog with one of his sisters. Marco, a spaniel, the 'top dog' in the household, above Mina, a Cairn terrier — but Elgar commemorated the latter in his last completed work, the delightful, wistful orchestral elegy *Mina*. The death of his sister's dog Juno upset him greatly, and so did an accident to his daughter's dog, who was run over and killed in a road accident ('I cannot keep back the tears & am not ashamed'). Meg, an Aberdeen terrier, was killed by a passing motor car. His best-loved dog was a spaniel, Marco (pedigree name Cooden Rajah), whom he owned from his (the dog's) birth in 1924 to his (Elgar's) death, and who outlived him by five years. When Marco was still a puppy, in 1925, the dog was taken ill, and Elgar cancelled London engagements to be with him. After he got better the dog wrote a letter on paper headed 'Master of the King's Musick, Ceremonial Department, St James's Palace, SW1', to thank Percy Hull, the Hereford Organist, for some curative powders. This time it was Marco's turn to report that that his master had been ill:

Memorandum from Marco

Dear Dr Hull,
I, Marco, am very grateful to you for the powders; my master has not been quite well for a long time & I propose to give him a course of powders as the instructions advise. The next time I bring Sir Edward to Hereford you will find him improved.
I do not complain of my reception in the [Hereford Cathedral] Close [where the Hulls' dog Harry had attacked Marco]; I will only say that if my casual acquaintance, Mr Harry Hull, ever comes here he will receive a warm reception; (NB there are *two* of us here).
With respect to Mrs Hull, Cedric & yourself
Believe me to be
Your devoted
Marco

Although the letter was signed by Marco, research has proved that it is actually in Elgar's hand. When Elgar dined, Marco and Mina had places laid for them at table (presumably without the cutlery). Variation XI, 'G.R.S.' (Dr G.R. Sinclair, the Hereford organist) in the *Enigma Variations* portrays the organist's big bulldog Dan: falling down the bank of the River Wye in the first bar, paddling upstream in bars 2 and 3 and his rejoicing bark when he finally gets out of the water in bar 5. A theme Elgar annotated with the word 'Dan triumphant' later turned into the great Straussian upward-leaping opening of his Overture *In the South*, subtitled *Alassio*, thus evoking the spirit of Italy with music portraying an English bulldog. So much for the power of music to paint pictures. When Dan died on the 1st of July 1903 Sinclair informed Elgar immediately: 'Poor dear old Dan died an hour ago. He was my best friend. . . . He has a quiet little grave under the big apple tree.' I have seen no reference to any Elgar cats, but he was concerned for all animals. At the outbreak of World War I he made an extraordinary remark in a letter to his friend Frank Schuster (25th of August 1914): 'Concerning the war I say nothing — the only thing that wrings my heart & soul is the thought of the horses — oh! my beloved animals — the men and women can go to hell — but my horses; I walk round and round this room cursing God for allowing dumb beasts to be tortured — let Him kill his human beings but how CAN HE? Oh my horses.'

FAURÉ's *Dolly* Suite was published in 1897 by Hamelle, who (says Robert Orledge) seems to have had something of a cat fixation. The *Kitty Valse* was originally the *Ketty Valse* — Ketty being the name of Raoul Bardac's pet *dog*; Raoul was the original Dolly's brother, and his nickname was '*Messieu Aoul*' — which was the original title of the movement published by the cat-loving Hamelle as *Mi-a-ou.*

GOUNOD shared with his mistress Georgina Weldon her monkeys and parrots. Also her aptly-named dog Whiddles, for whom she cared more than for her besotted friend and whose sudden fit in a carriage played a part in the break-up of their relationship.

HAYDN would have seen many 'dancing' bears coming up into Austria from Turkey and the Balkans — cruel regions where to this day these beautiful animals are tortured by being taught to associate music with having to walk on heated irons. Then, when they hear the music, they go through the same motions. This is supposed to entertain tourists. An eighteenth-century dancing bear might account for the *Bear* Symphony in C major of 1786 (although most such namings must be taken with a pinch of salt). Some people even detect certain growling noises in the basses, both in the finale. No. 83 in G minor of 1785 is called the *Hen*, probably from the pecking quavers in the first movement. There is the *Farmyard* Quartet Op.76 No.1 in G; the *Bird* Quartet Op.33 No.3; the *Frog*, Op. 50 No.6; and the *Lark*, Op.64, No.5. In the summer of 1794 Haydn visited the composer and castrato Venanzio Rauzzini (b.Italy 1746, d. Bath 1810) in Bath. In Rauzzini's garden there was a stone erected to his dog Turk, with the inscription:

> Turk was a Faithful Dog
> And not a man.

Haydn was touched by the words and made them into a four-part canon. In Vienna he owned a parrot, who survived him and is described in the catalogue, dated 26th December 1809, of the composer's effects, which was compiled for auction by the valuer Ignaz Sauer. The final item in the long list of priceless manuscripts, printed music, pictures and instruments is 'No. 614: A LIVING PARROT. From the breed of teachable Jacos, the size of a pigeon, grey with a red tail. Since according to all natural historians parrots attain a high age of about 100 years this one is still young. Herr Haydn bought him 19 years ago, not fully grown, in London, for a high price, and taught him himself. Lives, as is customary, in a metal cage.' Professor H. C. Robbins Landon, who kindly informed me of Jaco's existence, said that Jaco used to greet Haydn's guests at Gumpendorf, near Vienna, and when the auction took place fetched a large sum, so keen was someone to own a creature which had spoken to Haydn. I wonder what became of the bird? If he did not succumb to psittacosis he would have been the longest-surviving Haydn pupil, might have talked to Schumann and Brahms and outlived Wagner. Frau Haydn went in for dogs, cats — and pet priests.

LIZA LEHMANN (1862–1918), the celebrated English composer of drawing-room songs, including the self-parodying *There are Fairies at the Bottom of Our Garden*, set to music two delightful poems by Rudyard Kipling which warm the hearts of animal-lovers who protest at the clubbing-to-death of baby seals. The first of her *Two Seal Songs* starts —

> You must't swim till you're six weeks old
> Or your head will be sunk by your heels;
> For summer gales and killer whales
> Are bad for baby seals.

CONSTANT LAMBERT (1905–1951) was a renowned cat-lover and prolific cat-owner, and gave several talks on the BBC Third Programme about Cats in Music.

Without an exhaustive reading of MAHLER's correspondence and other documents I have not come across any reference to pets belonging to him, except for a passing statement in one of the biographies that before going off to one of his 'composing huts', where he was not to be disturbed, he would 'stuff a pair of kittens into his overcoat pockets to keep him company'.

When the boy MOZART was being exhibited in London in November 1769 at the age of eight, an eyewitness, Daines Barrington, published a lengthy report of the child's musical prowess, but his performance was not without interruptions '. . . while he was playing to me, a favourite cat came in, upon which he immediately left his harpsichord, nor could we bring him back for a considerable time.' The Mozarts' dog, Bimperl, often figures in the family letters and is always described with love and affection. As she was an English-style fox terrier she also enjoyed the alternative name 'Miss Bimpes'. The Mozarts delighted in telling each other about her droll doings, her food intake and (else the Mozarts wouldn't be Mozarts) her defacations, in colourful language. Bimperl also appears in a sketch of a fugue-subject: perhaps a companion to Scarlatti's fugue-writing cat. Bimperl is a corruption of the word Pimperl — in Austrian speech P and B sounds are often interchangeable — and means pimple — indeed Spot, a favourite name for English dogs, too (Mozart prided himself on his slight knowledge of English). Mozart's favourite terms of abuse, which he bestowed on anyone who displeased him, including his superiors and the Archbishop and his courtiers, was *'Hundsfott'*, or 'Dog's C*nt'. It is not generally known that Mozart wrote part of a Cats' Duet, *Nun, liebes Weibchen*, K.529a, the text by Schikaneder (the *Magic Flute* librettist) and the vocal line and string parts by Benedikt Schack. 'The baritone, a Magician, has turned the soprano into a Cat. He keeps singing endearments to her, she replies only with "Miau-miau" . . . .' The four-part Canon K. Anh.195, also to the words 'Miau-miau', formerly ascribed to Mozart, is thought to be by a composer named Brixi. On the 27th of May 1784, Mozart noted down the sum of 34 kreutzer he spent on *Vogel Stahrl*, a starling, which he bought because it could sing an approximation of the Rondo theme from his G major Piano Concerto K.453. He sang for the Mozarts for nearly three years, until the 4th of June 1787, when they had to bury him in the garden of his Vienna residence in the Landstraße. He composed an epitaph, *'Hier ruht ein lieber Narr, Ein Vogel Star . . . .'* ('Here lies a foolish darling, a little bird called Starling'), and insisted on his friends' joining a solemn funeral procession round the garden, ' . . . while singing a Requiem, a kind of Verse Epitaph.' The starling seems to have been replaced by a canary, because Mozart's sister-in-law Sophie Haibel (or Haibl — Austrian spelling varies in this respect, too) reported that when Mozart was dying '. . . he asked that his darling, a canary, be removed from the adjoining room because he affected him too strongly.' Sophie supposed that the singing annoyed Mozart's acute hearing, but who knows, he might have found it too sad to bear. One of his short dances, with piccolo obbligato, is called *Der Kanarienvogel.* Mozart's mother, in a letter home from Paris, dated 14th May 1778 (one of the last, for she died at the beginning of July) wrote a PS: 'I send my greetings to Theresa [the maid] and a kiss to Bimperl. Is the grasshopper still alive?'

RAVEL introduced amorous cats in his ballet with voices, *L'enfant et les sortilèges* (the part of the tomcat-on-heat taken by a baritone, the innocent kitten by a soprano).

SATIE had a way of attracting stray dogs in the street and taking them home to feed them. Robert Orledge says they were the only living things that gained entrance to his living-quarters (presumably apart from the dogs' fleas). As Satie never cleaned his rooms dried dog turds were found there after his death. One of these dogs might have been the lucky dedicatee of his *Trois Préludes Flasques pour un chien.* ('Three limp Preludes for a Dog').

DOMENICO SCARLATTI (1685–1757) had a cat which is credited with the composition — *recte* improvisation — of the subject of his Cat's Fugue (Sonata in G minor, Kk 30), by walking over the keyboard, as cats often do when their master tries to play. Attempts to persuade a modern cat to go over the same theme as Scarlatti's, notably those by Professor Edward J. Dent, have ignominiously failed: cats have their own minds.

The British composer, travelwriter and champion of women's rights DAME ETHEL SMYTH (1858–1944) appears not to have felt much love for men but found a faithful companion in her dog, who (like one of Elgar's) answered to the name of Marco. He travelled with her everywhere, even abroad — that was before rabies caused Britain to pass quarantine laws — though he had to endure European indifference or hostility, as well as the inhumane dog kennels provided on German trains, outside, between the wheels! In her memoirs she tells how in 1889 she was made to pay for Marco's *dégats causés par le chien* to her landlady when he resented being left alone in her apartment and demolished it while she went to the Paris Exhibition; and how he failed to save her when she fell into an icy river: he just 'sat down and watched the proceedings dispassionately': fortunately the water was only four-and-a-half feet deep. Having established what her dog was called we can reveal that she pronounced her name like 'Smith', for she entitled a section of her autobiography 'The Smyth Family Robinson' — a joke which would not stand up with the pseudo-genteel BBC-recommended pronunciation which rhymes it with 'tithe'.

SIR ARTHUR SULLIVAN had a dog called Tommy, which he acquired as part-settlement of a debt from his stockbroker friend Edward Hall, whose firm had gone bankrupt owing Sullivan a large sum of money.

> (Diary, 31st of December 1890) Poor old Tommy died during the night. He came to me in November 1882 from Edward Hall from whom I claimed him as 'assets' for the £7,000 lost through Cooper, Hall and Co. Never will be seen such a dear, loving, intelligent dog again.

Yet *seen* he was, though only in a glass case, and thanks to the taxidermist's art. For Sullivan could not bear to have the animal buried and had him stuffed. One might suppose that he felt like doing the same to his stockbroker, but the dog-repayment must have been a good-humoured restitution, not a snarling one involving solicitors or bailiffs, because Sullivan and Hall remained on good terms. He could well afford to lose such a huge sum, but grieved at the loss of Tommy. Arthur Jacobs, in his Sullivan biography, says it is not known whether the part of the debt not covered by the dog was ever repaid.

Perhaps not surprisingly TCHAIKOVSKY was a cat man. In a *pas de deux* of the ballet *The Sleeping Beauty* he affectionately portrayed two amorous cats and, had he been English, would doubtless have called his cat Pushkin (after the man whose novel became *Eugene Onegin*): instead he called it 'Midnight', because it was black. Less affectionately he nicknamed his young violinist-friend Iosif Kotek 'the tomcat', because he was 'too fond of women' to respond to Tchaikovsky's advances.

In 1737, TELEMANN immortalized in song a little domestic tragedy, when his cat ate his canary. He composed a solemn *Trauer-Musik eines kunsterfahrenen Kanarienvogels*, or 'Funeral Ode on a Talented Canary', for countertenor or alto, to commemorate the event, pay homage to the bird and berate the cat. With different words the final *arioso* number might pass for a valedictory aria from one of J. S. Bach's Passions: 'My Canary, good Night'.

VERDI had a modest love life, both conjugal and extramarital, which probably does not warrant a chapter, but he was a dog-lover. His biographer Julian Budden says he owned at least two dogs, a Maltese spaniel Lulù, and another dog called Blach, of unspecified breed; as well as a kitten, as described in the letter below. Blach wrote to Count Arrivabene's dog Ron-ron on the 28th of August 1856:

> Blach to his brother-dog Ron-ron:
> Greetings: You did quite wrong, my most beloved brother, in not coming to see me, for I would have received you with open paws and wide-open jaws, and my little snout would have shown you all my canine brotherly love — with four tooth-marks on your furry cheeks. You certainly wouldn't run the risk of cholera here, nor of meeting any metropolitan nutcases. There are, however, a good number of imbeciles whom we keep in order with a cuff from time to time. My butler and secretary-factotum — he of the little hooks — leaves me wanting for nothing; amaretti pour into my mouth, all the big bones go to me, my soup is ready when I awake, the entire household is at my disposal, and; the moment it gets too hot I change my room and bed at whim and no-one stands in my way. In my spare time I look after the education of a young kitten, whose progress is very satisfactory and who will gain herself a reputation as a cunning thief, if she isn't throttled first. So you see, my dearest brother, everything is running smoothly here, in accordance with my suggestions and my wishes, and if you do come, my paws, my teeth, my tail, are all ready to receive an honoured relative in a fitting manner. My male and female secretaries [i.e. the Verdis] send you greetings. Talking of my secretary, I read in some newspaper that he is about to make some more hooks [Verdi was working on *Don Carlos*]. I shall rate him among the metropolitan nutcases. If this is so I shall inform you. Meanwhile I send you a doggy, brotherly hug.
> Greetings.
> Blach

Budden says the 'little hooks' (Italian *rampini*) refer to a remark made by one of Verdi's servants, who declared it strange that the master became so rich when all he did was make little hooks on paper.

WAGNER's dragon in the Ring Cycle does not come within the scope of this Pets' Corner, and the swan in *Lohengrin* is merely a form of transport; but the composer was genuinely fond of animals. In 1863, he wrote to his mistress Mathilde Maier, 'Look after your little dog. These animals were given to us purposely by a benevolent power, so as to comfort us' (but then Hitler felt the same about *his* dog and treated him kindly). In July 1855 Wagner wrote about his dog Peps to Otto von Wesendonk, the husband of his mistress Mathilde (a different Mathilde from the above, for his turn-over in mistresses was greater than that in pets). Peps had been taken ill during Wagner's absence in London, and died shortly after his return:

> I fear that my good, old, faithful friend Peps is going to die on me today. It is impossible for me to abandon the poor animal in its last moments. Don't be cross if we ask you to dine without us . . . you won't laugh at me if I cry? Your R.W.

Wagner shared Peps with his first wife Minna: another of their dogs was called Robber. He and Minna also had two parrots, consecutively, Papo and Jaco. Minna, or somebody (it would not have been Wagner, for whom jokes were no laughing matter), taught Papo to say, 'Naughty Mr Wagner — Poor Minna!', which he did, ceaselessly (and never was a truer word spoken by a parrot). In 1866, another of Wagner's dogs, Pohl, died while he was away, and, on his return, he found that his landlord had buried the animal in the vegetable garden. Wagner had it exhumed, wrapped in the rug on which the dog had always slept, and reburied it in a wooden coffin. Over the grave he had a marble table erected, 'To his Pohl — R.W.'

Pohl was replaced by Russ, a big Newfoundland. He died in the spring of 1874. Cosima wrote: 'Yesterday he was still running behind our carriage on the way to the theatre, happily leaping around and barking. With him a good spirit has left our house. Tomorrow our old friend is to be buried at the foot of our grave . . . .' (the plot in Bayreuth which Cosima and Wagner reserved for their own burial and where Russ has his own headstone). Not all the Wagners' pets returned his love. One dog is said to have hated him so much that when Wagner called him in the street the animal ignored him and pointedly walked straight past his master. Intelligent beings, dogs.

Finally, there was a 'WELL-KNOWN MUSICAL SAVANT' (his name unfortunately withheld by the newspaper report quoted in the *Musical Times* in 1886), who educated 'his favourite monkey to become a good pianist. After only 48 lessons, the monkey Tabitha, who is a real ornament to her sex, could play scales with surprising dexterity. The suppleness of their fingers, their agility, their strength, all tend to show that most monkeys are born pianists. Patience is the only thing required to bring out this hidden faculty . . . .' The *MT* added an editorial comment: 'We can scarce, perhaps, imagine that expression will be the strong point of the animal's performance; but if she can run up the scales as rapidly as she can run up a tree, there will most assuredly be people ready and willing to make such a show remunerative to a smart speculator.'

INDEX